PRAISE FOR KIRSTEN

French Trysts

"Charming and friendly . . . readers who are fans of all things Parisian are sure to enjoy this novel, which delights in its setting and offers up the world of French seduction to playful examination." —*RT Book Reviews*

"A steamy peek inside the life of a modern-day courtesan." —*Kirkus Reviews*

"Adds a new twist to the traditional American-in-Paris tale. Alexandra is a charming heroine. Laugh-out-loud funny." —*Booklist*

Paris Hangover

"Gucci bags, Jimmy Choo shoes, and now a copy of *Paris Hangover* are all essential items for the upwardly mobile young woman." —Sylvia Beach Whiteman, owner of Shakespeare & Co. (Paris)

"Women . . . will be champagne-tickled by this sexy chic lit *du jour*." —*Playgirl*

"Strong debut . . . there's something for everyone in this witty novel: red-hot love scenes, glorious depictions of Parisian sights, and a snappy story." —*Kirkus Reviews*

"Wickedly entertaining paean to the delights of living in Paris." —*Chicago Tribune*

"A great novel with a lot of heart." —*Fresh Fiction*

"This is a witty mousse, yet it also is unsparing, without cruelty, ambitious, not vicious, chic, without the inevitable creak of a writer trying too hard. *Paris Hangover* will hang around your dreams long after Klein kisses you good-bye—on both cheeks, of course." —Jacquelyn Mitchard, author of *The Deep End of the Ocean* and *A Theory of Relativity*

"The decadent, sexy journal of a New Yorker chasing a dream in Paris. Her tales of looking for Monsieur Right are controversial, hilarious, and poignant. A fresh new voice in fiction." —Frédéric Beigbeder, author of *99 Francs* and *L'Égoïste Romantique*

ALSO BY KIRSTEN LOBE

French Trysts
Paris Hangover

Paris, Baby!

Kirsten Lobe

St. Martin's Griffin
New York

Note to the reader: Some names and identifying characteristics have been changed.

PARIS, BABY! Copyright © 2011 by Kirsten Lobe. All rights reserved. Printed in the United States of America. For information, address St. Martin's Press, 175 Fifth Avenue, New York, N.Y. 10010.

www.stmartins.com

Design by Kathryn Parise

LIBRARY OF CONGRESS CATALOGING-IN-PUBLICATION DATA

Lobe, Kirsten.
   Paris, baby! / Kirsten Lobe. — 1st ed.
       p. cm.
   ISBN 978-0-312-60532-2
   1. Lobe, Kirsten.   2. Authors, American—21st century—
Biography.   3. Americans—France—Paris—Biography.
4. Single mothers—Biography.   5. Life change events—
Humor.   6. Homecoming.   I. Title.
   PS3612.O235Z46 2011
   813'.6—dc22
   [B]

First Edition: May 2011

10 9 8 7 6 5 4 3 2 1

For my parents, the heroes of my magical childhood, my
loving best friends in adulthood, and my extraordinary role models
in parenthood, who together, each in their own unique
way, brilliantly offered me the following:

"There are two lasting bequests we can give our children.
One is roots. The other is wings."
—Hodding Carter, Jr.

America is my country, but Paris is my hometown.

—GERTRUDE STEIN

Prologue

"*Be faithful to that which exists within yourself.*"

—ANDRÉ GIDE

Cut to Paris, St. Germain, Sunday, early afternoon in June . . . warm golden sun and light breeze off the Seine.

There I am, standing ridiculously, anxiously in the queue ("line" for those of you not fluent in Euro-speak), at the magnificent renowned French pastry shop Ladurée, on rue Jacob. Clad in what can best be described as a getup. And I mean that not in the literal sense of having just *got up* and tossed something on . . . Oh nooo, *au contraire,* that notion has long been strangled off. Frankly, I don't even know if the "casual-wear-whatever" thing was ever in my DNA. What I mean by "getup" is the maximum sartorial effort that one must *always* make in Paris.

Particularly *as a woman,* an expat, in St. Germain, a *single* woman . . . and a blonde (FYI—they don't love blondes here; to clarify, *playboy men* do, but the rest of the culture, not so much).

Ouch, that's a lot of wardrobe pressure, *n'est-ce pas?* But this all goes with the whole deal of living here: insanely beautiful aesthetics are the law, without exception, for every storefront, man, woman, child, piece of clothing, tea bag, and handbag. I am used to it and therefore take a particular delight in abiding by said law. To define this strict decree further: its essence is to find and create just the right mélange of "chic-elegant-effortless-cool"—that also should be a mix of new elements AND something with family history or a story and an anecdote (as in, "Got this at Les Puces from an old woman who told me she wore it to dinner with de Gaulle"). Further to that point, head-to-toe Chanel is as wrong as having flat, one-color hair.

You get it. One doesn't schlep on some sweats and Converse tennis shoes. You may be stoned in the streets; god, you'd have to *be stoned* to consider it. Thus, I sport a loose low chignon that's meant to look haphazard but took four good goes to get right, a pair of low-waisted white capris from Agnès B, with a distressed-to-the-nth brown studded belt bought off some gypsy in the Marais and a classic Kenzo chiffon floral blouse sprinkled with tiny "tête-à-tête daffodils," tulip green espadrilles from a street market in Biarritz, and my beloved beige leather doctor-bag-style purse from a trip to London's Portobello Road. Pretentious? Oh, *bien sûr.* But, listen, as I don't want to have to say this again: it's *required* here or you will be 1) Eaten alive with visual condemnation that will make the taunting of middle school girls in your youth seem like a coronation or, worse, 2) ignored as if invisible waste matter, thereby given horrific service or none at all (as in, denied access).

If you're currently packing for Paris, just get one damn outfit that's spot-on perfect, and you're all set. The flip side of having to get it right, right, right is that Europeans often wear the same outfit again and again. I once worked for Diane von Furstenberg and that woman, with all her millions and closets the size of airplane hangars, would wear the same getup day after day, right down to the necklace. (Come to think of it, maybe you can do that and pull it off better when you're hyperfamous and the jacket is Yves Saint Laurent Couture, $55,000.)

Enough of the clothes chatter . . . back to Ladurée and the divine pastries. Anxiously shifting from one foot to the other, I peek over the shoulders of the herd of Japanese tourists in front of me. Snapping photos, bustling about with mouths agape, ordering dozens of Ladurée's lusciously packaged sumptuous chocolates, satin-ribbon-bound tins of Lapsang souchong tea, and regal framboise patisserie. Despite being summer, tourists in the adjoining tea room faithfully order cup after cup of the coveted Ladurée's hot chocolate, famed for being so deliciously creamy-thick, a spoon will stand in it. Thus, the fragrance of rich *chocolat chaud* dances into the foyer, embraces the scent of butter crème, and waltzes into one's senses, evoking a lulling cloak of hedonistic swooning. Too deliciously descriptive? *Pas du tout.* And get this: I am still possibly *even understating* the delight of it all. And the anticipation for consuming these lavish desserts is exponentially multiplied by the fact that today—*I will be eating for two!*

It occurs to me while waiting in line: Early pregnancy cravings + French patisserie + 20 euros burning hole in pocket + the ability to purchase in such quantities that may look like "fixins for a party" but in reality are for being devoured in the complete total blissful privacy *chez moi* (without onlookers looking askance—and the French do this SO well—at calorie intake or ravenous delight in what can only be described as gobbling) = SHEER PURE *BEURRE* HEAVEN!

Despite living in Paris for eight years and knowing with total certainty that, once it is my turn, I can take as damn long as I want without a need to rush my order, I cannot stop myself from mentally compiling a list of my desired wants . . . no, make that *needs*.

Deux flaky golden *croissants,* shimmering with a buttery shell; *deux petites tartes des fruits* glistening with ruby-red raspberries under an umbrella of dark chocolate shavings; *une religeuse* in whisper-light pale green *pistache* frosting that swells to a dome peaked with a dollop of pure crème dotted with a silver *bonbon; une tarte aux fraises*; *un palmier* with the gentle crispness like a sliver of gossamer; *une grande meringue au chocolat*; and a trio of macaroons loaded with creamy ganache: *ré-glisse* ("licorice"), *citron* ("lemon"), *et vanille*.

I make my way through the ordering process in what can only be described as heady delirium. Finally, after decades of battling to keep reed thin under the pressure of the discerning-to-the-point-of-ruthless mass of Parisians, I am going to eat every damn thing I ever wanted to and, you know what, I am allowed. I am pregnant!! And I just realized that I can also, *enfin,* take *carte blanche* in not giving a major hoot what any man thinks about me, physically, in this city. Oh la la, I don't know which is a greater pleasure! Pastries galore or that I can finally relax, since, after years of whittling self down to resemble a *gamine* and then still hearing every bit of unsolicited criticism (they call it *counseil*—counsel!) from the droves of sexy hipster Frenchmen, I am officially off the market and free from the endless sea of critiques that come with dating.

Unconciously, a quick, terribly unflattering snort bursts from my mouth as I recall a smattering of comments from my amours that have stuck with me over the years:

"You have a pimple, what a pity . . . *for us both.* You should have
  considered canceling."—Jean, on a blind date, at the first minute of meeting

(And the following critiques from a single summer):

"Kiki, you should really dress more boho."—Olivier

"You should really dress more like a butch chick."—Renaud

"You should really dress more refined and pared down."—Thierry

"You took kilos [gained weight], *non,* Kiki?"—Alain

"Your hair is the color of *frites* ['French fries']."—François

"It is too long"—Georges . . . "too short"—Bernard . . . "too straight."—Paul

Talk about making my head spin with varied demands galore! Oops, sorry, I have serious mental files of the legions of charming comments from my suitors. Clearly, once I open that door, it's like fighting a tsunami to shut me up again. But now . . . *now,* I can chill! Finally! At thirty-nine years old, I have found one of the most sublime delights yet—here, at Ladurée, in this singular moment of anticipation, self-prescribed dashing of willpower and guilt-free indulgence, all tied up into one afternoon, because of the greatest gift ever given to me—a baby!

After reading every printed book, guide, and medical journal on pregnancy, I know full well, at this early stage of three weeks, it's (he? she?) still as small as a grain of rice, as they say, but it will be treated to one hundred times its weight in gold, if I gorge on that *mousse au chocolat* sprinkled with gold foil! What divine pleasure—and trust me, this girl, *moi,* has turned over every stone and leapt into every . . . possibility, on my "pleasure search" through life.

So, now you are up to speed on the big issues: I'm thirty-nine, a blond American who's been living in Paris for eight years, an avid fan of clothes, and pregnant with pastry and chocolate issues. Oh, and a single mom-to-be. Yes, from the get-go. I better rewind here a smidge or your head is going to fall off.

I guess you could say, until I got pregnant, I was a serial dater.

I always hated that term, since it does sound slightly criminal—as in serial murderer, and, frankly, I could've murdered some of my French exes for flagrant cheating, but as we all know, for them that's more of a goal than a crime punishable by death. Alas, I never got married but thought I was wanting to, yet curiously never really allowing myself to get to the altar. (Freud? Jung? Anyone?) I just adore Frenchmen and love serious long-term relationships. Have been in big, beautiful love stories of three, five, and seven years . . . *and then I moved to Paris*! (Where, need it be said, it is quite remarkable and rare to find a solid, honest love story.) It is so bloody difficult here to find—how shall I put this?—men who are faithful and have all the integrity that our fathers had and (hmm, this may be it) the ability to really connect, to give himself to a woman with honest authenticity and sincerity.

Oh, that's big! That's really the deal. A revelation. Seriously, I know the stereotype is that Frenchmen are smarmy snobs, selfish and shallow. I am always arguing *against* that image with my friends in the States who have not yet or have vowed against dallying in dating Frenchmen. I waffle between defending them and condemning them. Depends on the day, actually. Truthfully, Frenchmen are so damn fascinating, since they are exceptionally well read, innately elegant, can cook exceptionally well, make love like iconic fantasies, are witty and playful . . . and, well, maybe *too playful*. And so you find yourself falling for them hook, line, and stinker, and then a waft of reality hits and you accept that, because of the cultural and social framework in which he was raised and educated, this man is going to be apt to stray, flirt, and otherwise generally drive me completely bonkers. Or some variation on that. To clarify—Frenchwomen know all of this, don't care, and are fine with it, knowing precisely how to deal with it *all* by birthright and luck. God, how many times I wished I had that gene.

American women don't. We freak out, panic, take it personally, and think we can be the one that changes them. It's all quite complicated, and yet, once you've lived in Paris and dated the French, you are forever changed. You can't go back and date a guy from Boise who loves his job selling gravel, eating TV dinners, reading *Popular Mechanics,* and wearing poly-blend suits or basketball shorts (which are so unattractive they should be illegal outside a professional court).

So, to the point. A few months ago, by luck, at my best friend Zola's birthday dinner at the sha-sha hipster resto Calvados, I met a marvelous British man who lived in London. It wasn't a love-at-first-sight cliché exactly, but by night's end, after dancing for hours at Castel, four of us—Zola, Sabina, Mister Brit-o-Honey, and I—headed to a cheesy resto, Café Mabillon, at 2 A.M. to snarf *croque monsieurs et frites.* After watching this man all night, marveling at his wit and very unFrench way of quietly enjoying the evening while allowing us all to be ourselves, in a way that was almost magical, it suddenly hit me as I devoured my fries—You know what, Kiki? This is a great man . . . perfect for you and, though not a Gallic god as per your usual *tasse du thé* ("cup of tea"), I felt my heart race as I realized: I had happened upon a man unlike any I had known, who intrigued me to no end. He seemed in every way the full spectrum of a real man and made me think that so many of the Frenchmen I had previously loved were essentially two-dimensional. Seriously, they were like life-size poster images and, of course, with the whole hit-list markers of charming, literary, and sexy that I always sought like a religion . . . and yet they were often like movie characters that you could feel and touch but not truly affect. They liked to decide everything, moved the relationship at their will and whim, and, even after years together, there was still an unknown that plagued a true level of trust and equality. Or, more to the point, they sucked at communicating in a sincere, genuine, give-and-take way. Was this new Brit Mister Right? Ohhh . . . you bet.

Fast-forward three months: he and I are madly in love and zipping around Europe, crazy for each other. Thrilling to the core! Me, patting myself on the back a bit for finally having the wisdom to choose the one man in the room NOT dancing until dawn with his skinny hips being one of the top three things I love about him. What an idiot I have been!

Blake, as my lovely divorced Brit is known, was capturing my heart with all his emotional honesty, thoughtfulness, and love. He loved his kids, and, when I asked him on our first date if he wanted more, he smiled broadly and replied, "Never say never." Our time together was like, say, flying on cloud nine on Ecstasy while being bathed in kisses. Divine!

Then we got in one stupid argument and split up. Still, afterward we e-mailed and chatted a bit, even if there had been a gentle tap at the pause button on high romance. And then I realized I was *avec enfant*—pregnant.

Let's just say, it was dicey timing for us, and, as you can imagine, this detail added a certain and assured drama to all involved. (Understatement of the millennium!) I can't begin to express how much I wish it would've worked out in another way, but he decided the timing wasn't right to have a baby and, well, I was pretty damn sure, despite the surprise offer, I did. And being a woman who just two weeks before had been showered with love by my amour, I was foolishly optimistic that he was just overwhelmed and stunned but would surely come around.

All this brewing, when I got a phone call from the States. My sister

Lily, who had been trying every fertility treatment from Clomid to acupuncture to eating mass quantities of yams . . . garf! I was eager to get her opinion and advice, if not support. First, though, we do our family version of round-robin (there are five kids), where we pass family gossip and news back and forth by phone, somehow always butchering the content—like news went out my brother "Mark went on a vacation and caught a Man-of-War"—somehow got back to me as "Mark went on vacation and bought a Manet in Singapore." Or Marisa said, "I love a good gin and tonic and I heard, " I love a good high colonic."

Then Lily, who, by the way, resembles Meryl Streep twenty years ago and has this butter-smooth sweet voice, says, "Kiki . . . Corbin and I are done. Years of trying and all the emotional upheaval and hopes . . . I can't do it anymore. My doctor says there is just no chance I can get pregnant . . ." her voice trailing off into a gentle sob.

"Sweetie, why not adopt! C'mon Lily, there are so many . . ." I interrupt, trying to steer toward hopefulness. *It's a habit.*

"I don't think so. I can't even think about it right now . . . I'm spent, but I think if you want to have a baby one day, Kiki, you should really get on it. That whole fallacy that women can easily get pregnant after thirty-five has just shot my life all to hell," she says, with a gentle authority that has always both commanded me to listen and let me know she truly cares. I divulge that I am, by luck, fate, and surreal timing, already three weeks pregnant and that Blake is telling me that I'm on my own. I confess to her that I'm terrified, happy, missing him, anxious, and mad at him, all at the same time.

"You are strong as nails, Kiki. Look how you set off for life and design school in NYC all by yourself and then set sail for an unknown future in Paris without knowing a soul there. You *can* do anything and this . . . you can do it alone. To be honest, at your age, this may be your only chance to have a child . . . Or better still, have the baby and give it to me!" she adds, joking and lightening the gravity of this intense situation.

I get off the phone, feeling amazed at the serendipitious timing of Lily's torturous ending of trying desperately to have a child—*just as I become pregnant.* At any other time in our lives this conversation and her advice would've been surely more convoluted. It seems to me to be a fatalistic moment and not for nothing did these two events over-lap. I now feel that much more confident and sure and, of course, adoring the permission and buttressing of the idea of keeping this baby, who, I must state and will always find solace in, was created by two people wildly in love and connected in spirit.

So there it is, the biggest most important decision of my life hang-ing in the air—Could I possibly consider having and raising this baby alone?

I go back and forth, weighing all the issues into the wee hours. With the exception of speaking to my sister Lily, I want to make this decision privately. It's not something you just throw out at a brunch with friends to get feedback, like, "Should I buy a leopard trench from the new Lanvin collection?" Nope. *Pas du tout.*

I desperately want to speak to Blake and see how he feels. I call him and he says, "Tell your family and friends that I am trying to wrap my head around this." I joke that our child will surely have a great sense of humor, and he jokes, "He will need it!"

Yet the life force inside me gets its voice, and all I hear is, "Come on, Momma, we can do this," from my much yearned-for child. Every mother in this precarious scenario, undoubtedly, knows this unique experience and the inescapable power of it. A man, probably, would not. It defines what it is to be a mother. And there was no more self-questioning. I firmly decided that even with Blake's nonpasticipation, I was going to have this child "all by me ownself," as I used to say as a kid.

This is huge. This is both strangely freeing and, frankly, a tinge sad. On one side I feel very pleased to be living in a modern era where this is accepted and possible. And yet, good god, just where did I go so off-the-charts wrong that I am going it alone and making this monumental leap? And, more to that, is it entirely selfish of me to have a child from the outset, without a father figure in place?

I lean on my knowledge and certainty that I will shower this child with all the love that I have so deeply held for him *or her* through the, literally, decades of dreaming of becoming a mother. For I am one of those women who—call me a total sap, it's fair—has written reams of poetry over the years about my longing for a child. In the name of full disclosure, I am also one of those women who chooses new baby names every few years (at eighteen, I was sold on Jessie and Ryan), and, god, I can't believe I'm admitting this, I even bought a tiny Bonpoint sweater and bonnet set when I was twenty-five, for the child I wanted to one day have. It's now been dragged around the world and is ragged and quite dusty and smells like a young cow since it's sat in my Louis Vuitton (*vache*-lined) train case for nearly fifteen years. At any rate, I am feeling confident I can do this; I can be totally giving, committed, and nurturing. I am confident all my friends will bolster my decision because, frankly, it's not that astonishing, since I have always been very nontraditional, to put it nicely.

The clincher is my mother, Susan. Who, I must state, is my hero and the most amazing woman I've ever known. Brilliant, beautiful, the most wonderful mother, and, simultaneously, a well-known and successful artist.

My mother is a phenomenon, unparalleled in all arenas—great cook, extraordinarily elegant, brilliant, hilarious, an expert on the Florentine Medici, the most giving and loving mother one could hope for or imagine and now, tragically, in the last stages of Alzheimer's.

I know. Gutting. The once most vibrantly alive, ravishing woman, the toast of the town and the best friend to all of us five kids, has been ruthlessly diminished to a mere shell of her self. Unable now to walk, feed, or dress herself, she lingers on in a private world where she can barely express herself. To see this decline in anyone you know is devastating, and to have it be your mother cruelly lashes at your sense of a loving god or even a just world. My dear momma is *living,* if you can call it that, in my hometown of Lake Geneva, Wisconsin, where she is adored and endlessly nurtured by her devoted husband, my stepfather, as well as tended to at home by a nurse.

Momma rarely speaks, especially into the phone, but this is all we have when I'm so far away. It kills me. I was the baby and she was my best friend, mentor, therapist, and champion at every turn. To see this vivacious and dazzling woman so terribly weakened and to not even be able to *really* talk with her is the greatest tragedy of my life. Especially now at this crossroads, when I find myself old enough to truly appreciate my parents but still young enough to want their advice and wisdom.

Thus, I try to reach her; seeking somehow to find her, in that husk that is her body and mind shutting down. She can *listen* as someone holds the phone to her ear but will often just start to cry or say, "Tony!" her husband's name, over and over. It's wrenching. I make the call and, as ever, begin to tell her about my life and try to find the words, any words, that might bring her out. My brother Andy holds the phone for her since her hands can no longer grasp and are curling up into fists; those hands that once painted with such precision, gorgeous children's books of exquisite detail. Vicious disease!

I'm her youngest; she has to remember my voice, right? I ramble on and tell her about Blake. I go on and on, that he was fascinating, successful as hell, hilarious, so not the playboy type; how, adorably, on our first date, his voice and hand quivered with nervousness and how I loved that he had a strong silent nature. Finally, I just blurt out to my mom that it is now confirmed that I am pregnant and that Blake, despite having sired our baby, isn't exactly popping champagne in celebration. "Momma, my time to have a baby is just running out, and I feel like this happened for a reason now, and I am going to keep it even if he apparently isn't interested in participating on a daily basis."

I blather on, though the words really hang in the air as there is no hope for a response. "I think I can have a baby alone. I can't fathom my life without a child, and you showed me, *all of us,* that it's pure magic. The best that life offers. Momma, you set the bar so high as an extraordinary mother. If I can take some of all that you taught me, I will be a good mother bear. I should do it, right?" I trail off as she starts to murmur inaudibly.

Then, "There is no right man . . . so, yes," she says, and I am dumbfounded. Flabbergasted. I can't believe my ears. She hasn't really spoken or made any rational comments since Christmas two years ago, when she looped all her hoop earrings onto her sweater (which was cool, actually) and said nothing save for pronouncing the stuffing "foul!" which made us all fall down laughing. So *her.* Always a surprising, witty woman. And now she had said this to me. As a child of a mother with Alzheimer's, you leap at this, you feel honored she spoke to *you*. You cling to this as though she will keep speaking . . . and you take it as gold.

I did. And I felt her full consent, her approval swept up with her wisdom. And I felt her holding my hand all through the process that followed.

Chapter 1

"Childhood is the sleep of reason."

—Jean-Jacques Rousseau

I am SO NOT one of those people who can wait until the precious and precarious first three months pass to tell people I am having a baby. After making my life-changing and monumental decision, I call my *copine* Zola here in Paris, call back my sister Lily, and call my BFF (friends since we were twelve) in Los Angeles, Kathy. There's lots of howling with joy interspersed with plenty of serious candor. My euphoria has even affected my beloved cat, Verdi, who is ricocheting off the walls and virtually up to the seventeenth-century *poutres* ("exposed beams") with shared enthusiasm, which I find endearingly empathetic.

With so much to think about, plan, and ponder, I can't even stay in my apartment. Too much energy coursing through me to be contained in these four walls. I race over to Zola's flat—amazingly, one street away—since I feel like I'm going to explode with pure joy if I don't have an outlet to revel in this, the most marvelous of events. (Mental block on baby's father exit? Oh yes. Coping tools working at precision efficiency, thanks.)

My *chère amie* Zola is just, hands down, the most loyal friend and while we are opposites in a lot of ways, we get on like a house on fire. She's funny, smart, and, while sometimes she could be accused of dressing a bit like a secretary, she's an amazing partner in crime. Read: she will meet me for drinks at Café de Flore after work on a Wednesday night and bounce around St. Germain until we end the night having danced until 3 A.M. Some could even say we are each other's surrogate family or even act like a couple, since we buy each other heaps of birthday and Christmas gifts, celebrate New Year's Eve by making an elegant dinner *chez elle* and going out *après*. Every Saturday we window shop, lunch *en plein air,* and run errands like an old couple.

She is so *in* as godmother for my baby, since she will be wonderfully doting and a great counterbalance to my influences. And on a silly note, I love her name (I think people often evolve into the name they are given, and that's why I'm choosing my baby's name with the greatest care). Zola was named by her parents for the writer, Émile Zola. How elegant is that? Yet, I am eternally grateful that my mother didn't name me after her favorite writer, Dostoevsky. Without doubt, I would've been doomed to a life of bad teeth and chin hair.

Zola is a petite, red-haired, porcelain-skinned beauty if ever there was one; part Debra Messing and part Vargas calendar girl. Interesting footnote—for some totally absurd reason there is a French myth that women with red hair smell particularly bad. And in the always twisted way that the Gallic put their spin on an idea, the not-so-appealing smell is supposedly from redheads' nether regions, or, as they say in slang, from *en bas* ("downstairs"). What a crazy crock, huh? And even sillier, this odd belief *still* permeates the minds of some of the less educated souls of France. I know this because of many a story from Zola, where she regales me with tales of ex-boyfriends being pleasantly surprised that she is as fresh and fragrant as an orchid.

Alas, after door codes galore and passing by the concierge, who always glares at me like she's been reading my diary or something, I burst through the door of Zola's tiny jewel box of an apartment and we grab arms and dance in circles, chanting, "No way!! No way! A baby!" I'm seriously relieved she is being so supportive and open-minded about all this, since she is more than a bit conservative and a smidge religious—*when she wants to be*. I am beginning to accept that this whole "baby solo" idea is really out there for some people.

We sit down on her canopied bed, the only place for two people to sit together in the three-hundred-square-foot studio apartment.

"Wine? Champagne? Maybe just a sip?" she asks, since we are the most faithful drinking compatriots and always start off every rendez-vous with a glass in hand.

"No thanks, I am drunk on bliss and I am not going to risk anything with this baby. I'm going to stop my daily runs, I'm even going to stop riding on scooters . . . Oh god, I'm going to be a mom . . . Do you believe it? Strangely, I'm not even nervous, I'm just so excited to be pregnant. Do you think Blake will come around? Truthfully, he speaks so glowingly about his kids, it's just endearing beyond words," I say, falling back into the masses of silk pillows and shams.

"You know, it's impossible to say, but I've seen you two together; you are an amazing couple and he clearly loved you. But you can't bet on it or hope for it, since it would be agony if it wasn't to happen. You sure you want to do this, Kiki? It's going to be really hard sometimes . . . more than we can imagine, probably. You know you won't really have a framework of help in family close at hand. I will always be there for you, but I know you, you like your freedom, and your whole life will change. What will your father say?" she asks, pouring herself a second glass of the pretty decent Aligoté from the Nicolas wine shop on rue du Bac (4.20 euros a bottle, *pas mal*).

"I know . . . *I know*. I am ready to do this solo if need be. I've wanted to be a mother since I was twenty-two, and I am so bored with all the self-focus. With only having my own little life to think of. God knows, you'd agree, I've been killing relationships left and right for years by trying to push silly Frenchmen too quickly to the let's-move-in-marry-and-have-a-baby stage, when all they want is to have an affair with an American girl for the unique experience of it. Let's face it, when you're careening toward forty, you know who you are, what you are capable of, your strengths, weaknesses, and what you really hold dear and precious. Hell, I truly believe this happened now because it was meant to be. And let's face it, I am not going to let the sea of waffly Frenchmen ruin my shot at motherhood. Frankly, most of the men I've dated here are too immature emotionally to become great fathers and husbands. Not a one of them I have known since I moved here eight years ago has ever gone on to a monogamous relationship, let alone marriage." We nod, after briefly running through mental files and realizing this is true for us both. Bizarre.

I continue with my defensive diatribe. "And eventually when I *do* get to date again, having a child by myself will weed out those flakes and only leave men with integrity and decency. Right or *non*?" I say, with assuredness. That way of rationalizing every detail to my point of view is a big part of me, I fully admit.

Zola smiles slightly but her eyes quickly dart out the window, revealing a tinge of doubt at that last point. True enough, but I let it go. I'm swimming in blissful la-la land and nobody is going to squelch the joy of motherhood for me! I am not some wishy-washy twenty-something trying to find myself or thinking a child is a great accessory. I am probably more passionate about wanting a child than anyone I have known, and I am ready for the judgments and even the scorn that I may encounter. Bottom line, if I listened to everyone else's opinion my whole life, I would never have the life I do have. I'd be back in Wisconsin, working in, hmm, retail? Or as a bank teller? Oh god, horrors.

Zola and I wrap up the night taking another pee test (positive again, hip hip hurrah!) and making a list of what to do next. Blood test for true confirmation and go see her OB-GYN; as a self-employed artist, I am not—and this isn't very clever of me—in the French health-care system, so I only see doctors in the US when I go back for annual visits. This means that my pregnancy and the birth will all be out of pocket for me, but get this? It's still about half to a third as expensive as having a child in the US—even when you're laying out the cash as a foreigner. And I am dead set on an American hospital as the birth place since no way am I going to have my baby in one of the dozens of hospitals in Paris that don't even have air-conditioning—not to mention that I need to know 100% of what the hell the doctors are saying. Dilated to six centimeters and in the final hours of giving birth is not a time to be asking for a translator. Once I fainted while running, and the ambulance doctor kept saying, "*Bouge pas!*" ("Don't move!") as I wrestled to sit up while he was taking my blood pressure. Alone and terrified, I thought he was saying "*bougie pas,*" which translates, sort of, to "no candles." Point made.

With energy to burn, Zola and I dashed out to an invite-only cocktail party at the Armani boutique on the *coin* ("corner") of boulevard St. Germain and boulevard Raspail. Never a bad idea to celebrate something momentous in a divine setting and surrounded by glamour and beauty. Honestly, I would've been just as tickled to loiter around a Greyhound bus station in Detroit for all my happiness, but you work with what ya got, right? Of course, I found it not at all difficult to pass on the champagne and still have a great time. Nevertheless, it should be noted, this is landmark HUGE for me, *très* shocking, since I think of champagne as one of my four food groups, the others far less glam, one being baguettes, another, tuna.

The tiny baby inside me had already taken hold and was spreading the joy. That night, I was, *dare I say* (and I can, because it is so bloody rare)—I was unstoppable! Met a flurry of new interesting women friends, a bevy of handsome successful men. A few of us zipped off in a friend's Maserati to a dinner for twelve at Société, and I was . . . well, what we all want to be at a party—our best selves *ever,* fun, clever, and fabulously happy. To crown the evening, the king of the Parisian social world, Daniel Marie Rouyer, saw me leaving after we finished dinner, stood up, blew me a kiss, and said, "*Bonsoir,* Kiki, the Queen of St. Germain!" This fleeting annointment (and maybe he says it to every girl) was like a kiss good-bye to the brow of the girl I wanted to be when I moved here, became if only for a blink, and now was very quietly leaving to become a mother. Indeed, it was my quintessential last grand soiree: a final hurrah and, paradoxically, the first magical evening of what I consider my new life.

My new life *avec bébé* was cooking along beautifully, if you don't linger too long on the fact there are generally two people sharing the extraordinary joys of pending parenthood. (Though, thankfully Blake has stepped up and done a great many things for this baby's future.) And I say that not carelessly, since I won't dwell on it again, but Blake's absence was heartbreaking and not just for the innocent child we created but also for me—I loved him terribly and mourned losing him with great seriousness. But I am a woman who picks up and carries on. I have had my heart broken before, and I survived, and now I need to be everything stable, healthy, and good for this baby.

Zola was my rock through this tenuous period. Ever at the ready with an ear, a hug, and support as the weeks passed. She was a freaking saint to offer not just to accompany me to my first OB-GYN appointment in three weeks but also to be with me during the birth. That is a true and rare friend. To have a child alone is one thing, but to imagine giving birth alone with no one to share that experience? Oh god, that would feel really heartbreaking. As this pregnancy pushes forward, I'm starting to really see that unquestionably sad moments will occur. I just want to sidestep as many as is feasible and make this unique adventure as joyful as possible. As the pregnancy books say, the fetus can be influenced by your hormonal mood swings as well as the happiness-inducing cortisones your body releases.

Mental note—in short, don't cry or stress. This proves excruciatingly hard at the five-week mark, when my adored cat of fifteen years, Verdi, falls ill with a stomach tumor and dies. Fuckity, fuck, fuck. I'm shaken to my core since suddenly I'm really, really alone in my tiny world. No man, no family, no faithful cat that I adore. Her presence in my life was incredibly like a ballast, and here I had to kiss her goodbye as she struggled for her last breath? Torture. I battled for the baby inside me *not* to sob and wail with the crushing sadness. Verdi was so magnificent, she deserved to be mourned with a full emotional tribute, and yet I couldn't allow myself to go there. I stifled my grief as best I could. I could hardly breathe that day she died as I operated in a trance, tossing out her toys, litter box, and blankets. The apartment felt empty without her, and I didn't even want to leave it, to avoid experiencing at my return the absence of her delightful meow that had always greeted my every arrival. I will always feel that this cat, *who knew me better than most people,* took her quick and quiet departure sensing that I was going to have a baby and that she and I were closing the chapter of life as the best of buddies.

After that bleak week, I had a trip to the French OB-GYN, who confirmed by sonogram that there was a baby in our midst. Hurrah all over again!!

Only in France do you sit in the waiting room and read a selection of magazines like *Paris Match, Uomo Vogue,* and *Gala* while sipping espresso, before being told by the female doctor, "Indeed, you are *enceinte.* I advise you to feel free to drink a bit of wine each day to relax, and if you smoke, cut down to four cigarettes a day. You need not worry about soft cheese or sushi but *mon dieu,* don't gain more than twelve kilos during the pregnancy!" (That's a skimpy twenty-six pounds.) She followed up by showing me exhibit A; a photo of her own darling child and saying with that Gallic pride that is generally-to-always tiresome, "I myself, gained only six kilos and was in my favorite Chanel skirt the day after giving birth." I must add she looked at my already burgeoning belly with a raised eyebrow, as if to say, "Oh, you Americans really let yourselves go when you get pregnant." Ei yi yi.

Staggered and stunned by this whole experience, I vowed to stick with American doctors from that day forward, since this is not a time to *feign* embracing the French way; I can adhere to all the French rules here, like "a woman never pours herself wine at a party or a dinner out" and the rigid, "arrive no sooner than twenty minutes late for a dinner as a courtesy to the host," but I think I will stick with some of the good ole USA's pregnancy advisements, *merci.*

Humorous detail I shan't soon forget: on the way to the doctor's office, I was hotly pursued by a fairly attractive businessman, who essentially chased me down to the very door of the doctor's office and said, "I really like your skirt." (Italian eyelet in virginal white, thanks. Color chosen intentionally to counteract new awareness that single motherhood may be odd or racy to my new doctor). "May I have your cell number?"

As ever, I always ask that a man gives me his number so as to not be put in the position of waiting for a call or giving out my number. (Control issues much? Oh yes!) Anyway, this was more to ditch him politely, but love this reply of his, without missing a beat, "I am afraid that would be a bad idea as I am married, so I would rather take yours to avoid complications."

Only in France! Complications? It was almost like a sign that going it alone into pregnancy with the crop of absurd men out there was a mighty fine idea after all! But truthfully, despite the exhilarating news that I was absolutely preggers, I was starting to reel emotionally from all the stress of losing Verdi and the lonely path that lay ahead. So when Zola suggested we take a short holiday together to have fun, get away, and *tourner la page,* as they say, I was game. Entirely.

"Kiki, we could go to St. Trop, I know all the right people to go to Rex . . . blah blah," she puts out there, as for unknown reasons she loves St. Tropez madly. Sitting by the pool at Nikki Beach or Club 55 in Chanel head-to-toe is her complete bliss. I am the dead opposite in every respect. I prefer a week on the tiny island of Île d'Yeu, off the coast of Nantes, watching, in rain slickers, as the first fishermen set off in their tuna boats on cold wet mornings. Voraciously reading books, devouring the local fig tarts, and scooting around on bikes in the classic French striped tees that are worn like uniforms on the island. Despite loving glam events I believe vacations should be just that; the antithesis of regular life.

"Ah, that would be a *big fat* no, as one, I am a *big fat* cow now that I stopped running and am eating like a wildebeest and two, you know

I loathe places like that. Never have been and never want to go to St. Tropez. I'm sure it was amazing in the fifties, but it's really nouveau riche now, *non?*" I reply, trying to just murder off that discussion, as I unexpectedly catch a glimpse of my new chubby face in the mirror over her fireplace. Jawline? Gone. That was frigging fast. Just how fat will I get? I always thought I could keep it together and be fit and chic when I got pregnant, and I was dead wrong. I'm already falling apart physically. Lovely.

"Well then, where? Maybe London again? We always have a rage in London," she counters.

"Oh dear, no London. I would surely try to show up at Blake's doorstep, which is ridiculous. No, I'm in no shape—*literally*—or mood for a 'rage.' Doll, why don't we just go to a château in the country somewhere? Or a spa? Isn't there a chic Givenchy spa in Versailles?" I ask, clearly assuming the air of my once far wealthier self as I struggle with grasping my new identity.

"Cool idea. Okay. As you like, I'm in. But maybe Hubert can come by for a night or two?" she says, referring to her aristo-rat boyfriend.

I nod. But I hope she can take a break from him for more than a day or two. I know she is afraid he will go to some club and replace her in an instant—since that's exactly how they met. That fear always goes hand in hand with the relationship when you've met your amour in a club at 1:00 A.M.

We plop down on the floor and go online to book a reservation. Not so fast, since it's like 320 euros a night and that's all I could possibly spare for an *entire* holiday. After more searching, we blow off the beautiful beach towns in Brittany and Normandy, like Deauville and La Baule, which are almost all fully booked, scary pricey, and long train rides. We settle on a charming castle, Château Hotel Mont Royal, just thirty-five minutes from Paris in Chantilly. *Parfait!* At just

90 euros a night, with a posh buffet each morning, the price is a total steal in August. (Reason being all of France flocks to the beaches and it's just a nineteenth-century castle, not seventeenth-century, for example, so it's considered not exactly high end—so many castles, so little time.)

That settled, I find I'm positively elated to take a break from my apartment, where I miss Verdi madly and where worries plague me for the future. *Au revoir* reality.

The château does not disappoint; set on a high hill overlooking a lush forest below, it's sublime to just, well, eat ghastly decadent breakfasts, swim in the pool, hang poolside . . . and luxuriate in some peace. It's divine to just dial down the constant need to be self-aware, and, indeed, I end up wearing the same cotton sundress for days, soaking in the ability to just *be,* to not be seen or on display, as one feels compelled to in St. Germain.

Like a bit of a kook, Zola can't bear it, and with a suitcase of strapless dresses, a toilet bag full of makeup, and wildly eager to go show Hubert her new slimmer body care of a rigid protein-only diet, she flees back to Paris after a day. I stay on alone. This is fine. Solo is my new world, and this is a great time to embrace it. Not to mention, as we had traveled to the château by train and taxi, we had no means of leaving the grounds, so I was finding it none too thrilling to be trapped in a castle with a girlfriend whose whole agenda was refusing great food in lieu of boiled eggs and sending texts to her boyfriend. (Insert catty hiss.)

These last few weeks, despite her help and friendship, it's quickly becoming apparent to me that Zola and I are going in different directions in life and there is no denying that this pregnancy, this baby is going to be a personal journey and I won't be the same person in even five months' time. Already, there is this palpable shift in my ability to deal with the superficial—and that entails watching Zola starve herself and play all the necessary games to simply intrigue a French boyfriend. Now it irks me. All the catering to men and the back-and-forth manipulation that is so integral to relationships in France seems so absurd once you step away from it for a reprieve. Amazingly, now pregnant, away from Paris, and alone, I can extract myself from the mentality that one has to adopt on every level to live as an expat in Paris, and it's an eye opener. The fog has cleared, it is refreshing as hell.

In my days at the château, I find immeasurable solace in walking through the woods, listening to the varied calls of the birds, noticing the different songs that wake you at dawn versus the soothing symphony of the whippoorwills in the evening. I watch the rain-filled storm clouds gather at sunset, and, with my hand on my small belly, I smile at the wind that whips my hair into loose tangles. Mornings are spent picking wildflowers to put by my bedside and afternoons are whiled away with book in hand. The fresh air is like an elixir and the smell of blooming lilacs and lavender quiet all the worries and sadness that were so in step with my daily life in the city. It's good to be alone, hear the quiet voices in me that are drowned out by the drama of Paris.

Living in a big city, it's easy to forget that time spent solitary in the midst of nature's offerings is truly enchanting, moments that are completely free, private, and revitalizing to your spirit. I needed this break more than I knew, as instantly this reconnection with the exquisite beauty of the wilderness brings me back to my own childhood in Wisconsin. Recollections of myself as a wily ten-year-old tomboy climbing cliffs, discovering mossy caves, and building tree forts in the forest of our summer home flood my thoughts. They were the times that gave me the elements of *self* that are my true core. I am not the equivalent of my closet's contents nor even the image I present. I am still that tomboy kid who just thought it might be great to see what being a glam diva in Paris might feel like. And I guess, unlike some people, I just went for it and, by sheer luck, it came to be my reality. But now, as I embark on being a *maman,* I wonder if I want to keep being this hipster chic person or if I could, even if I wanted to? Paris was a dream the way I had lived it, but my images of motherhood aren't as connected to living in Paris. It's more about being a parent who can offer walks through the woods than dragging my child to Café de Flore while I try to keep up a social life. Being here, getting dirt under my nails and thistles on my pant cuffs, reminds me how terribly precious and vital playing in nature is to a child's soul—building curiosity, independence, and imagination.

In this day and age, of a global need for preservation and awareness of our environment, do I really want to raise my child in a busy city in the midst of car exhaust and car alarms? And in a small apartment? Are the advantages of life in Paris more valuable than those of the midwestern countryside? I really don't know. And since I am the only one who has to make all these monumental decisions, I start to feel the extreme weight of responsibility. Scary as hell. I welcome accountability, but it is daunting after so many years alone *and* becoming a parent alone.

Watching a dandelion teeter under the weight of a lusciously fat bumble bee, suddenly, I hear a new voice of calming intuition pipe up, "You have to take it slow, let things unfold, and listen to your heart. As long as there is a healthy child who is lavished with love, the pieces will fall into place . . . *souffle.*" (BTW, that doesn't mean "go make a soufflé"; it actually translates to "exhale," . . . seems my intuition is fairly fluent, cool.) Exactly what my mother would say, holding my hand and with a gentle caress of my furrowed brow. What I would give to speak with her about all of this.

Amid all these heady thoughts, I feel a tinge of morning sickness cresting. What the F?

I am—or this baby is—craving, of all things, circus peanuts. Yeah, the barfo neon orange candy of pure puffy sugar that not so shockingly isn't on the room service menu. Proving you can take the girl out of the Midwest but you can't take the lowbrow palate out of the . . . good god. This kid in my belly is already making me laugh out loud.

Chapter 2

"Children and drunks always speak the truth."

—PROVERB

Back in St. Germain. Four months pregnant!

No doubt about it, pregnancy does a lot of wack-a-doodle things to your body, your skin, your hair . . . your mind!

Case in point: This morning I managed to rally out of this new tired-to-the-bone phase to *attempt* to plod through my daily yoga stretches. Frankly, "pregnancy yoga stretching" is more of a name I've given to my ritual of trying on my increasingly tight running tank top and shorts to see my ever-growing belly. I sort of look at it from all angles, mentally chart the thrilling changes, and wrap up with casually taking a pass on the grueling process of exerting any energy. Folding my body into an origami swan is a nice idea, but somehow having purchased *and* thumbed through the *Pregnancy Yoga* coffee table book *and* changing out of pajamas feels like enough.

And let me just say, I laughed uproariously today as said shorts now look so ridiculously tight, I thought I had them on backwards. Literally took them off and tried them on again. Nope. Just stomach and bum shape shifting into the unrecognizable. But today, I kid you not, my belly is square. I have seen low bellies and high bellies but never angular. Is this at all normal? Maybe this is just another one of those zillion details to being pregnant that no one ever tells you about and you just discover by yourself as you go, and think, "No way! Say it's not so!" Much like the unwelcome news that your nipples will get bigger *and* darker (does anyone ever want *either*?) or that your hair gets as greasy as if you're conditioning it with olive oil. And then there's the fact that your sweat kind of smells less than lovely. Hilarious, when you think about it; you're damn lucky you are *already* pregnant since nobody would even want to f#@k you now!

But back to being square-bellied—a wave of slight concern takes hold that something is going wrong with my pregnancy. Not unusual. As any mother-to-be knows, new and irrational worries spring up through any *and every* given day—that taking an aspirin will give baby a cleft palate, that eating lobster may result in a baby with swimmerets and gills. Even after the precarious first trimester, the worries go on and on! Or maybe it's just me. I always tend to anticipate the worst so as to not be sideswiped by bad news. Yep, set the bar low and you're never disappointed. That self-hatched philosophy can be applied to everything, from dinner parties to a blind date!

Anyway, pooped-tired today and level-4 worried, I opted out of washing my hair. Looking to take a page from what I like to think was my previous occasionally glam self, I grabbed a fabulous vintage Pucci scarf to wrap around my hair, in what *had been* a very St. Tropez or vacationing-in-Capri style. Tossed on some slim silver hoops and glanced in the mirror before heading out the door. HOLY . . . crap!

What the . . . ?

I was a dead ringer for an old fortune-teller!

This "look" isn't working *at all*. This must be part of that transitioning-to-motherhood process, where you stop wearing even remotely sexy clothes because they simply feel *and look* ridiculous. Cue: suddenly starting to resemble your mother. Hmm.

Okay. Noted, guess this all goes in the "pregnancy changes" category as surely as my miniskirts and trendy sassy camisoles go in the *poubelle* ("trash"). Some of these changes you anticipate and revel in, like the glowing radiant happiness that makes you exude an internal light like a beacon, and then there's the swelled, bigger breasts that are so firm you think, "Well, I'm just *lov*-ing this." And then the not so fabulous, like, in tandem with my cubist belly, I have instantly acquired what can only be described as a huge monkey butt.

No, really, all of a sudden I am sporting a caboose that is not at all booty-licious but more orangutan hindquarters in both size and shape. *Thankfully not in color! Good lord!* Who knew I would be bursting out front and back? Maybe it's nature's way of counterbalancing the burgeoning stomach. Beats me, but it's weird as hell, and since I obviously haven't yet acquired a truly obvious state of round baby belly, I am looking an awful lot like I just let myself go terribly. Call me shallow—*and you wouldn't be the first*—but sometimes I wish I could sport a sash that says, *Je suis enceinte, je ne suis pas une vache* ("I am pregnant, I am not a cow").

Silly of me to be self-conscious but pretty much everyone in my neighborhood is well aware I have neither a husband nor even a boyfriend, so I am surely becoming the subject of gossip. By the way, a hint of both thinking you are the first woman to ever have a baby and a tinge of paranoia is yet another fun, fun, fun aspect of pending-motherhood behavior.

On the gossip and judgment front: Lord knows the hypersnooty *femme* that owns the *boulangerie* on rue de l'Université is blatantly appalled to see my girth expanding so rapidly, as yesterday, when I ordered up *deux baguettes avec jambon et gruyère,* a mere appetizer to my lunch these days, as ghastly as that is, Madame de Bakery Bitch pointed to my gaping jeans waistband (albeit hooked with a rubber band as I saw in some magazine and thought quite a cool way to buy some time before elastic pants from hell) and bellowed, "*Mon dieu, attention! Ce n'est pas très elegante!*"

I was stunned. For starters, no one in the USA would ever make such a comment, second, she should be *hyper*sweet to me since I drop, like, 15 euros a day at her bakery, trying to keep up with my voracious hunger (very likely paying for her fat baker sons' numerous tattoos). And third, who are you to critique me, you weird old bird who dyes her hair Ronald McDonald red and wears perfume that smells like an old folks' home!

I unleash hell *here*—in written form—as for some reason ever since I moved to Paris I just cannot go off on the locals with some clever quip as I might be inclined when one of the vast sea of injustices is thrust upon me. I guess it's because I think I will get a past participle or tense wrong and will be made the fool *twice* over. (A perfect example of this was when I was living in NYC and my boyfriend and I passed a construction site where two workers were in a full-on argument. One Armenian-looking guy yelled at the other, "Mother fucker YOU!" My boyfriend and I fell apart laughing, suggesting to the guy, "It's, 'you motherfucker.'" You gotta get the pronouns in the right place, cowboy, or you look like the idiot. Mental note cemented, so it's kind of a drag, really, to feel possibly inept at slandering the guilty. So I simply took

the high road, as I like to rationalize it, and replied curtly that I was
pregnant. She glared at me as though she didn't believe me and snorted
off aghast. Fun. Way to rejoice in the thrilling marvel of the glory of
life growing inside me, lady. Whatever. That's the thing about the rare
French snob, you cannot ever decipher where the elitism springs from,
so just write it off to DNA and move on or you'll drive yourself batty.

But back to this pregnancy of mine already in progress. Let's just talk
a minute about the wild changes in your skin. Day and night, I slather on
huile d'amande all over my belly like I'm basting a turkey in major hope of
avoiding those vicious stretch marks that I am so prone to. FYI, during
my college years, I gained the infamous freshman fifteen and then *another*
five pounds to set myself apart from the norm, as has always been my
way, and, mother of god, I still have the battle marks on my hips of gaining and losing those Pepperidge Farm pounds. Side note: Once, I dated a
man twelve years younger than I, and he noticed them in the morning
light *après un soir d'amour* and gasped, "Jesus, what happened to you?!"

Oh lovely. Nothing like having to explain them to a man so young
and naive that 1) I had both shoes AND jeans older than him and 2) he
thinks Daniel Craig is the *first* James Bond.

At any rate, even the skin on my face is starting to loosen and sag,
and I keep catching glimpses of my new Sharpay-esque crow's-feet and
think, What the hell, I am taking the best care of myself of my life! I
don't drink at all, I'm being ridiculously healthy, and now I have aged a
virtual decade since that pee'd-on pregnancy stick came back positive
four months ago.

For me, still theoretically single, though when baby arrives will be
a *maman plus une,* I don't think I can quite fall apart yet. Damn, for as
much as I am so terrifically elated to become a mother, sometimes the
pending single mother aspect is quite daunting. I know I already hashed
this all out months ago—I had to make that, I like to think, courageous

decision to say, single or not, I was going to be a mother. For all the details that I have come to terms with in going it alone on this magical path of parenthood, I know how vital daily contact with an adoring father is to all children, and to start out this child's life without that is a gnawing ache. To be honest, I can only hope that some lovely man will take us on one day, and that to worry about it all my waking hours now is just negative energy. So I hit a mental pause on that monumental worry and look ahead to the future . . . I must continue with my life-long running theme of eternal optimism! Does that sound in staunch opposition to my previous mantra of setting the bar low? Fine, let's write it off to hormones. If changing one's mind is a woman's prerogative, when pregnant, that should be times one hundred, or one big fat free ride on all behavioral mood swings! So then, wrapping up my laundry list of "baby on board" (and god don't you loathe those signs in the back of cars? They are as tiresome as people who say the cliché, "to put it in a nutshell") changes—I now crave, of all things . . . the smell of toilet paper. And yes, I am deadly aware that this is *so* not chic, barely a step above those circus peanuts, *and* terribly bizarre. Hey, at least it's not as wacky as some women, who I've read actually crave dirt. Eating dirt? Surely high in fiber but *come on.*

So there I am, strolling down boulevard St. Germain on a sunny afternoon with the slight fall chill of an autumn wind—what I call football weather from my days growing up in Wisconsin—and I am literally carrying a huge wad of toilet tissue in my pocket that I sneak sniffs of . . . oh, about every ten steps. Obviously ditched the old fortune-teller look and opted for the more anonymous: beret with a black turtleneck, a pair of black wool leggings, and the Max Mara trench coat I got for a steal at a sample sale in NYC fifteen years ago. Damn! You know you're getting old when you realize that half your wardrobe is the same age as the models on the cover of *Cosmopolitan.*

Snorting up more of the fresh fragrance as I pass by Brasserie Lipp, it occurs to me that Martha Stewart cultists would probably find this T.P. obsession an appealing neat freak notion, but as I literally slept last night passionately groping a roll of Charmin as if it were a lover trying to flee, I did thank the lord that I haven't a husband who is observing all my ever-surprising new activities.

Side note anecdote on Martha Stewart: Back in my NYC days, when I somehow managed to intrigue an amazing, famous Frenchman for, well, an incredible five years, Martha Stewart became a fixture in my social world. Which I have to say wasn't heaps of fun but always provided me with plenty of Martha stories that amused my design world coworkers. I first met her at my boyfriend's ten-year anniversary dinner at Nobu. Truth be told, he and I had been together two months by then and this was our first big outing in the milieu of the grand world of successful people known worldwide by first name only. I was freaking nervous as hell to see the dinner was about sixteen guests and all of them über famous but me. Lovely when one is forty years old and secure, but at the time I was twenty-nine and feeling overwhelmed by it all; I was trying to appear cool but was, frankly, a total wreck. My boyfriend sat next to me, which I thought was going to be calming yet turned out to be painful as he chatted away to his ex, Diandra Douglas, in French all night long, which at the time, I couldn't understand. Annoying, with a capital *A*. So, I sat there, smiling and attempting to keep up conversation with the likes of the architect Richard Meier and the master photographer Victor Skrebneski. For about five whole minutes, I was thinking I was holding my own and starting to feel some peace at the dinner. In retrospect, I think there was only about three hundred seconds of my feeling calm all evening.

I must confess, having only—in my previously normal, struggling designer lifestyle—walked past Nobu wishing I could even see in, let alone dine there, I was rather a Japanese dining novice. With my new feigned façade of appearing cavalier, I poured my tiny clay carafe of soy sauce into a tiny sake cup and drank it in a flourish when a toast was being made. Lo and behold, I sooo didn't expect to be imbibing a lifetime quota of salty soy sauce in one gulp and was overtaken by a biting gag-grimace that only massive fermented sodium can create—an "I could well vomit" expression. Unpleasant but unnoticed by all, I told myself, putting the tiny cup down. Until . . . Martha Stewart in all her "sisterhood with women is clearly bullshit" glory, sitting across from me, chose to laugh uproariously and announce with a booming voice to the ENTIRE table, "Kiki just poured a big cup of soy sauce and drank the whole thing . . . Oh my goodness, I am sorry, Kiki . . . I couldn't take my eyes off the sight." Everyone was fairly amused as I gushed, red-faced, blabbering about the clay pot resembling the sake one . . . and blah, blah blah.

My boyfriend was clearly embarrassed for me (and for himself). He smiled faintly and falsely and swung back to the infinitely more sophisticated Diandra. I clearly failed the dinner with the grown-ups . . . and I decided then and there, Martha Stewart is a fucking bitch. I can support that—not so uncommon—opinion by her continued constant need at every social event, to get in the four-inch personal space reserved for lovers only of my then boyfriend. Every damn time we would be at the same party or dinner, she was on him like a magnet, so close her shadow was yards behind him, for god's sakes. Honestly, it freaked me out every time, and, like clockwork, I would make a scene in the car ride home about how much I loathed that sow. Dumb youth on my part. I only wish I hadn't been so young and made nervous by that world; if it all happened to me now, I would let it roll off my back.

But back to my new man-free, Martha-free life, where such matters need not concern me. Thank god.

Ahhh, it's a virtual delight to be able to crawl into bed at 8:00 P.M., the same hour when my previous self would just be picking out an over-the-top outfit for some madcap adventure into the wee hours. And how cool to not have to adhere to the rigors of upkeep that having a man in your life, or more so, *looking for one,* requires. I get to sport gigantic white grandma underwear, shave my legs once a week, let the bikini wax and pedicure appointments peter out to the occasional, wear sensible shoes and flannel pajamas, and basically take a welcome pass on dolling up every day, on the off chance I will run into the man of my dreams.

On that note—with my constant evil heartburn—it's a huge relief there is no lover/husband to sneak in for a smooch when horrific hormones are busy kicking back up dinner's curry shrimp. Yecch, I even repulse myself with the following confession. How do I put this? I chomp Siligaz, the equivalent of French Gas-X, by the handful since I am forever virtually propelled down the grand boulevards of Paris by what my grandma would call a spell of intestinal discomfort and the French call *ballonnement.* Yes, I am marching around with a balloon in my pants. You have to agree, the term *ballonnement* is hilarious and dead on. Frankly, I am getting more than a little tired of making my thrice-weekly trip to the *pharmacie* and having my pharmacist made all too aware that I need, once again, a huge box of the inelegant Senekot (laxatives), Siligaz, and six-pack of *papier hygiénique.* Chicer moments I have had.

Today, my thoughts race as I ignore that my beret is starting to make my head itch like the dickens. Oh, bloody hell, I forgot this chapeau-o-mine is wool and I cannot bear the feeling of wool since I got pregnant. Chalk that up with my new total disgust at the idea of eating eggs. If you think about it, it really is appalling. I mean, eating embryos. Blaargh . . . I could be sick right here. Absolutely not. I refuse to puke in front of the glorious St. Sulpice church. That would be as unchic as you can get. You know what? I am sick of trying to be chic all the time. It's exhausting. But Paris demands it. Surely it is no great shock that the level of service you get when sporting some slap-dash jeans and sneakers pales enormously to that when dressed to the nines.

I kick through the crackling red maple leaves that scatter underfoot and think, Oh my god, I cannot believe that this time next year I will be kicking through these leaves with *my* darling child in tow, giddily wading through, chattering away. Heaven! I can't wait to meet this little treasure . . . Wait, I guess he won't be walking by then, will he? There I go again, getting ahead of myself. Maybe motherhood will calm this ever-present constant impatience that is . . . Aagghh!

A gnarled tree root snags my shoe and sends me flying. "*Merde!*" I unconsciously yell out like a truck driver who has no sense of etiquette, as I feel my ankle twist like a weathervane in a storm. Shooting pain goes from zero to ninety and I damn near buckle trying to right myself and slog into something *semi-resembling* walking. Alrighty then, this is that softening muscle crap I read about. I grimace and feebly turn and drag myself toward home, abandoning my daily ritual of touring the fantastical, beyond your dreams baby store Bonpoint, on rue de Tournon. Pity, since, for any soon-to-be *maman,* it is like pure sweet heroin for an addict.

Halfway on my lumber-stagger home, I pass my beloved Café de Flore, longing to pop in for my once habitual *verre de sauvignon* but knowing a healthy baby is far more vital, even if all the French doctors I have met with say a few glasses of wine a day are okay. A *few.* They do draw the line at a bottle a day though. That's bananas! I'm so not going to grow this baby in an alcoholic amniotic bath, even if it would ease some of the anxiousness. FYI—I think this counts as my first unselfish act. Hurrah!

Surprise—musical interlude of Mozart's *Requiem*. I know, seems odd, but it's my cell phone ringtone. Going into the second stanza, my Nokia simultaneously vibrates in my breast pocket. (And that's about all the fun the neglected girls get these days.) I slide it open and check who the hell might be calling old abandoned *moi*. Frankly, since my days of jaunting about at the hot nightspots and fabulous art openings have ceased entirely, I am not so popular anymore. I don't mind. I am hatching a baby, my life dream has come true, so who needs that pack of raging hipsters. (Note—more rationalizing going on here, big time.)

Incoming call from Zola. I hit "answer" and say by way of greeting, "Girl! I miss you!" just as the clock of the St. Germain chimes noon, in its magical sonorous way that makes you question if it isn't really 1785.

"I know, me too. How are you feeling these days, Kiki? Still off to bed before I even get home from work? You know you could still go out . . . even date. In fact, sadly, the grand affair with Hubert is *fini*. He says I am *trop americane,* do you believe it? Come back and be my wing man—I need to find Mister Right pronto," she says, not so sad, but with a smile in her voice. This girl moves on quickly and with focus. I tend to linger and am way more nostalgic and reflective when a relationship ends. Even if I'm the one who chose to leave!

"No way, you're kidding. Over for sure? Half the time, men like Hubert just need some space. Though I do have to say, 'aristo' men do tend to feel family pressure to pair off with other French nobility. I know it's your thing to wish to marry into it, but I think they generally do opt for French wives," I say, having seen it spin out as such, dozens of times.

"I know, you're right, time to face the reality of it . . . tough to let the dream die and date commoners again!" she says, laughing. "But really, *how are you,* Kiki?"

"I'm pretty good. *Merci,* sweet girl. But regarding going out at night? I can't even fathom it; I'm so tired all the time. And as for *dating?!* You have got to be kidding! *Please.* Surely, you recall I accidentally tried that. You remember, that guy François-Olivier I met at the Armani party, we made plans for a dinner and eventually got to it when I was two months pregnant? Remember? I thought he knew I was pregnant and was chatting me up as a new friend and fellow painter. Arriving with flowers at the outset, all coo-coo for cocoa puffs over me with the first course, inviting me to the Maldives during *le plat,* and when I told him over *crème brulée* that I was *deux mois enceinte,* he gasped so deeply he almost inhaled the silverware off the table. Then he announced, 'If you are so independent, Kiki, then you can pay for yourself . . . and pay for wasting my evening.' And with that, he left me at the door of the restaurant. In the Marais! Charmer. No, I don't see dating in the cards right now," I reply, thinking back to what a staggering bummer that was. I mean I know it was awkward for him but he didn't have to be so rude! Frankly, I guess I can't imagine how bizarre that must've been for him.

"Oh, come on. You still look great . . . and why not stay in the game? Remember, Heidi Klum met Seal when she was pregnant and Linda Evangelista hooked up with Peter Morton of the Hard Rock Café when she was, like, eight months pregnant," Zola counters. (Zola has a curious trait; for all her analytical intelligence, she is strangely intrigued by inconsequential trivia. If you ever want to know who Lindsay Lohan is dating or the latest plastic surgery endeavor Nicole Kidman has partaken in, Zola is your girl.)

"Zola, you're nuts. Perhaps you are forgetting a crucial detail here; I am not, nor ever have been, a supermodel, which I think doesn't exactly help me in that *dating-while-pregnant* arena. And since having gained a mighty twelve pounds already, I have noticed that I attract only garbage men and the odd obese German tourist. And seriously, how do you ever have the time to keep abreast of these celebrity gossip bits, my dear?"

"Oh, I know. You, who shuns the pop icons of the modern world. I know you'd rather live trapped in a Merchant Ivory film, but these are modern times. Surely you can find a great man still. Belly and all. What about that hot British guy we met last time we went to London together? Ian of the sexy sideburns, right? You never told me if you spoke to him again," she adds.

"Oh, god. That was like a year ago, girl. Yes, he was beyond handsome and very funny, which I love, but check this out. Do you possibly recollect, when we met and I asked what he did for a living, he replied with that wicked saucy British accent and I took him to answer, 'I'm a barrister'? Which of course, is just beyond charming and highbrow, right? After a month of texting across the Channel like mad and a bevy of racy e-mails that had me swooning, I got him on the phone and when I asked, 'Do you wear those proper regal wigs and gowns to work?' he replied, laughing, 'No, we can wear anything we want, just not baseball caps.' I was like, 'What?' He said, 'You know, I told you I am a *barrista*. I work the night shift at Starbucks on Carnaby Street.' I died. Hello? I thought he was an intelligentsia wizard and turns out he is a latte half-caf maker. God, I can pick 'em . . ."

"Get out! A barrista? That's insanity. Hey, what are you up to today? Doing your daily baby store junket?" she roars, still giggling.

"*Bonjour, monsieur. Tout va bien?*" I slide the phone away from my mouth and tack in a quick hello to my favorite newspaper dealer at the *presse* stand on rue des Saints-Pères. He is such a dead ringer for Saddam Hussein, it's uncanny, and it has to be such a drag for this really sweet man.

Back to Zola . . . who knows me so well. "Well, I just took a massive digger near St. Sulpice. Really screwed up my ankle, so I am traipsing home to ice it. Hey, do you think I should call S.O.S. Médecin to have a doctor come look at it?" It's a very cool French service: you can summon a doctor twenty-four hours a day for a pittance. Since France is hypochondriac world headquarters, this has got to be a team of thousands.

"Oh, no no no. You have to see my *kinestherapiste*; he is sub-*lime*. He can cure any pain, any illness, and he can certainly help you with that vile heartburn you endlessly complain about. Half his clients are pregnant women who get everything treated, from morning sickness to hemorrhoids. Seriously, he is booked solid, he has such incredible talents. Everyone sees him from the aristos to the rock stars! I am pretty sure I can get you a rendezvous. I will call him right now. When are you free?" she leaps in without even letting me argue this out.

"Ah, that would be *anytime*. My social schedule is rather open of late, shall we say. But are you sure? I don't even know what a *kinestherapiste* is. Is it like a chiropractor or physical therapist? I am such a nonbeliever in chiropractors," I add, totally dubious but thinking that losing this killer heartburn and shrieking ankle pain would be amazing.

"You need not worry, I will text you with the details *tout de suite*. And Kiki, naming the baby after me will be payback enough!"

"You know, I might just do that. *Merci,* angel. Chat soon. *Bisous.*" I click off the phone to fish for the keys to my flat as I punch in the code to my building. Hmm, a doctor so heralded for his healing and magic medicinal powers, he was booked months in advance and would only see new clients based on a referral from existing followers? Okay, I'm always up for a good referral.

THE FOLLOWING DAY

Zola made the call as promised and arranged that emergency rendezvous for me a mere eighteen hours after the ankle incident. *Grâce à dieu,* since the pain in my ankle was so great I was virtually dragging myself around the apartment on my hands à la Daniel Day Lewis in *My Left Foot.* Convinced self it was useful training for teaching my future son the crab walk.

In a quick chat before heading out for the so-called big healing event, Zola made a point of going on the record:

"I know you, Kiki, you'll wig out. His office is in a shitty area of Paris, but don't think that means he's not a genius. He just doesn't go for the pretension that one with his talent could employ."

Fine. The days of my previous doctors' offices in New York, which were so chic with their fireplaces and art deco furniture that you actually *looked forward to going there,* are a sad distant memory. I was ready for the French version. Desperation can be quite motivating!

Unquestionably, this would be a divine time to treat oneself to a taxi ride, but I just cannot do it as I keep thinking, Listen girl, that would be one less toy you could buy your baby. (Possibly could be counted as selfless act number two.) So, being newly self-appointed Madamoiselle Budget, I drag out the *métro* map and plot my strategy for the adventure. The nineteenth arrondissement, eh? That's two subway changes and a long hike. Better allow an hour to get there and some extra time to shuffle around in search mode. Oh, aces. This is where I try to convince myself that in medieval times people used to traverse *all over* Europe to have their ailments healed so I should consider myself quite *fortunate* to be able to take the speedy subway for the pittance of 1.40 euros. Not to mention, there will be none of that unseemly leeching and bloodletting with warm glass cups. (I am eternally able to rationalize any scenario for the best, and if that skill should elude me one day, I will be so screwed. A lot of people say reality is what you make it, and my twist is reality is what you make it *into*. One glass of wine and I can convincingly argue the value of buying a Birkin bag when you cannot even pay your rent.)

Hobbling along, plugged into a soothing Norah Jones tune on my iPod, I journey from the chic sixth arrondissement to the nineteenth— from the fur-collar neighborhood through the white-collar to the progressively blue-collar . . . verging into the "I wish I had a shirt with a collar" area of Paris. To clarify the step down, I passed Louis Vuitton on my way down into the *métro* at Place Mabillion, and when I ascend the *métro* station Pré St.-Gervais, two disheveled teenagers immediately corner and harass me for my wallet (I blaze by, ignoring them) as I quickly realize I am very likely the only person around who bathes regularly, didn't have dirt encrusted under the nails, and has teeth.

Guarding my teeth and purse, I wander past a vast array of kebab shops and wholesalers of what appear to be slabs of compressed meat, but just as easily could've been dashboards. Finally, I spot the correct address and find myself in front of the cement, Bolshevik-style building of the famous healer genius. What a ramshackle dive! Oh, he'd better be good. Grimacing and now yearning again for the distant days of going to my NYC doctor's office, a chic Stanford White brownstone, complete with trays of Carr's crackers and Perrier in the lobby, I plunge ahead with my French adventure into medicine, *or some variation thereof.* Type in the door code. Pointless, really, since I notice the door's lock has been pried off and is swinging open with the wind. After initially reeling back from a waft of what was surely someone cooking odiferous cabbage, I follow a long corridor, the color of dried mustard, to a laminate wood door with a hand-scrawled note on cardboard, CLAUDE PINOCHET, KINESTHERAPISTE.

This is insanity.

The doorknob almost falls off in my hand as I reluctantly enter what is clearly a studio apartment so pathetically feigning to be a doctor's office. Let it be known, sheer awe and fascination kept me from turning on my heel and heading for home. Upon entering the faux doctor's office, I find I've stepped directly into a tiny two-by-four-foot entrance/lobby/waiting room/hall with two orange plastic folding chairs jammed in facing the door.

Oh god. Is this for real? No receptionist. *Hell no.* Where would she have *stood*? Or sat? On the pile of *Le Monde* all yellowed and dog-eared beneath the plastic chairs? I am about to take a seat when I realize that, once again, since I am quite possibly the Olympic champion of constantly needing to pee when in places where it's scary as all hell, my bladder insists I seek proper accommodations ASAP. Super duper.

I catch a glimpse of an open door to the right, with the sound of a toilet running. Yuck, I should just start wearing diapers as I forever have to delve into ghastly bathrooms all over this elegant city. (Like the *toilette* last week, on the rue des Beaux Arts, with the nineteenth-century hole in the floor and the filthy foot grates to squat on. With my tremendous *malchance* ("bad luck"), as I looked up to the leaky ceiling, my brand-new Dior—I call anything purchased since the millennium "new"—sunglasses slipped off my head into the black slimy dank hole. I admit to momentarily debating a nauseating reach into the *maison de fèces* for my precious glasses and then thought, No, I could never use that hand again, and certainly will need both for child rearing!) Somehow just remembering that event makes this place seem less appalling. So I run my hands up and down the interior wall in the darkness (And what's with French light switches anyway? They are always in bonkers locations.) and finally discover the switch behind a crunchy dirty towel on a nail. Gag.

Bathroom now illuminated and cue gag evolving to gasp! Voilà, Claude *le kinestherapiste*'s private grungy toilet is, as you can imagine, failing miserably in its half-assed ruse as public facilities. Oh geez. Is that really his razor on the sink and whiskers on the floor? Fuck, here's an idea, mister: look up the word *hygiene* and do some work here. Turning a blind eye to the less than spiffy WC, I, in my urination desperation, relieve myself, doing the hover-craft technique, *bien sûr*. I don't even want to use the toilet paper, since it's all so dirty and bizarre. Hey, terrific. I *have* my own toilet paper . . . right here in my pocket. Many thanks to my constant craving, since I have inadvertently saved myself from what is surely a petri dish of multiplying bacteria aplenty!

This brief high note of self-preservation passes as I rear back from the sink, noticing out of the corner of my eye—and you are never going to believe this—dirty dishes piled in the shower! Mismatched plates and a calcium-stained wineglass, all encrusted in an array of short hairs and baguette crumbs.

Can you fathom that I still stayed *chez* doctor? I don't know . . . the hope of walking again without pure agony and curing my heartburn had mysteriously bound me to endure this whole surreal experience.

Just as I am returning to the waiting room/lobby/corridor space, lo and behold, Claude the Genius (though clearly not with dishes!) appears and gestures me to follow him into the adjoining room. Hmm . . . he looks a lot like a French Billy Bob Thornton. Think part used-car salesman and part homeless man. Like a walking-breathing mug shot, more or less. Add the French-no-deodorant aspect and some intense after-lunch bad breath and you get the overall offending-*all-the-senses* feel.

Going into this next, tiny, windowless room—his so-called office/actual bedroom (complete with *très* obvious fold-out couch)/treatment area—I saddle up on the circa 1946 doctor's-type table. Clearly purchased second- or thirdhand at some flea market and don't even allow yourself to envision there's a fresh banner of tissue paper atop to welcome me aboard. *Pas du tout.*

Claude just stands silent staring at me, so I launch into my spiel of the ankle-twist maneuver, the extreme pain, and the violent heartburn as he intermittently takes notes on yet another of those cardboard squares that strangely also double for him as office door plaques. On the desk behind him sits a huge primitive computer, a gigantic jar of body oil, piles and piles of bills in their torn-open envelopes, a weathered postcard of a fat Buddha, and a Charles Aznavour CD. Professional? Reassuring? Oh, I think not. Generally I prefer, say, a wall adorned with magna cum laude certificates from Harvard Medical School and a photo of said doctor with famous political figures thanking him for saving his life.

Claude asks me to take off my socks, lay on my back, and remove my earrings. *Almost* normal until he tells me I have *très belles pieds* ("very pretty feet") and begins tapping them in random places. I lie there thinking, C'mon, Zola even said it'd be weird but will assuredly prove effective, so just chill out, Kiki. Imagine you're in Nepal getting blessed by the Dalai Lama. Claude, masquerading as a doctor, gets busy poking around on my ankle, asking where it hurts as I yelp, "*OUI, LÀ!*" every few taps. Then I feel him stop and back away. Are we done? That seriously didn't help. I crane my neck to see that he has scooted off to a bookshelf and begun silently perusing through a collection of three-ring binders. Long story *long,* he whips frantically through one, as quite obviously he needs a visual refresher on just exactly what the inside of an ankle looks like. What follows is a request to see if I might be willing to have a go at acupuncture.

Gagging on breakfast for, like, the third time, I throw all reason out the *fenêtre*. All knowledge of his extreme neglect to hygiene, interiors, having a personality, medical training. And I foolishly reply, *"pourquoi pas."* Whatever, I'm clearly trapped here for the duration, so just do your hocus-pocus and let me get out of here, kiddo.

You are so gonna love this—he goes to his desk and takes out a slim object I'm convinced is going to be an acupuncture needle and we're gonna solve all this *tout de suite*. Nope, he grabs a gnawed-on, short yellow pencil. Exactly like the kind they give you at mini golf or IKEA, and he proceeds to press it quite forcefully into my ankle. What the hell!? I'm on the verge of laughing and/or screaming at the absurdity of this whole scenario when he yanks my entire foot toward him with such force I'm convinced he's ripped my foot right off my body in some snatch-and-jerk move. Though in this case, I'm the jerk.

"Motherfucker!" I yell out in English, and somehow, *for some reason,* I feel this huge surge of electricity pulsing through my body, as though I'm possibly healing in some zen universe previously unknown to me OR the nerve endings in my foot are simply just ripped clean in half. Still being the optimistic fool, I stay reclined and virtually catatonic in my energy-surge-fest, while he proceeds to tell me when precisely to breathe in and breathe out . . . *"Souffle . . . inhale."* I'm following his instructions like a Jim Jones cult member with no will of my own. He commands I lay still while he covers my legs with some beyond filthy pilled acrylic blanket in what was possibly once the color pink.

Claude *le génie* pours some of that eucalyptus body oil on his hands after stealing another quick glance at the drawing of an ankle from the three-ring binder and lunges at me with greasy hands to begin an ear massage, stating this is for the heartburn. Is there any flow to that process? Drawing of ankle + ear massage = heartburn cure? Yeah, I know you're asking yourself what the hell is going on. Exactly! The cartilage in my ears and lobes is getting a serious rubdown as he continues to tell me when to breathe and occasionally gets so lost in his slimy ear manipulation that he forgets to tell me to exhale. Is depriving oxygen to my brain part of the healing process?!

This is all complete nonsense, I'm hip to that by this point. I've got a French snake oil salesman over here slathering my ears, sneaking peeks at a book—not even bound—for guidance, I'm covered in smelly pseudo-pink acrylic (that in itself is a horror, *non*?) after being prodded with a short golf pencil. When does the actual medicine start? Next, to be frank, I get a butt massage over my jeans. (And *thank god, over* my jeans! No way my huge monkey butt is making an appearance in this venue.) Derriere manipulation is done in tandem with him telling me I must avoid all dairy products. (But isn't it common knowledge that dairy is good for bones? I guess not in hocus-pocus short-pencil-medicine land.) And that I must eat a lot of rice—"*Riz pour petit déjeuner, déjeuner et dîner!!*"—and drink lots of wine, *Bordeaux,* to be specific. That kills me. How French!

With a happy butt and my mind reeling, I groggily sit up, put my earrings back in my glistening, oil-drenched ears, noting that one ear is clogged with oil and I can't hear anything on that side. Of course, I let that slide. Wise choice, don't you think, at that juncture? A smattering of sense returns and I plop down the fee of 40 euros just to hightail it outta there before he comes up with any other wild-ass treatments. I bid him adieu and *merci* with the speed of someone running out of a burning house. His final parting words are, "Eat rice!" Sure. Right on, Claude. You poor sod.

As I'm walking back to the subway, shaking my head in awe of just exactly how nuts my life has become and what a fucking hoax that was, I realize . . . no way, the pain in my ankle is gone. Poof! I swallow hard to test the burning esophagus. *Rien!* The burning rawness is nonexistent. Unreal. Yippee! I plop my happy monkey butt down on a seat in the subway, realizing I am now one of those odd souls that you see who just sit alone on the train with a goofy grin. Generally I find them curious to the point of irritating. But I can't contain myself.

I am elated.

Again, more of that reassuring, soothing hope and calm bathe me in their peace. As with all pregnant women, my hands unconsciously glide to caress my swollen belly, and a fog of near delirium washes over me, like only a healthy pregnancy can give rise to. I think to myself that maybe, just maybe, I can make this "single mother in a foreign country plan" all work as I dream it.

Chapter 3

"Every child is an artist.
The problem is to remain an artist
once he grows up."

—Pablo Picasso

"You have to go, it's *your* art opening!" commands David.

Pacing around my apartment, cell phone in one hand and the other cracking open the French windows for some air, I moan by way of a response, "Ugghh, I *know,* I am being too bizarre here but I don't want to be the center of attention tonight. I feel like every damn person will just be saying under their breath, 'Oh god, she looks like hell, only a few months pregnant and what's happened to her?!'"

"You are being so shallow and absurd. You look fine and it's not supposed to be about how you look, but how *your art* looks, you stupid ass," he yells back.

My best male *ami* in Paris, David, seemingly won't let me continue to stay in and eat my way through this pregnancy. Bastard. *Kidding.* I love this man and as a fellow American expat and a gay man, he gets to speak to me with a frankness I wouldn't permit a French straight man. We've been dear friends since design school in NYC, and, as luck would have it, he is now in Paris for a two-year stint setting up a new division for L'Oréal Paris, which is fucking fantastic. To have someone around who I cherish and knows me from ye olde college days—days we'd scramble and scrape together five dollars each and take the subway to Central Park to "picnic" with our deli sandwiches and wine coolers (like that's chic?) in Sheep Meadow and while the afternoons away chatting about how we were going to be hugely famous fashion designers, of course, millionaires by twenty-five and own New York. *Yeesh,* youthful naïveté at its best, I guess. We were wildly passionate young designers and, to our credit, the only two students who created our own collections while still in school, sold them in boutiques, and fought for the Yves Saint Laurent award. We both lost out to some chick from Long Island and we drowned our sorrows in Little Debbie snacks. And I will admit to our riding the elevator of our dorm for hours, sitting on the floor, stoned, thinking it was a hilarious ride. Then again, maybe it just seemed like hours.

Like me, David quickly bored of the NYC design world, made a clever exit, and now is a big shot in the beauty business, not to mention happens to be one of the most lovely men I have ever known. Incredibly handsome, and, well, he could be Marc Jacobs's twin in every aspect—hip, chic, and hilarious *all* the time. I love this man.

He works like a demon these days, so we generally meet up just on Sunday for brunch at Flore, dishing on men while eating club sandwiches (no more $5 deli options; at Flore it will set you back three times that but the ambiance is about three hundred times better), then we saunter about, shop, see exhibits at the Louvre. We *always* have each other howling with such gut-wrenching laughter, tears streaming down our faces, laughing so hard that we literally have to stop walking from almost collapsing. Obviously this isn't "done" in Paris and that makes it all the more over the top and fun. When it comes to gut-wrenching laughter, Paris etiquette goes out the window, there is no way I will ever abide by that social rule.

Anyways, I always come home half in love with him, sides aching, and so grateful to know someone so bright, gallant, and well read. I love that I can bring up any writer of any era and he's raring to go with opinions and ideas. And here, I know he is right to push me to attend my own art *vernissage*. Hell, it is in a gallery just round the corner on the rue des Beaux Arts. And I should be beaming with pride and glowing with pending mommahood, and yet somehow I'm stupidly struggling with how pregnancy is just annihilating my body and thus my self-image. Despite the massive and boundless joy I feel to be making a baby, I can't quite accept that, since I stopped running and the pounds just keep piling on, I feel like a squishy fat mess. (Body issues? Yes, add that to my list, on equal footing with control, as I previously mentioned.)

David continues to berate me, "Okay, Kiki, that's it. Enough! I have to say, you are forbidden to spend another minute worrying about how you look! You probably are only going to get to have this *one* child, this *one* pregnancy, and you sure as hell better pull up your knee socks and cherish every second and every kilo from this point forward! You are going to the *vernissage,* I'm leaving work early, picking you up at 18.30h and marching you over there. Wear the gunmetal grey empire dress and your grey snakeskin knee-high boots with those damn knee socks pulled high, girl! See you then. *À tout,"* and he hangs up.

He is right, dead on. I have been an asshole. My obsession with aesthetics is so hard-wired. How dumb of me to focus on how my arms are becoming all flabby flags a wavin'. Who cares. These damned hormones are shaking my confidence and making my brain go all wonky and emotional. Christ, I even put eye cream on my toothbrush, forgot to lock my door when I left today, and threw my purse in the trash and carried the garbage bag as my purse for three blocks. It's a damn good thing I don't have a job as an air traffic controller, huh? I vowed from that moment forward to let go of all the body image worries and just celebrate the baby inside me, and I really have David to thank for that wisdom. Interesting that this reality check is not from a woman but from a gay man. I know my mother would've said it to me as well and I guess that is also something I need to rely on and trust— that her infinite wisdom does still live on in my consciousness and that I have to listen closely to hear those voices. That was her life's work, to prepare and support me to know inherently and unquestionably that I am capable of anything I wish to do. *And to do it with great passion and commitment.*

Damn, it's hard without her. When I see mothers and daughters lunching together on sunny café terraces or out shopping, hand in hand, as they do in Paris, I feel such a physical ache for her, it's staggering. There is no way to get over, around, or through the pain of losing her in this way. It's always raw and just beneath the surface of my conscience thoughts. For her, for me, and for this baby (who is going to be pretty frigging expensive in Paris so I better sell some work ASAP!), I pull myself together and go off to get ready for the evening. I haven't really dressed up for an evening since this belly and grand derriere burst forth onto the scene and, well, it's a regular riot choosing underwear. The fave standby La Perla lace bra isn't going to fly with these bad boys spilling over the top and, frankly, out the bottom. If my boobs get any bigger, they could officially be referred to as jugs and that's just frightful. Looks like we are opting for a running bra that will smash them down to pancakes and the string (thong *en français*) is getting stored for now, since it's feeling more like butt floss—with a lot more butt than lace going on down there. Dear god, it's time for the gigantic mom underwear to make a night *soiree* in all their glory. So, then, over the belly or under? *Over* hides the belly button poking out like a turkey thermometer but *under* feels a smidge more sexy. I go with under the belly and jam on some (super unsexy) super-padded gym socks to ease the trauma of my too-tight snakeskin knee-high boots. But hopefully no one will suspect this ghastly fashion crime and these boots demand it, since after two steps I feel 1) I'd be a lot more comfortable if I took my nail file and sliced off a few toes and 2) like I'm walking on pirate peg legs and really want to just fling the boots into the Seine. Any woman will tell you there are a few pairs of heels in their closet that are just so damn fabulous that they will endure the horrific pain and all. And these beauties, a gift from an ex, my first pair of Michel Perrys, hold that position. Killer boots indeed; I never leave a night in them unscathed or unfucked. Hmmm, cancel that. Tonight will surely be the exception to the latter. Though, I have to say, it's been several months now, man-*men*-sex-free and it's kind of getting arduous since my body is just screaming for a shag *all the time.*

Factoid—I think Frenchmen are seriously, I kid you not, *in the know* on this hormone-induced mad sexual desire of pregnant women, since I am still getting hit on, leered, and eye-fucked on the streets of Paris and, I'd be the first to say, it's not like I'm looking all that sassy. On one hand, it's kind of great to still feel desired and sexually appealing, but on another, it's different enough of a look and a smile to make you know these men aren't trying to meet you to *date* (as, unlike *moi,* 99% of them are married!). It's feral, animalistic, and surely a pheromone thing. An in your face "I'm clearly sexual since I am clearly pregnant" banner that Frenchmen are so brazenly attracted to. I know I have said it before, but man does this country fuel itself on sex and sensual delights. It's just the scrim and the underlay of everything— a walk down the street, a trip to the *théâtre,* a magnificent meal, the way cologne and *parfum* hang in the air everywhere one goes. In short, Paris is laden with tantalizing temptation and it's a hard place to be single and flooded with wanton desire . . . especially when you can't really partake.

In truth, I have had a few exes offer, as they put it, "their services"; obviously they are wildly and weirdly curious as to how different it would be. And, need I say, I don't imagine a lot of American men would make the same offer. As for Frenchmen; I think they just want to add yet another sexual variation to their experience archives. Nevertheless, I feel this unique total commitment to my baby to just be a good girl, safe, and I guess you could say madonna-and-child saintly.

Off I go to the gallery opening with a six-pack of Perrier in my purse and lovely David on my arm. It's a wonderful, warm evening and the crowd spills out onto the street since the gallery is packed to its rafters. Funny to see how all my dear friends make the pilgrimage to see my little show. I am really touched—*literally.* Everyone, including a lot of my old boyfriends, arrive (and stagger around in shock for a while that I am much to their amazement independently *enceinte*) and then feel compelled to ask to touch my belly. The awe on their faces at the sensation and idea that there is a baby in there is enchanting. Since I don't have a husband or family to share this experience with, I realize my friends, god love them, are my precious alliances in which to share this pregnancy. Indeed, it becomes a dream of a night for me, and amazingly less about my art on the walls (which I loathe to chat about) and more about celebrating the new life inside me and *ahead of me.* I come away from it *elated*—sold a painting to a big-shot dealer with a breathtaking *hôtel particulier* on quai Voltaire; *dying to pee*—drank all the Perrier since, I have to admit, it was quite hard not to imbibe my beloved social elixir, champagne; and *amused*—watching everyone I know get falling-down drunk while I stayed sober—I could've charted the IQ drop rate that occurred with every drink! What a massively surprising take on what I had previously been doing virtually every night with abandon (as is par for a social life in St. Germain) and with that sloshy certainty that with every drink I was becoming funnier and *more* sharp-witted. *Au contraire.* Messy-silly is hardly attractive. I have to say, this baby, this pregnancy is giving me many life lessons every day.

I pull David aside as I pack up to leave and tell him, "Darling, I can't thank you enough for kicking my ass into coming tonight but more so, to have really opened my eyes to enjoying each and every second of this pregnancy. It's been kind of hard to adjust without a mate to hash it all through in the moments of hormone-surge self-doubts. Thanks for being my sounding board and the calm in the storm of my trying to wrap my head around the enormity of going through all this alone."

"Kiki, think nothing of it. You're not alone. See all your fans?" he says, sweeping his hands through the air at the gaggle of hipsters.

"You and I both know, half of these people are here because I am just another spoke in the machine of St. Germain. A novelty, a blond American chick who laughs louder than anyone. And the other half are here for the free champagne and to critique my art with wild abandon," I reply, realizing the statement that started out as a quip is entirely true.

"Hmm. True, I suppose. But I am always *here* to ream you out and hold a mirror to your constant ever-loving insanity. Very few others dare!" he roars. "Hey, listen, you are going to be a great *maman* and I'm hoping to be the first to give your baby a present," he says, reaching into his Prada briefcase and pulling out a pretty fuchsia-wrapped package tied with a silver satin ribbon.

"Really?! How great! You are the best! And, I have to say, you are absolutely the first gift giver . . . how damn sweet." And I rip open the gift as a few onlookers glance over.

An adorable teensie-tiny newborn onesie slides out onto my palm, barely big enough to cover it. With a growing audience of curious observers, I unfold the tiny shirt, hold it up, and show the word "REBEL" emblazoned in pale grey type on the charming tee to all. Cheers, *parfait!, bien sûr,* and laughs abound. Triple-cheek kisses to David, and I feel my eyes well up. Hormones have me such a sap these days, *mon dieu.*

I make the long gamut-run of good-byes and bid David and the crowd a happy adieu by 9:00 P.M. Walking home under a full moon along rue de Seine, the golden light reflecting off the cobblestones, I feel lucky and blessed and exhausted. Just now noting my feet are throbbing in my boots and yet, I don't feel any pain, since the night was such a surprising total delight. Sometimes the planets align and life just delivers you the greatest and most precise medicine for your soul, when everything seems fluid and positive. When you are my age, you are wise enough to know this is a truly divine moment; thus there is a lovely awareness to be consciously celebratory—exalting in the rare synchronicity of all the pieces coming together.

Delicious to be able to slide into cool sheets alone and so content. The swarm of delightful chats with dear friends swept away all the worries that might have kept me lying awake otherwise, as tomorrow is a big day:

AMNIOCENTESIS DAY

I am ecstatic for this day. Take great effort to wear something pretty, since lately I have been feeling as attractive as a sloth, though it turns out my belly and ass are even bigger than I thought and all efforts to become *becoming* are misfiring. I feel kind of like Humpty Dumpty jamming into my old "fat jeans," and with these big hips, I am the dead opposite of "hip" and am looking a lot like my home ec teacher from fourth grade, who we used to call Harriet Humungous Hips Lybeck. Not a hot look.

All the same, the so-called huge needle that is to be inserted into my belly to check that my little sea horse has now spawned into a healthy webbed-foot baby is a landmark rite of passage I welcome gladly. With my new social calendar of nothing ahead, I am frankly just loving reading, nesting, and following my baby's constant growth and development. Any new mom has to agree, it's positively thrilling to see with each week how the life inside you magically evolves and what new body part or skill your baby has acquired. The phrase, "He has ears now, no more gills!" is splendidly fun to hear fall out of one's mouth. Obviously, I can't wait until I can see my little vertebrate again on the *échographie* ("sonogram").

Last time, the vile wicked witch of a technician was clearly so rushed for lunch, she hurriedly took the *de rigeur* quickie black-and-white print as mere protocol, and sadly you can't make out—as I used to say in seventh grade—jack iguana. Meaning, I can't tell if that's a foot or an ear and I curse the woman all to hell for not taking the extra thirty seconds to let me see my baby as anything more defined than what looks like a Rorschach test of a rabbit playing the flute. Not to mention, in contrast, I have seen many an e-mailed video from my American mom friends of actual DVDs in action of their tiny embryos doing backflips! *And in 3-D color,* I might add. Screw these old-school Frenchies with their primitive machines. Grrr.

But now it's back to the American Hospital for the amnio and I get another chance to see my darling baby, which as a new mom without a job or husband is all I think about! (Hello, department of redundancy department.) Happily marching into the doctor's office, cool as a cucumber, my mood gets hideously whiplashed as I realize upon entering that I am the only mom *alone.* In all my worrying about the big needle, I hadn't thought of that. Had not anticipated the scene I was going to be delving into. But of course, any and all husbands with a shred of decency would accompany their wives for this big event. Instantly, I am blindsided with loneliness and doubt. Is this how it will always be? Me alone, while other mothers get their hands held and cheeks kissed as I teeter on the edge of heartbreak by the stark contrast? I have surrounded myself with so many other single women friends, I forgot there are loving couples and the mentality of "we are in this together and twice as happy since we are *both* so tickled to be parents." I am seriously shaken. I want my mom. I didn't, in any way, expect to feel so *solitaire,* and somehow, in this country, that idea isn't all that modern; I feel like a failure to be going it alone. I know no one can see by looking at me, but I feel like I am wearing a sign that says, "Blake isn't exactly rushing back to me ASAP with engagement ring in hand, and no one else on the planet wanted to marry me so I am pathetically a single parent by choice!" And yet, I have had almost twenty marriage proposals and wouldn't want to be married to *any* of the men I see here (except maybe the hot older man who resembles Sarkozy—I have a hideous crush on him).

Still, I can't shake the desire to get the hell out of here. In the down time to wait to be called to be stabbed in the belly (clearly the elation has evaporated now), I eat from the basket of free patisserie set out for the anxious moms. I don't care that I am the only one, obviously, grabbing at brownies and brioches and cookies and croissants— all individually wrapped in plastic—fueled less by hunger than pure, unexpected mental trauma. No truly elegant Parisian woman would partake—*nor is,* apparently—especially in public, of such subpar fare

(I think they are made for kids or for those country folk living far from fresh *boulangeries*), but frankly, I don't care a whit right now what anyone thinks! I am sad and not *Parisienne* and somehow mad. My mind is playing some evil game of warring factions that I had felt thirty minutes ago were peaceful allies. I can't stop feeling overwhelmed by the fear that I can't manage this single mother job as well as I had thought I could. I have no family, just a mere handful of "call in the middle of the night" friends to lean on. Is that enough with what lies ahead? The up-down and whirling of hormones is no help when I need to be the rock of stability and self-assurance. Did I mention I want my mommy? Wait, I am the mommy! Arghggh!

I gorge on pastries, mentally cursing all these women to hell for having lovely husbands, making a visual check that, *oui,* they all have wedding rings on. Should I just wear one to see if it feels better? *Please.* How dumb. I jam empty snack wrappers in my bag one after another and pass the time comparing my bump to the other moms, who, for once, I can be assured are all the exact same stage in their pregnancy. Verdict: mine is about normal, save the squareness, and all in all I win for best dressed. No great consolation since that shallow side of me is dying off and I shut her down when she still yammers on occasionally.

After signing a stack of formal disclaimers *en français*—which isn't all that fun when you don't know what the technical words are—I get called in. Finally. It's been one hour there I would like not to remember. Let's get to the big show! In truth, the actual needle to tummy isn't that painful. I look away as the nurse unsheathes the damn thing—I have no need to really hold that image in my memory. To be sure, the only thing that can *or possibly could* lift my spirits is seeing my baby, and god, please tell me if it's a boy or girl. I don't have a preference at all and actually detest people who do—how ghastly, just be happy your child is healthy. But I want to see him or her, and I know that would sweep away all my sadness. The nurse shows me my baby for all of, I swear to god, ten seconds since the waiting room is backed up and she is all about "move 'em in and move 'em out." She says, "Mmmm, the baby has turned its back now and I cannot tell you which sex it is. *Désolée.*" And I'm dismissed.

I walk out of the office drained and limp. Like I've suddenly seen into a window of how being a parent alone *could be* and it ain't going to be a cakewalk by any means. No man there to more or less tell the nurse that we aren't leaving until we see that baby full frontal. No one to fight for us as a family *but me*. No one to giddily share the baby's first steps or first words. No one to cry tears of joy with me when the baby is born and say, "This is the happiest day of my life." Men! Once again causing me anguish and there isn't even one around. I guess it's somehow a good thing that Blake is not a Frenchman or living in Paris, since that would cause me about a hundred times more grief on about a hundred different fronts. *Ça suffit!* I have enough to think about today.

Honestly, it's all rather wonderful to be pregnant, if you take away the fears that are loaded in when one is forty. I have never been much for loving statistics and the odds and to read the possibilities of having a child with Down syndrome or spina bifida; lordy, it's terrifying. I always felt I couldn't possibly bring a child into this world with such a deck stacked against him, yet it's almost scary how, at this stage, after such an intense emotional connection to your child, you can't fathom saying, "Oh, a chance at birth of Down syndrome, well, let's end this child's life now." I am amazed to realize that, even with my full-stop passionate pro-choice stance and belief that women are free to make their own decisions (across the board, concerning their lives and their children), now, with the baby in my belly, I know I would have to either have the baby and devote my entire life to caretaking of my precious child or, if swayed *somehow* to terminate, would without question lose my ever-loving mind.

I think only when you become a mother, whether by the process of being pregnant or adopting, do you finally gauge the emotional agony of what it *might* be to lose a child, to see your baby very ill, or, horrors, kidnapped. For years you see the accounts and news reports of such sad tales and injustices and you feel empathy but—and maybe I am wrong here—only when you have a child does the extreme reality and horror slice at your soul. One thing I know for sure, if anything ever happened to this child of mine, I know I would not want to continue to walk the planet, simple as that. I bet it's a rare father who would say the same . . . *it's a mom thing.*

Après l' amnio, lying flat on my back in the rear seat of a hired car heading back to Paris (doctor insists on no vertical movement and total bed rest for three days after the procedure so as to avoid amniotic sac rupture), I realize, Wow, fuck bugger! (Mental note—clean up even cerebral swearing auto-pilot.) Perhaps, more effectively put, "This is indeed time not only to be mature on all fronts by fully blossoming into all I saw my mother be for us but also to create an eternal armature of strength or I will have to endure this emotional battering at many an unexpected turn. I have to be both mother and father and find my own depths of power to remain stable, self-reliant, and consistently resilient." Fuck bugger, indeed. I have less than five months. I am *too* alone.

Zola is so busy with her new love, Jean-Pierre. Yep, as expected, the previous suitor, Hubert, more or less disappeared, as they tend to do with the poor girl. This new amour of hers is sounding more substantial; neither a ladies' man nor an aristo-rat. I think he sells insurance or something or other and he lives in the *banlieue* (suburbs of

Paris). Moreover, he, lo and behold, seems after a month to be still holding the title really terrific guy, which is about twenty-four days longer than most Frenchmen.

No Frenchmen for me, thanks. I need to find other single mothers in Paris, and American expats would be the best. Is there such a thing? Of course there is, in this day and age; hell, you can find someone to come over and teach your dog how to mime. *Et voilà,* the Web doesn't disappoint. I find Message Moms—expat mothers in France, and there's even a sublisting for single mothers. Genius. I have always been one to smirk at any organized groups, especially organized group meetings, but this new me is shedding my old skin and kicking new doors open (and clearly hooked on cheesy metaphors!). It's just that I've never been much of a girls' girl (*par example*—cell phone contacts register a count of seven women to sixty-eight men), but I am feeling a new wave of sisterhood with all women lately, a kinship of understanding. I am seriously grateful to go meet, seek advice, and discover women who are on the same journey. The biggest journey of my life . . .

Chapter 4

"For truly it is to be noted that children's play is not sport and should be deemed as their most serious actions."

—MICHEL EYQUEM DE MONTAIGNE

Septembre–Octobre

I'm a strange bird, this I know, but I felt like a *total* loon tonight. I received a beautiful congrats card from my childhood friend Kathy in L.A., and, while visually devouring the lovely Anne Geddes photo of ravishing pregnant women looking all ethereal and peaceful, it hit me—I have to get a photo of this belly-o-mine!

Oh, come on, there isn't a pregnant woman out there who doesn't feel like a blob but wants just one photo to represent this magnificent experience—and makes it appear like she was just a vision of serenity and beyond stunning the whole way through. A total charade to be sure, but it can all be blamed on that famous pic of Demi Moore gracing the cover of *Vanity Fair,* in diamonds and couture. She set the bar high— that bitch who just won't age and gets to sleep with that silly-sexy Ashton Kutcher—and while I can't match her on any of that, I am damn sure going to get at least a *low-brow* snapshot of my belly.

Plopped on my Wassily Kandinsky chair with the sun beginning to set, wishing I had just one comfortable place to sit in my damn apartment, I do a check around the room for a possible photographer to shoot this belly-o-mine. Nope, no Annie Leibowitz. Not a soul here to help me get this shot. I am dead set on this, have to make it happen, and can't be stopped. Don't feel like bothering Zola to be photographer in question. She's too busy pressuring her new boyfriend to propose. And, frankly, I'm weirdly shy and not really able to exhibit naked self to other women, which is hardly an option as I really don't have any other good girlfriends in town. As ever, looks like I'm going to go solo on this task and, well, no better time than the present. Hmm. This is going to be *très* tricky, since all I can figure out is I have a self-timer on my digital camera and have to somehow balance it on something and skooch 100mph back into the frame and hastily assume tranquil and radiant image. Holy Christ, this is next to impossible. Looks like the bathroom shower curtain rod will serve as backdrop, but I definitely need to make that matte black so as to have belly silhouette "pop." Okay, better slip off snaggily huge bra and huge undies to lose any imprints on this flesh that's all a-blazing with swelling.

I slip into a robe and decide maybe I should start with my face and try to see if a spackle job of makeup and a blow out is going to be in *any* way attractive. It's been so long since I wore makeup, I almost feel like a preteen playing dress up, since I take such delight in all the process. Mascara? How fun, it does really make your eyes bigger! And pressed powder is a miracle worker at toning down the red flush on my cheeks. How neato! God, what a dope. I'm having a baby in a few months and my brain is working at age eleven. Terrific.

I get way carried away with the whole makeup thing and doll up in red lips like I *never* normally wear. Blow hair into a gentle wave attempting to emulate 1930s pinup Veronica Lake but it comes out more like a 1985 prom coif. Toss on a few of my bigger diamonds (thanks again, ex-boyfriends!) and I'm thinking I don't know who the moon-faced trollop in the mirror is but she's entertaining me through another night of nothing to do but read baby books. Fun!

I stand on a kitchen chair, safety-pinning a black pashmina to the shower curtain for the desired backdrop. Talk about feeling lame?! Crap. Making huge pin holes in scarf from the weight of it dragging down. Oh, whatever, far more important documentation of life event here going on, and pashminas have seen their day, right? Okay, things are coming together. Overhead lighting? Evil. I Scotch tape a bit of an old Wolford stocking over the blaring ceiling light, again teetering on kitchen chair, one foot on windowsill, thinking this would be a very stupid way to fall. Not to mention, this all by no means feels the slightest bit glamourous and I'm fairly sure this wasn't the way the Demi Moore shot was set up. Not by a long shot.

Okay, here goes, a test shot. Place camera on stack of books sitting on chair, facing me and said backdrop. Nope, no way, this is definitely *not* a horizontal shot. Have to balance camera on its side, flip the timer ever so carefully to not tip camera over onto floor shattering into smithereens and now dash back into frame, *or where I think frame is.* Click!

Crud. No flash. Gotta put that on "auto" but leave self-timer. Done.

Flip, dash, pose! Okay, anytime now . . . take the fucking picture already, hurry up, I feel soooo stupid posing in my bathroom, the sound of the upstairs neighbors' TV droning on and people out on the street laughing as they leave a restaurant. Get a load of me. *Merde!* Didn't flip the self-timer, I guess. Hustle back. Click! Damnit. Missed the shot.

Retry 3: Click! Check image. I am beheaded and slipping on bath-mat.

Retry 4: Click! Oh, bugger, I moved too far forward and am like all hair on a sphere of flesh. Camera needs to be higher. Race to grab another book to put under camera, rebalance, sweat starting to set in motion a landslide of makeup.

Push timer, twenty-three more attempts at self-placement in screen and altering angles and expressions. And, click! Got it!!! A very fine photo of me (or someone who vaguely resembles me) and baby, cropped perfectly at what was once a slim hip bone, with hands on breasts, dia-monds a-shimmerin', and only the slightest bit of shower curtain peek-ing around pashmina. That's a wrap, folks!

Like a pregnant single girl with a purpose and mission—*and very little else*—I am over-the-top pleased with my little photo. And for reasons unbeknownst to my sense of privacy and personal pride, I go to the computer and fire off said image to my closest friends and fam-ily. Having a baby alone does that to a lady. You are just exceptionally eager to share it with *someone,* and taking a moment to consider how wacked it is to put it out into cyberworld just isn't in the cards. It was a success, actually, since it did reap a dozen kind and complimentary replies, as well as create the illusion, for those in the USA, that I was looking about a hundred times better than I was in reality. I'm all for that; nobody is seeing these stretch marks and swollen ankles. It's kind of like my own personal take on the age-old question, "If a tree falls in the forest and no one is there to hear it, does it make a sound?" Tweaked for me to, "If a stretch mark and a spider vein grow brightly red and no one is there to see it, do they really exist?" See, I am completely mad. Yes, but a completely mad girl with a very fine photo to show to her child one day and enjoy recapping the adventure!!

With that endeavor under my belt, I felt really excited for making the adventure today to meet up with the single expat mothers group. Wasn't the slightest bit deterred to wake to a rainy mist, since I always have felt a fondness for the way a sprinkle of rain pattering at your cheeks makes you feel truly alive. Ever since I was a child, I'd set out once the rain *started* to fall, finding the way everyone else scatters for cover rather amusing since it would leave me a private world to enjoy. When you think of it, it's just water, and people freak out and scamper to keep dry as if it's acid falling from the sky. So, needless to say, I thought a mist of cool rain would be a memorable delight to share with my baby.

Wrong.

As the time to scoot off to the noon rendezvous drew closer, the light showers turned to such a vicious storm that it was blowing garbage cans down the cobblestone streets and ripping flowers right out of their window boxes.

Okay, I have no option (which I am starting to notice is a running theme to my life in Paris) but to walk to my meeting, since standing outside in this hurricane to wait for one of the six taxis in town is going to be an exercise in frustration *and* saturation. Nor is there a bus or *métro* that would bring me anywhere near the Île St. Louis, where one of the single moms has offered her flat for our brunch rendezvous. *On foot* it is, and with my semi-desperation to seek advice and the wisdom of these women, nothin' is going to keep me from getting there. Time to cloak self in the ever-at-hand shield of mental perseverance and determination that one must don *so* often in this town. Two steps out the door, umbrella inside out. Four strides, umbrella whipped to smithereens, would dump in a trashcan if they all hadn't blown down to another arrondissement. Pelting rain and lightning escort me the mile or so as I walk along the Seine seeing people hauled up in the alcoves at the Academie Française like refugees, a huddled pack clinging together with expressions of fear. Maybe I should turn back? This is bonkers and now with water squishing between my toes in my shoes and having beaten my bouquet of yellow tulips to mere stems, my arrival is going to be as pathetic as my mood.

Nah, I'm just passing Notre Dame now, and turning back is as far as going forward and I fucking have to make it there. This is a test—of my will and my ability to make it over all the hurdles that will be popping up constantly as a single mom. Right. Think "it's just water" and endure. Except for the pebble that's just flown into my eye and is grinding away layers of my cornea, *it's all good.* Pfff-ff.

Just as I find the building—which I was so ill-prepared to imagine as being an absolutely stunning, medieval, half-timber mansion—the rain abates and the sun peers through as if to say, "Okay, you've arrived, cue rainstorm-attack test completed." I glance at my watch and notice I am, despite the beating and walking against the wind with such force as to be almost forty-five degrees in a hunch, early again. I'm always early! Which doesn't go over so well in France. Whatever. The guests are all going to be expats; they get it. I punch in the door code and announce myself to the welcoming greeting—so rare in Paris—of, "Hey, come on up, it's the second floor!"

I pass on ringing out my pants hems that are spewing water like a rain gutter, since bending over is starting to hurt these days and, unless there is a 500 euro note on the ground, it ain't gonna happen. Make my way through another enormous oak door and into a vestibule that is astonishing. Talk about stepping back into time! This is a stained glass illuminated turret with huge stone tiles leading up a winding plank-laid staircase, precisely of the fifteenth-century châ-teau or cathedral variety. Obviously in France, it becomes nothing to see or live, as I do, in a seventeenth-century building, so rich in his-tory and with wood-beamed cellings that were living four hundred years ago. Yet this building of some unknown single mom was posi-tively around when Notre Dame was getting the finishing touches! Zounds. Once a single-family home, to be sure, still gorgeous and smelling marvelous in its weathered stone and oak carapace. I love Paris for this shit. This is the kind of orgasmicly thrilling sights and discoveries that enchant you every day and make you think, "I could never live anywhere else!"

The fact that my hair is glued to my neck and my underwear are falling down to my knees with the weight of rainwater is long-lost as I hurriedly make my way to the door on the second floor, studded with nailheads. What would I give to live here? Wonder if she is game for being two lesbian single moms? For this home, I would gladly switch orientations!

A pretty brunette in her early forties sweeps the door open and with a gentle smile says, "You must be Kiki. Did you walk here in this torrential downpour? Oh, goodness, let's get you inside."

Needless to say, I'm struck speechless upon seeing that the flat is just enormous—with fifteen-foot ceilings and a view directly out to the Seine rushing by below. Center stage is a vast dinner table (could've been at the Last Supper, as is clearly uber-antique) overflowing with a beautiful brunch buffet situated in front of an immense marble fireplace so large you could walk into it and have a musical quartet join you! I'm the first one there, no surprise. Save the host, Marie, and her mother, who is there to help set out a truly bountiful array of France's all-star brunch fare. Shimmering salmon *fumé*, toasts, crème fraiche, golden brioche, black-as-tar olive tapenade, fragrant tarama on baguette rounds sprinkled with fresh chives, canapés of tiny quiche *au chevre et épinards* and an array of *pâtisserie*—*pain aux raisins, pain au chocolat,* and *tarte au pommes.* Divinity!

With an eye on the apartment of my dreams and the buffet of my fantasies, I must make small talk before plowing through both with joyous abandon. Turns out Marie is half-French, half-Brit, and her lovely willow of a *maman* is the French end of the influence. Thus, Marie is fluent, well-traveled, and holds a seriously top-dog position as an ambassador to England, consequently the flat that is—get this—*given* to her to live in. I am rarely jealous. Even in Paris, with all the lovely bewitching and chic women. But now I am sitting there, all wet, fat, and *dying* of jealousy. Real estate envy is my Achilles' heel and here there is even more to be jealous about than I can bear. Marie has this house, this great French mom, a great job and is, honestly, like everything I wish I was, *had, or could be,* and, more than that, she can offer her little three-year-old daughter, Solange, the greatest lifestyle and opportunities.

Until about five minutes ago, I was sure I was all set up and in a good place and situation for my child, and now I feel like crap. Sad-sack poster girl. Marie is lovely enough with her niceties, but just French enough that she's not really open or warm. Thankfully other single moms start streaming in. Dry and happy for it, I might add, and clearly have previously been through this awe-envy trauma I currently have in my lap. Sitting drinking a warm cup of cider, which has about the same alcohol as light beer with ice chips, I feel it's kind of decadent for me but sadly not enough alcohol to ease the old self-doubt that's creeping up. It's rapidly becoming clear to me that *rendezvous sans* alcohol are really surprisingly tough. That's Paris for you. In NYC, I never needed a *coupe de champagne* for chatting at parties and such, and now I am like,

"Well, this is sheer hell. Sober chatting is hard, since I'm a squirrelly mess of nervous energy and my conversation has all the charm of toenail clippings. Lovely."

All the other mothers have met up before, and I am the new one, so there is a lot of my recapping my scenario and introductions with each new mom. The whole lot turns out to be about ten mothers, many with children in tow and who I didn't suspect would *not* be a gaggle of Americans, since there is only one American among them. The rest are Portuguese, Irish, British, Spanish, and another half-French/half-Brit like Marie. It occurs to me, Why the hell does Marie need this—us? A team of single, familyless women who haven't a drip of French blood in our veins? Maybe she just likes holding gatherings in her amazing home. Hell, I would invite over the postal workers just to revel in living like this.

I'm eating everything in sight, which is clearly my new coping mechanism for anxiousness as I give out my spiel over and over. I find myself feeling too weird; it's pretty bizarre trying to tell your story in fragmented answers as the children all run riot and you're there half-yelling, "I used to be a fashion designer!" like it's relevant or matters. I feel like I'm not even sure how much to say. Are you required to give your history of your dating failures and family fertility issues when you present yourself as a single mom-to-be? How much are we putting out on the table here, ladies? It all feels very weird to be so honest with strangers, so I segue to just pummeling them all with the innumerable questions that are stockpiled in my mind.

Me, between bites of brioche slathered with *confiture aux framboises*, "Is there a stigma in France to being a single mother?"

Overall consensus, "Yes, a bit, unless you have the father recognize the child at the *mairie* ["city hall"] after the birth. Birth lineage is important to the French; a child without a documented father *could* be scorned." (Reeling information *pour moi* indeed—would like to raid liquor cabinet and slip out of reality now, thanks.)

Me, trying to find inner strength, "Do you think that the French government will allow my child into the French system without a French father?"

Consensus: "Better hire a lawyer and find out quick or consider moving back to the USA." Ugh.

On one hand it's just cool to be around a ton of mothers for whom one could say no husband is necessary or wanted. Indeed, only one of them is even dating, which I find amazing, since I already feel massive pressure to find my baby a great father ASAP. But, and god will strike me for saying this, with the exception of three of them, I don't really see how they could date the local cruelly discerning male population, since they are just really, really Rubenesque. That's not mean if it's factual, right? The gig is, I am wondering if this weight thing *came* from the insanely isolating pressure of single motherhood or were they like that from the start. Not exactly a question you can ask. Troubles me; if the insta-ample curvaciousness goes along with single *maman*-dom, I am terrified.

Note to self: stop gorging like a maniac or you will get as big as the Hindenberg and you too will go down in flames!

The afternoon passes quickly and not without highlights: turns out I am fond enough of a couple of the moms to want to see them again. Interestingly, they are both Irish and funny as hell. Verania and Paula win the cool prize; they are warm, open, and super-clever. Cell phone numbers are exchanged as I try in vain to dust the ocean of crumbs and bits of salmon off my belly. Loads to digest here, literally and figuratively, so I amble off to steal a peek alone off the balcony.

Staring out over the waves as a *pelouche* passes by, crowds of tourists looking up at me, in this magnificent building, thinking I live here. Pfff. I wish. Damn, Marie has *the* choice setup here. I am going to want to go home and set my apartment aflame. I guess if I had to move back to the USA (shudder in horror), I could get a nice house and a big yard for my baby for the ridiculous cost of a tiny flat here. Not in NYC, though; after thirteen years there I know I could neither afford nor would I want to raise a child there. Could go to Wisconsin again and thereby give baby a trove of family—uncles, cousins, aunts, grandparents. Course not my mom, that would be excruciating all the more to place my baby in her arms and have her not even be able to speak. Ah, forget it, there's nothing to do there. I can barely tolerate the town during short visits for Christmas. And my life is here.

Blip of musing over "Option B" aborted and deleted.

Children are packed up to be taken home for naps, the table is cleared, and hey, I guess I better go. Didn't quite realize, I was the first to arrive and the last to leave (appallingly bad form) until I thanked Marie profusely for the lovely afternoon and headed back home. Hmm. Seems despite the general bad news and information about my status in France, I did enjoy being around moms. Men-free moms. After so many years of endless chatter with girlfriends about men, what they want, how they are great or are crap, etc., it's nice as hell to have the center of focus be about our babies. Learned a lot, and I will absolutely show up at the next Sunday meeting this week.

THE FOLLOWING *DIMANCHE*

I went.

It sucked.

Paula and Verania couldn't come because their kids had obligations, not to mention, they both live in the suburbs of Paris, so it is rather rare they can make it into the city for meetings. *Merde* news. I seriously felt so disappointed; it was almost like a wished-for hot man I was dying to flirt with hadn't arrived. No Marie of the fab mansion either—word has it she only is available for her own hosted events (I was right!)—leaving me with a bevy of heavy, crabby single moms I didn't know yet. And didn't much want to.

This single mom Expat meeting was SINGular, EXtremely PATHetic. No delight on any level. The children were all bonkers misbehaved; one boy slamming a three-year-old girl's hand in the door *on purpose,* which resulted in her shrieking, all moms sent into ice-pack-search panic, shrill scolding of devil boy, ending in hysteria on his end. This is enough to make one question the very notion of having kids! To be fair, no one could hold up to the bar set so brutally high the week previous by the wonderful house, buffet, comfort, and elegance of that lucky bitch Marie, but whoa Nelly, this whole affair was painfully evil in its juxtaposition. Almost like an episode of *Candid Camera,* in its contrast and comedic nightmare of boring, tedious, and cringe inducing. Fact— I vow never to host one of these fetes until I get the whole sha-sha apartment and have cash coming out of my ears, which will probably be never but, come on, if you haven't a flat that can hold fifteen kids and adults, don't offer. I dressed up—as you do only when going somewhere by invite when pregnant—and made a huge effort to bring fresh petit fours from Le Nôtre *pâtisserie.* Not cheap and, with my cash flow, I don't do this for just everyday people. And they turned out to be people I didn't want to see *everyday,* or ever again.

The gang of moms had really outdone themselves—*stink of sarcasm.* The spread was potato chips, store-bought cupcakes, Coke in a two-liter bottle, and pretzels, popcorn, etc. Very midwestern garbage and a setting that, dare I say, oh bugger, I've already got a reserved parking space in hell, was tiny, dirty, and dismal. A cold chicken cadaver devoured down to the bone marrow—god knows when—sat on the stove ignored for how many days? The bathroom towels so gnarly and crunchy, I dried my hands on my ample belly? It couldn't have been more depressing. Is this my future life as an expat single mother in Paris?

The bountiful Rubenesque women splayed themselves across a couch, in sweats *and sweating*. Chaos reigned as kids threw cupcakes and used the frosting for face painting. The friendly if odd mothers sat and ate and ate and set forth on cursing Frenchmen, filling their sadness with terrible food for their terrible moods. I learned quickly that, for these women caught in their mindsets of *victim,* every major holiday and child's birthday party is spent in this tight-knit group, escaping into this world where men don't exist except to be criticized. I am horrified by the idea that this could happen to me—*by osmosis*—if I continue to hang out with the chubby crabsters.

For whatever reason, this group was jam-packed with mothers who had been left, cheated on, or otherwise blindsided by divorce. Sad and inevitable tales. I think my distaste for the group is certainly driven by "misery loves company" and I loathe misery, so, see ya! I have enough on my plate to try to stay positive and fully optimistic, passionately adhering (read, *clinging*) to the classic French phrase *tout est possible* ("all is possible"), since all that happens in one's life affects or limits you as much as you choose to let it. Obviously, for the immediate future, I'm ditching this group and hanging my hopes on the other option from the message group: expat mothers who live in *my arrondissement*. I have to have more in common with that pack and, frankly, I don't think I was fitting in so great with the singletons.

Hip-hip-hurrah! News came in on the amnio; all good, zip-a-do chance of any real genetic problems. The American Hospital called today and confirmed I, make that we, are in the clear! This is such thrilling news and vaporizes that nagging anxiety that followed me around the last three weeks like a murmuring whisper: you know, your luck may have run out here and in your selfishness to have a baby, you may have created a child that will suffer forever. Phew. A greater sense of relief I have not known. Oh la la. Then the nurse said, "*Et aussi, c'est un garçon.*" IT'S A BOY!!!!

Victory dance around the apartment, calls put out to Zola, Kathy, David, and *all* my family. Everyone always said it was going to be a boy and I felt so as well, but it's for sure. A boy, a son! I instantly think of my mother and how thrilled she would be. How she would surely play the Christmas carol that she so loves, "Unto Us a Child Is Born," sung by Kiri Te Kanawa, and we would cry together with shared joy. As ever with thoughts of my mother, I have to subsume them and march on or I will stagger and collapse with the reality of it. I have a son and I am going to be his mom. He will be my boy, and I'm "Mommy." He will be my momma's boy and I will be the "she spoils him too much" mom. *En français—maman! Magnifique!* This is the kind of silly gibberish you say to yourself over and over when pregnant and over the moon. I don't know if it ever stops, actually.

A million things to do now, since I have been literally waiting for this good health report to buy any clothes, toys, or nursery furniture. Now I can let loose and spend the next four months going ape shit decorating and nesting.

I blow off a phone message from Gilbert, a man I met a year ago on a blind date. Kind of impossible to imagine showing up pregnant again for a date after that last debacle with François-Olivier. I may not know much on the etiquette of dating, but I think carrying another person with you in your belly does tend to add a dimension to the evening your date wasn't banking on. Even if he was a *banker,* like Gilbert. Come to think of it, Gilbert was great and we had a smashing good time. I was just in my *constant* idiot mindset of only dating hot playboys who like to dance all night but to whom I like to pressure into a rapid fire "let's have a serious relationship." (And yes, I now see the absurdity in it all, it's like looking at a red ladybug and yelling, "Turn green damnit, now!" Ridiculous.) Gilbert was also just coming out of a divorce and didn't seem that keen on another immediate long-term "story," as they refer to relationships here. Interestingly put, huh? So after one date of fabulous conversation and lightning quick banter, I, clever girl, moved on to the next reluctant hot shot for me to lose massive time and energy on. Alas, Gilbert was sadly just a case of bad timing, I guess. And still is. *C'est la vie.*

I have another man, albeit tiny, who is going to be the center of my universe, and now I can start picking out baby names and nursery furniture. For once I have an "in my favor" zinger to those married moms: *I* get to choose whatever the hell I want on all fronts. In the words of that inarticulate warmonger George Bush, "I'm the decider." Which turns out to be marvelous in the making choices arena but not too marvelous when I am standing there at the darling baby boutique Natalys and realizing as I sign the *carte de crédit* bill that I'm also the only one paying, the one who has to get all these things home, and the one who gets to put the furniture together. Fuck bugger. The option of paying insane fees for assembly and delivery later this month is in no way going to happen, since budget and impatience won't permit. I am realizing impatience is expensive and I fall victim to it every time as equally as I martyr on with determination in the face of obstacles.

Okay, so I have just bought one sublime, pale oak baby crib with the *de rigeur* canopied *rideau* ("drape") of beige linen bordered with crème piqué, lined inside with an adorable bumper of same crème piqué edged in white rick-rack and an appliqué of a perfect teddy bear in cotton embroidery. Add a two-season mattress, linens, matching duvet blanket and pillow shams, *and* the accompanying waist-high three-tiered *table à langer* ("changing table") and an armoire with castlelike trim and cream muslin-lined wicker baskets. So French. Total fantasy baby nursery of my dreams! Now, I have to get them home and set them up, *alone*. Okay. This is going to take some doing as I am massively pregnant and have no strength, car, or even a taxi. Crapper, really? No one to call? Nope. David is traveling again. Can't ring Zola, since she is still full-swing in that new love story with Jean-Pierre and that means romantic late nights and cozy duvet days, as the Brits call them. (Read, stumbling home and falling into bed together and waking at 3:00 P.M. for brunch.)

So, Project One: hail taxi and get boutique staff to help me load the two boxes for armoire, mattress, and bed. Right. This is not done in Paris, since the mere suggestion of help on any of these tasks is met with rolled eyes and scorn. Whatever, ladies. Exert some effort for once.

Twenty minutes later, finally I get a taxi, the driver balks at the load and demands I pay him double for it "might scratch his trunk." Fine, *putain,* more waiting I cannot do. Taxi driver screams at me the whole ride to my apartment. (Hell-*o*, I'm pregnant, can you have some scrimpet of decency in your Gallic DNA?) He clearly isn't one of the fans of the rights all pregnant women gain in France. (You can move to the front of the line anywhere. Instantly. *La Poste?* Buying groceries? Film tickets? Instant VIP access. I love that and with my lack of patience am just milking it for all it's worth.)

Anyway, I pay rude-to-core driver double, as demanded, and he still sits in his seat, pops the trunk, and makes me lug out all the mammoth boxes by myself. Luckily, a neighbor appears and helps me load them into my tiny building elevator, where I can't even fit it all in. I have to slide it in piece by piece, let the elevator door close, go dash upstairs, and "call it" from my floor by pushing the elevator button. Then drag it all into apartment and collapse with exhaustion.

Then it hits me—there is no time to nap—as I so desperately wish and need to—as I have to walk back to the boutique and claim the linens, canopy, and the box containing the changing table. No way am I taking another taxi; that was like the nastiest Frenchman ever. What now? Humming. Thinking Cap on: airport trolley—I can rig it all on my metal baggage cart! Genius. See, who needs a man or to ask for help? Sweating and, for maybe the first time in my life in St. Germain, I'm so focused and motivated that I don't give a fig what I look like or who I might run into.

Back at Natalys, the staff is just simply mouth agape at this effort by the pregnant American lady. I'd bet my life, I am the only woman who buys this type of a posh nursery and hasn't the real means to have someone else move or pick up it all. Ah-huh, I get it now; I have a bit too much of a Bonpoint taste level with an IKEA budget. That's not a good thing. Noted.

Staff Natalys watches me pack everything up with expressions as though it were a car accident. (I prefer not to be on the receiving end of this judgment as a rule.) It's crystal clear they are completely bewildered why I'm doing this all alone, pregnant, and why the hell, in this slapdash, hyper-inelegant way. For the second time, *as at the amnio,* I become aware of how curious I appear in doing it all alone, clearly unmarried. Does it appear sad to other people? Seriously hope not. As it isn't in the slightest. It's merely an adventure and I'm totally fine with it. Just don't look at me like I was looking at those blubbery bitter single moms I met last week. I am not that. Right? You all see that, *non?* Why do I care? I never used to care a whit what people think—cursed hormones. Of course, I jet out of there hastening to make my way home with my overpacked boxes and bags teetering dangerously on the trolley held by a multitude of bungee cords for full "abandoned pregnant street urchin moving to next under-bridge lodgings" effect. And, FYI, there is no secret, discreet street or route to get back home. I gotta take this load down boulevard St. Germain and through the chicest streets on earth, would you believe!?

Crr—aaa—ssshh—hhh!

The right wheel apparently couldn't endure the hideous weight endurance test and freaked out, blasting off and racing into the traffic. Entire array of purchases scatter on the pavement. Can I just sit down and cry? Would that be fine? Just ignore me please. NO really, let's all pretend I'm *as invisible* as I wish I was.

My hands are raw from all the heavy dragging and we—baby, boxes, and I—are only just at the corner of Église St. Germain, right smack dab in front of the crowded popular *crêperie* and across from the famous café Les Deux Magots, as bad luck would have it. You know what? Fine. I load everything back onto the cart, with the help of some passing *Germans* who are very kind. And I kiss good-bye the rogue wheel and drag the remains back the four streets to my flat, wheel-less metal bit scraping loudly like a dentist drill all the way, drawing further attention I'm so not up for. I steadfastly face forward, lug on, determined to ignore all the onlookers of mixed expressions and the strong possibility the metal bit is making sparks that will set the whole deal aflame. All this apparently is yet another test from the baby gods—*Ça va!* Bring it on. I have legions of inner will-under-fire munitions!

As I turn into my building and heave the cumbersome frigging cart into the foyer, I see the precious little pillow shams have also made an early departure and are no longer at the top o' the heap. I just start laughing. Can it get harder than this? Oh, I am sure it can and will.

Back in my apartment, I pile all the boxes *et al.* in the hall. They span so wide I can barely pass through. Not only do I have to put all this together "by me ownself," I have another slight predicament. I have a one-bedroom with a small bathroom. Where am I going to put all this? My father's voice, speaking the phrase, "Kiki, looks like, once again, you're biting off more than you can chew," echoes in my thoughts. The self-possessed single mother in me answers back, *"Circa trova"* ("seek and you shall find"). Followed by the teenager in me, taunted mercilessly for my big unattainable dreams, who quips with a sly smile, "Oh yeah, just watch me."

Chapter 5

"Your children are not your children.
They are the sons and daughters of
Life's longing for itself."
—KAHLIL GIBRAN

Novembre et Decembre, 6–7 months enciente . . .

I pulled it off. Way, way ahead of schedule, need, or even normal pregnancy nesting rituals: I have redesigned my apartment for baby's arrival, and it's only November. The teetering tall stacks of coffee table books and novels (*très* Euro style) that had bordered the four corners of *le salon* ("living room") have been moved to oak bookshelves secured to the wall and the *cabinet des curiousités* laden with my collections of flasks, pocketknives, and Maasai African art has been locked securely. The antique silver bins chock-full of poisonous paints and pigments are now packed away in the *cave* (storage in the building's basement), and the outlets are child proofed and all cleaning supplies out of harm's way.

My dearly loved apartment once teeming with flickering candles alit each night on every surface and champagne flutes in arm's reach has been transformed from *une palace d'amour* to *une maison de famille*. I organized the nursery/my bedroom/boudoir by moving out damn near anything that is mine and placing the charming princelike crib right next to my bed. Now, to fall asleep looking at this darling crib, imagining that in a few months, my son will be lying right there is almost too much to bear. I know that seeing as there are still three months until this miraculous experience, I definitively win the prize for early nesting and prepping.

Hey, I have waited all my life for this baby, so sue me for jumping the gun on decorating. It's so fun and while space will be tight—like a posh version of TV's *Sanford and Son*—it's not like I am going to have gatherings of dozens of people over. Like the singular soul I am, I even declined Zola's offer to host a baby shower for me. Most of my friends are ex-boyfriends, and, frankly, I hate a hokey "you must act like you're having the time of your life" party. So, I just celebrate by myself endlessly and daily. For the first time in my life it's so great to see other pregnant women and feel a sisterhood and shared joy. Though Frenchwomen can be nowhere near as cool as American women with this idea; case in point, the other day, I saw a lovely pregnant woman who looked a little sullen walking down rue Mazarine. I thought, I should just tell her how very beautiful she looks and remind her of it so, just in passing, I said softly, "*Vous êtes vraiment jolie enceinte.*" And she instantly took two steps back and glared at me like I was hitting on her. "Hell-o bitch, I'm pregnant too. Ah-duh. Trying to be nice here, heard of it?" Whatever. Nothing's getting me down these days. Not even the fact that the diaper table was in no way going to fit anywhere but possibly in the bathroom. I dragged the whole schmear in and painstakingly set it up. Which is no small feat, with directions in tech-French (not my speciality) on a Xerox that was half cut off and like milk-stained secret message it was printed so pale. After putting the top shelf on upside down and then the sides backwards, all while heaving heavy boards and my belly becoming a major obstacle, I stood a bit back *et voilà*. It's done; marvelous! Wait a minute, I can't physically pass by it. I am literally stuck behind it and standing in the tub. This is no good. I will have to leave my flat in the next few months. Fuck bugger. I cannot for the life of me, no matter how focused, master any furniture construction or repair without botching it, damn!

I tilt the bastard on its side, hurdle over it, and vow to fix it later. Desire for a man moment number three-*ish*. And not just for handyman skills. Truth be told, these hormones are locked into "insane sexual predator" mode and I am really cursing self for not being able to partake in the much touted fabulous sex that comes with pregnancy. Oh god, the nerve endings and privates are all throbbing with desire and sending me dangerous signals: "See that guy, standing by the housewares department, go up to him, seduce him, drag him home, and fuck like wildebeasts." Shussh, I answer, horny hormones. "Fine, then the waiter at Flore. Take him. Take him now. Go, you sassy minx. Go forward and shag with abandon!" Good god, I am literally vibrating over here with desire. My consciousness is battling the raging surges and it's all I can do to just gather my wits. And take it on home, to put it cryptically.

Of no help was a dash out to Monoprix on rue des Rennes the other morning and still buzzing with the same vivid fantasies *à la* waking from a dream I was with George Clooney, my eyes set upon a gorgeous—as in insanely handsome—man standing next to me. In the baby bassinette section, no less. He is visually the epitome of what

I wish the husband of my dreams looked like. Quite tall, dark mocha hair, sky-blue eyes, mid-forties, strong hands and shoulders. Think Hugh Jackman with a great Gallic nose. A neck that begs to be bitten and an insanely fit body, clearly lying beneath an exquisite outfit. Ahhh, god. Men like this, even in Paris, are rare. They are usually too skinny, too short, possess too wacky or discolored teeth, too uptight looking, etc. (Quite the critic, aren't I?)

But he of the optic-white smile is just knee-weakeningly hand-some. Smile? Did he just smile at me? I am wearing the same long-sleeved shirtdress belted above my belly that I have worn for, well, every outing this last week. I bought it in London when I was twenty-five, and with the dip-dye print and volume, I just held onto it in hopes of one day wearing it as a chic maternity dress. Thus the dress of choice every damn day. To be clear, I am not looking great—my long hair is up in a topknot, which can be sexy when on Kate Moss or can be grandma when on a woman whose silhouette resembles a bull standing on back legs—me. I have zip makeup on and zip appeal. Flat boots and am exposing only the skin on my neck and the rosy cheeks with a splatter of freckles that appeared this month. Whose face is this?

The perfect creature speaks. To me!

"*Bonjour,*" he continues in French. "Do you know anything about these bassinettes? My wife just gave birth six weeks early and I am scrambling to get everything! I am lost," he says with a broad smile, gesturing to his shopping cart loaded with everything baby, save an actual baby. And he is laughing, revealing the most delicious deep crow's-feet by his sparkling eyes. Oh dear, do I loo-ove that on men.

In the fifth of a second I have to respond without appearing an id-iot in awe, my thoughts race. Well, of course, he *is* married, Kiki. Surely, to some ravishing twenty-something model who gets to wake up next to this gorgeous man. And what are you doing salivating at men anyway? Enjoy this simple exchange with a man you would give your right arm to be married to and chill out. Right. Do I need to speak? Yes. That would be a yes, he asked a question. I spew out some foolish drivel, and he instantly answers in perfect English after noting my accent. He asks how far along I am and I don't even know if I answered, I just want to hear him speak, watch his mouth move, know every and anything about him. Sometimes just meeting someone amazing is enough. Oh la la, Mister Wonderful chatters away as I fall into his eyes and then fall into a reverie and then something like a swoon. He is apparently a new father of four days and his wife is now back from the hospital and he dashed out to retrieve everything for his precious little girl and to get things to make dinner for his wife.

I love him. I want him to be my husband. Rats.

I congratulate him and he congratulates me on the pregnancy. (Sure, it's ah, great *not* having a man like you. Oh yeah, I'm a genius, doing it alone, everything. Wanna hear how I trapped myself in the bathroom today behind the diaper table? Nah? I guess with your Pateke Philippe platinum watch shimmering on that tanned wrist, you don't live in a tiny apartment. We are kind of flirting, right? No, I'm all wrong. Desperate and alone and remember, Kiki, ya look like a concierge after a big Sunday lunch.) We bid adieu and I stagger back into the *pâtisserie* section, by mere hormonal magnetic pull.

It suddenly overwhelms me that there *are* men out there like this; so excited to be a father, a doting husband, and easy on the eyes to say the fucking least. I tear up, feeling very alone and very sad. *I* should've found someone like him. Not that I really know anything about him, but he seems so amazing. What a fool I am. No husband and no father for my baby. And him—so giddily happy that he will chat up fat strangers like me simply, since he is so beaming with pride and happiness. Real tears well up and are hastily held at bay, I'm in the bloody grocery store for Christ's sakes. Pull it together, you sad sack!

Somehow, Mister Perfect Husband and I end up in the same checkout lane and he introduces himself and says, "I'm Jacques . . . my friends call me Jack. I just wanted to say, I think you look so great and I am sure my wife would love to get to know you. She hasn't been living in Paris long and hasn't many friends here. Let me give you my cell number and maybe we can all meet up sometime for a coffee."

I am stunned to be invited to connect with this man in any way and how charming is he, gathering up women friends for his wife? I would love to see this woman . . . but then again, maybe not, as this little meeting *par hasard* left me gutted. Maybe it would be too much to see the perfect little French family living the life I thought I could find, *and didn't*. I take his number and he puts mine is his cell log and we share an actual double-cheek kiss at the top of the escalator as he heads back to the luckiest woman alive.

Mmm, he wears Viktor and Rolf cologne. How divine, elegant, cool. Bugger! I can't stand it. I wish I had never met him rather than suffer this "oh, but I want it, daddy" little monster girl in me, like that equally chubby beast wanting the golden egg from Willie Wonka. I head for home, dragging self and groceries that made it into my bag though I can't for the life of me remember choosing them or paying for them. I have a crap realization—pregnancy is bringing out the jealous girl in me. Bloody good thing I am *not* married, I would be a wreck of a nag to my poor husband!

I sort out my mind by exerting my faithful compulsive organization skills. Oh, I can get into this *deeply*, when stressed. During my parents' divorce at age twelve, I had my Izod and Fair Isle sweaters all wrapped in tissue and then in boxes labeled with Polaroid photos and stacked by color. Oh, you can bet, I was quite proud that my entire

closet was arranged by segregated possible ensemble options, complete
with accessory charts. Every day I wrote what I wore so I wouldn't
duplicate an outfit for an entire month, would you believe? It was my
way of exercising some control, and my parents thought it healthier
than smoking pot and joining the circus and dating twins from Puerto
Rico with missing front teeth—*as my sisters did!* Not to mention, it did
have a positive outcome—I was voted Best Dressed in high school, but
that was hardly fair to anyone, as my BFF Kathy and I went to different
schools and swapped clothes, so we both looked like we were children
of tycoons with our vast wardrobes. I digress . . .

I guess I am anxious to go to the new mothers meeting in my *arrondissement* today. Luckily, the seemingly friendly mother who is
hosting lives just a block away and I have done a reconnaissance mission to prefind and review the building. Really a great building.
Frankly, I live in a charming tiny flat in an area that is among the most
beautiful and elegant in Paris. This was not an accident. I am all for a
small space in a breathtaking area, instead of opting for a fab apartment in a hell zone. I dated a guy two years ago who lived on the edge
of Pigalle, the famous red-light district. A sexy Breton man who was
in M&A, the guy had nice enough taste and the apartment was just
gorgeous with its fireplaces, moldings floor to ceiling, and ample balconies. Thing is, right underneath his balcony, on the street below,
were dozens of women, at all hours of the day, offering blowjobs, sex
in the courtyard behind, probably even sex in the *behind*! It was more
than a little creepy. I am all for legalizing prostitution, actually, but to
leave his apartment at nine in the morning and see men with wedding
rings *on tight* sashaying the street for an early morning delight—garf!
Alas, never had to go to that flat again as the Breton man, who had
previously asked me to move in, did a psycho about-face when I told
him the futon covered in crap faux American Indian print was not go-

ing to stay if I moved in. He chose the futon. To be fair, he did bail on me, but it was more likely because we booked a romantic trip to Greece and then he invited all his friends. I wigged. He left. Then offered to come back for sex visits but no future relationship. So French. So tempting. I tried once and found myself wanting to barricade him in my home for, well, *for ever!* Sex with Frenchmen has that effect. They are innately more passionate, creative, adoring, and attending to every millimeter of your body and of the tantric sex mindset that *your* pleasure is their pleasure. (Who cares if it's about their ego feeling fulfilled by their sublime skills and the theoretical power shift that's attained by having such mind-blowing talents?)

That's all a million years ago now, though. Time to set off for this "pregnant and new *maman* group" rendezvous. Like a cheese ball, I'm wearing a could-be wedding ring, so as to avoid having to leap right into the single mom story. I'm aware it's not so clever to start out friendships with a false impression, but I also weighed in the reality that I don't want or need anything but support; a framework of people who can offer me wisdom, like the best pediatrician's number, the basics of hiring a babysitter or nanny (since on the Web it's looking like another foray into French bureaucratic insanity—you need to pay them for vacations and insurance and secure fixed hours and wages, all reported to government . . . on and on). Not to mention, I really want to fix a little world for my son to be welcomed into, from the outset.

March myself and baby boy in utero over to the meeting, wondering along the way if I'm wearing too much makeup. Will they all be stay-at-home moms, unlike the single-mom group that worked tooth and nail and barely got the bills paid? Will they speak English? That would be great, since my French is crap lately; when a tourist asked me the other day for directions, I felt so annoyed with their just blurting at

me, "Where's the Louvre?" that I snapped, *"Non, parlez vous!"* which
was to mean, "I don't wish to speak to you" (a classic Frenchwoman's
autoresponse, actually), but I actually, stupidly said, "No, you speak!"
which clearly means—just about nothing. I walked away red-faced and
cursing self for blowing a blow-off so miserably. That's one thing the
French are serious about; if you're going to assume an air of grandeur
and disapproval, do it with great style and eloquence. I came off like a
moron. Aces.

In the elevator going up to the host's, Bella's, flat, it's immediately
apparent, oh yes, this is going to be another venture into lives of the
wealthy and more fortunate parents *à la* Marie of the palace on Île St.
Louis. Okey doke, I prefer mouth watering over someone else's good
fortune to the gag reflex of the last single mom flat's filth fest with fat
attendees. Oh, Christ, I am so judgmental. Frankly, I think I just say
this stuff in my head to amuse myself; it's a rare person that can make
me laugh and I have a need to giggle every day. Which in theory, should
make me a fun playful mom, *but I'm not sure.*

The glass elevator with brass fittings opens on the *cinquième étage.*
They have the whole floor. No surprise. Before I can knock, a tiny Fili-
pino woman in the classic maid ensemble opens the door from inside.
"Bienvenue à la residence de la famille Possese."

Fair enough. Aristocracy does warrant a bit of a nod to old-world
customs. Though this is a sharp contrast to my front door with the
sign, BUZZER BROKEN, PLEASE KNOCK. I am swept into a warm and
gracious foyer and into the bustle of mothers' and children's chatter
bouncing off the walls. In French and the Queen's English. Bella, a
handsome British woman, approaches and is terribly polite, clasping
her hand around mine and introducing me about as she just purrs with
compliments about my *bump* being "positively darling." How sweet! I
love British women and though Bella is a new mom to her youngest,

Sloane, just five months, she is definitely a few years older than me and instantly feels very much like an older sister. *Had my father had a brief fling with a Brit in say, 1963, for instance.* I like her immediately. Bella is clearly not French and very much not trying to be. That's rather rare and very appealing. With her chic jaw-length bob flecked with a few greys, she looks pulled together but with that air of a casual mumsy you just want to hug because you know they are squishy-soft that the Brits do so well. In her allover floral print cotton shirt and tailored khakis with loafers, she is very polished but in a quiet, old money way.

She leads me by the hand through the flat and makes me feel so welcome and pleased I came. This is perfect. From trailing around with her through the mass of meeting other mothers and mothers-to-be, I take in the full story of her situation, as they say. Married to a well-placed government official, she is a stay-at-home mom (SAHM), that is, fully in charge of running the home. The older children are all schooled at the high-end and fashionable (bilingual) International School of Paris, and each plays the piano as well as *another* instrument.

"Eleanor will play us all a little vignette on the harp at half past noon!" she announces proudly. The children have a governess, Dotty, straight out of central casting with her blue hair set by rollers at 5:00 A.M., surely, rosy red cheeks, buttoned-up grey apron over shirtdress, and soft-soled shoes. She has nodded hello in her hastening about to corral all the children to the playroom and out of mummy's way. All the children are being ushered away to the playroom as the mothers gather in the *salon* and set about nibbling on biscuits and tea. With the wall-to-wall lush carpet in hunter green (rare in Paris, where everyone has parquet floors) and the fussy antique English paintings of horses, ascendants, and pug dogs, well placed over garnet velvet couches and crisp white marble fireplaces, this home could be smack dab in

Covington Garden. Not a French object to be seen. Interesting. Indeed, more people are speaking English than not. What a coup! A dozen new possible mom friends to meet all in one afternoon and all are my neighbors! Yippee! My son will have his little friends all in place so we don't have to be the kooky, sad single mom and child cast aside at the parks!

I busy myself trying to remember ñames—was it Celine who had the perfect white Dior blouse on? Or was that Hermine? A sea of women are met and it's bloody hard—as they'd say—to remember which perfectly coiffed, gloriously chic woman was which. All are in their mid-thirties, married, and *well* at that, it's clear. Diamonds are as big as my eyeballs that are about to roll out of my head in such awe of the clarity and sparkle, and I feel a bit the token Boho mom-to-be, standing there in my high black boots and, dare I admit, cheap black jersey cardigan and matching elastic-waist skinny jeans by Zara, with a lace-trimmed camisole underneath. It occurs to me, I kind of look like one of the aging fat sisters from the 1970s band Heart. Egads. With my dark roots coming in under the blond highlights (and as I haven't seen my natural hair color for years, was shocked it's streaming with silver!), I could be *either* one of those has-been haggard chicks. Nevertheless, all the moms are so pretty and polite and it is rather fun to be there, amid such a lovely setting and people for whom, well, life is a breeze.

Tea sandwiches are brought in by the Filipino maid while her husband, equally as tiny, scurries about with a tray offering sherry and Pimm's cups. Charming. The banter resumes among the mothers in the salon. Conversation is to indulge on as much as the trays of tea cakes and petit fours that are brought in and laid on the marble table in the bay window looking out over Paris's beloved and bedazzling St. Germain. It strikes me, wow, this is essentially a twenty-first-

century version of the women's *salons* that were born in this very arrondissement some four hundred years ago. Well-dressed, well-read
women, speaking about politics, literary pursuits, and art. How charming. Why do I have to be the out-of-place sow wearing this shabby
ensemble? Moreover, why is pregnancy making me so damn self-
conscious? I am hating that.

Back to the salon and guests all chatting away. Hermine of the
Dior blouse, "I really have to say, there is no better school for my boys
than Sherling Hall in Gloucheshire. I recommend it highly. My husband, Pascal, and I visit the children there twice a season and of
course we chat every fortnight. It's truly marvelous for its prepatory
curriculum and formal guidance. I *shan't* think what we would do
with the boys in Paris?"

Another mother, whose name I can't for the life of me remember
(but she looks like a Claire, if that helps), says, a bit sheepishly, "We have
botched it then. Sent our girls to Potsdam Academy in Geneva and they
have started to wear Goth makeup and listen to Marilyn Manson.
Whatever shall we do?"

"Horrors," Bella says, sipping tea, pinky finger up and lifted just so.

"Marilyn Manson is the Anti-Christ, I tell you," states Renée of
the upsweep and Chanel tweed bolero.

Celine of the cashmere sweater set and Cartier choker of pearls,
"Marilyn who? Oh, I couldn't say, as I haven't heard of her, I am only too
delighted to report. Indeed, I, too, am completely taken with the notion of boarding school, as I can't bear being required to look after the
children on the weekends when we are all going to the country house.
It's simply exhausting trying to entertain their endless questions."

A roar of polite laughter applauds her comment, as if she just
stated some Latin maxim that summarized the calamities of world
suffering.

Are these women serious?! As we all sit here, noshing and sipping, the children are sequestered out of sight. I don't get it, aren't they the joy and delight of life? A modern-day *salon* this is not. Maybe because I am not a mother yet, I don't get it. I can't sit here like a lump or more like the blob that I am. Should contribute something. My mouth opens and I haven't a clue what's coming, since pregnancy has deleted any edit mechanism, "Bella, do you, by chance know Marie Toulon? She works in the Ministry, like your husband. She also is British." Not so foolish a question, I'm thinking. Establishing I have *some* international chums.

"I am *English*, not *British*. And no, can't say that I have had the pleasure of making her acquaintance," she says, making a tortured expression, as though I have proved a disappointing guest at word one. Somehow, fresh out of the starting gate I have killed off any hope of being a woman of comparable ilk and character. I swear, her face said *all that*. She looks off toward the window rather than continue chatting with me.

Okey dokey. British is not English? And vice versa? Whatever. Who knew not knowing this distinction would be a terrible faux pas. I sense a distinct shift in the room, as though I have turned into a pile of steaming poop at this pretentious snoot fest. Conversation turns to where to "holiday" and the apparent new theme "grave concerns of the wealthy" resumes full-on.

Hermine: "We passed the last *Pâcques* ["Easter"] taking a sojourn through the Amazon, one of the Abercrombie and Kent getaways. Mind you, just the two of us, left the children with their nannies to have some romantic time. Well, it was simply a dream. Fully air-conditioned private bungalows with attached spa . . . heaven! A personal chef and a full team of butlers, one for each of us. Sublime! If you go, I have to say, you must buzz the tree canopies in a helicopter as the legions of exotic birds scatter and fill the sky with a myriad of colors!"

Claire or whoever the hell she is: "We are off to Patagonia with Abercrombie too! Jean-Pierre bought a thousand acres there last year and we haven't even set foot! Heard the village markets are just a trove of inexpensive treasures!"

"I am booking a return to Jodhpur, India. Back to place some couture orders with my genius of a seamstress there. You know, it is she who makes all the hand-beaded caftans and dresses I just positively *live in* when we are at the house in Saint Jean de Luz. Now I have her beading the table linens for the house in Marrakesh and making raw silk drapes for the boudoir and the best thing—*I only have to pay her the equivalent of just 11 euros a day! Can you imagine!?*"

It's crystal clear my tale of making living room drapes out of a tablecloth from a restaurant supply store in Neuilly isn't going to hit home with this crowd.

Eleanor is ushered in to play the piano by the Filipino maid at exactly 12:30, cutting short a discussion of which is the best face cream. FYI, something called L'Essential Essence Esthedrem, made with collagen extract of rooster necks, which, if you think about it for even one second, it's not like roosters are known for their smooth, baby-soft necks. Weird. Eleanor gets a silent, sober nod from her mother to begin. A Brahms concerto, if I am not mistaken. The mothers look slightly miffed to be interrupted and place their tea and Pimm's cups on their laps. Beautiful music and again I am briefly swept away with the sensation of being at a seventeenth-century salon. So charming, if you close your eyes and ignore all the guests, save for the child.

SAHMOTUE—Stay-At-Home Mothers of the Über Elite (those who apparently under no circumstances would mention stress or problems of any kind and whose children sleep through the night and take naps on demand)—clap halfheartedly, while making demi-smiles of dismissal to the homely, if utterly adorable little girl. My heart goes out to her. I've been that homely little girl. And frankly, am feeling like the older version of her now! I yell without a thought, "Bravo! That was terrific, Eleanor! Well done, young lady!" *Quelle* outburst. The mothers, including *her own mother,* look at me like I have been smoking pot or am a raving hysterical loon. It's called support/encouragement—anyone here able to take their head out of their ass and look into the idea? Clearly no.

The tea ran on until 1:00 P.M.—nap time for the children, at which time they were all gathered and escorted to their respective parents. I noted very little in the way of, "Mommy, I missed you!" reactions; more like they were being returned to their wardens. Bizarre. All of the toddlers had a new Bonpoint shopping bag on their arm and were busying themselves comparing the *nounous* ("stuffed animals") and other assorted loot that each had received apparently as parting gifts. The Filipino nanny/maid/server made a final appearance; now handing all the mothers bags from the *très* chic boutique Dyptique. I think I was the only one who actually took a peek in the bag and thanked Bella, the others jammed them in their Chanel and Ferragamo (I always wondered who wore that label) purses of the season. Cool, a boxed *lilas*-scented candle and a set of soaps of every pastel hue. Nice detail, actually, and seriously generous. Bella offered me a perfunctory handshake good-bye as a Brit, sorry, make that an *English* mum would. She distinctly thanked me for coming but didn't make much fuss to insist I come again.

Indeed, only one other mother asked me for my phone number, which I found surprising as we never really spoke. A very pretty thirty-something woman with a low ponytail of cornhusk blond hair, wearing zero makeup and one of those women, you imagine, who doesn't even own any. Clad in a grey long-sleeved tee shirt and slim jeans, a look that reads Seattle, come to think of it, and exudes an air of calm like I always wish I did or could! Standing together in the large foyer, she puts her hand gently on my arm and almost whispers, "Hi, I'm Tara. Also an American, obviously. My husband and I just moved here from Seattle"—I was right—"a month ago with our four-year-old, Sam, and, well, I was hoping maybe we could get together sometime. Not sure I will be coming to one of these meetings again; it was a bit too . . . grand, if that's the word. My husband and I are a lot more chilled."

"Yes, this was my first time and it was . . . ah . . . *informative,* I will say that." And we both laugh, realizing we aren't alone and thank god. We exchange numbers in the elevator going down and it's a delight to see her son, Sam, is so animated and vibrant. So un-French. He is all over her, clinging to her legs and recapping the playdate:

"We had cake but they didn't have any ice cream. Still we had a lot of fun playing puppets. Mom, they had a real stage with all these puppets, but I didn't know what the other kids were saying . . . talking *French.*"

Charming. I hope my son is as free in spirit and as fun a character as this little guy. Tara and I chat a bit until we reach boulevard St. Germain and she and Sam head down rue du Bac to their flat. We both are so clearly relieved to have found a sister in soul, that we ditch the double-cheek air kiss of Paris and share a quick hug good-bye, vowing to meet up again soon.

By luck, I have met a possible *amie,* Tara, but for the love of god, where do I fit in in this country? Two expat mom meetings and neither was my cup of Earl Grey. After my apparent indescretion of making a major *contretemps* ("an inopportune or embarrassing event"), I am feeling persona non grata at that *hacienda.* (Way to mix French, Latin, and Spanish, huh? See, I can be international!) It occurs to me, the only valuable thing I learned this afternoon—in yet another of my comical *poisson* out-of-water outings—is to make sure I sign up for perineal reeducation after I have this baby. Shock of shocks—the government pays for an afterbirth, ten-week perineal reeducation course to get women's uteruses back into sex-ready shape for their husbands! So French!

Chapter 6

*"Children enjoy the present because
they have neither a past nor a future."*
—Jean de La Bruyère

Christmas is mere weeks away and at almost eight months pregnant, I can no longer jump on a plane and fly home to Wisconsin, so looks like I will be spending the season in Paris. I can't get sad at the prospect of being all alone, as there are worse things in life than going to midnight mass at the magnificent Notre Dame with a baby in your tummy doing joyous backflips (baby doing gymnastics—*pas moi*). As much as it would be so great and comforting to be with family right now, knowing that next year I will bring my son "home" and have a long-dreamed-of *real* family Christmas, with three generations together, oh la la. Heaven.

In the meantime, I busy myself consoling Zola, who recently made the wild ultimatum to her boyfriend of a few months, Jean-Pierre, that he must either marry her or she will leave him. I have never been a fan of those pressure-packed demands; they never seem to work and Frenchmen abhor commitment under pressure. So, she is seriously suffering as they take two weeks apart to see if they "can't live without each other." Egads. But it's been a pleasure to have more time with her. Zola really is so incredibly helpful and dear, offering to take birth classes with me and, of course, that monumental gesture—to be with me when I have the baby.

I've got to admit, the whole notion of going into labor alone, in my apartment with no mate, no one who will giddily leap up and say, "Our baby's coming!" is pretty hard to wrap my head around. Then there is a long, forty-minute drive to the American Hospital and I have heard dozens of horror stories of *merde*-head taxi drivers who refuse to take heavily pregnant women to the hospital because they fear both having their backseats treated to "water-broke-placenta-baths" and the messy spontaneous *enfant* deliveries. Thus, now I have had to add to my long laundry list of fears the getting to hospital race, on top of the birth itself. Fook.

Somehow the birth is not the daunting part; the physical pain and labor will be a cinch compared to just managing to be a parent, all solo. Still, no regrets at going it alone, indeed, it's the best, most thrilling, and satisfying decision I've ever made. Not for a second have I *ever* had a doubt that this child is the most wonderful gift and I am terribly grateful and humbled to receive it.

Bon anniversaire . . . à moi!

It's my fortieth birthday today (zip-a-do freak out about it, amazingly enough), and Zola has arranged a table and will be my date for dinner at Ralphs, the *très* fashionable resto by Ralph Lauren, the new sha-sha joint in St. Germain. With my belly and ass battling for most ridiculously expansive surface area, I would kind of prefer to duck into some small bistro and not be smack dab in the center of the domain of reed-thin models and uber-chic Parisians, but I think it will also be good for me to dress like a girl rather than an old gym coach (I have been donning my black Adidas warmups day after day of late). And it will be fabulous to be out *past* sunset for once and eat something other than baguettes—I'm up to three a day and I am still hungry!

Zola made reservations for 8:00 P.M. for us, which is absurdly early here, since people generally don't even go for aperitifs until that hour. Very cool for this *maman*-to-be, because I can hardly keep my eyes open past 9:00 P.M. lately since I'm so tired to the bone. Alas, a hot, vibrant date I am not. I have nothing terribly dressy or cool to wear and, since I haven't the funds or need to shop for true maternity clothes, I find I revert to my eighteen-year-old self in pulling together an outfit that was meant for an entirely different look. Which at that time was wearing pillowcases as skirts (remember I was in design school, where there was an obligation to tweak stuff) or wearing a preteen's cardigan as a tiny shrug; or there's the season I wore huge chef pants, paperbag waist tied with a rope. Now that I am a mature forty years old, I can't exactly go full-hog absurd so the least cuckoo choice for the night was to take an old Missoni knit pencil skirt and pull it all the way up over boobs-n-belly *as a strapless dress*. Totally belly-hugging tight as skirt was meant for my old body—many many sizes smaller, but it worked and looked downright cool. *I think. Or so I convinced myself.* At this point in pregnancy I can no longer pull off caftans and drapey flowing tops, since they just go over belly to furthest point and drop, making a hippo-in-a-tarp-type silhouette; not very sassy! And frankly, with even the front of my thighs now chubby and mush,

I think sporting just calves and shoulders is enough exposure to this ruthlessly discerning crowd.

Zola popped by to pick me up and arrived at the door, hilariously as though it were a prom date, dressed to the nines, bearing flowers—rubrum lilies, a fav of mine—and packing a camera and a beautifully wrapped huge box.

"A gift?! You shouldn't have but I am damn glad you did, darling! You are so thoughtful," and we settle in to the couch to unwrap the box.

"Just a little something for you. I have been assembling it all since you got pregnant. I looked everywhere for just the perfect Kiki-ish things," she says, helping me rip into it.

I reach into the depths and pull out an object that feels like a tissue-wrapped laptop. A gorgeous black and white houndstooth diaper bag with a black leather shoulder strap slips out and onto my lap—*in the scant space available there.* "No way! It's divine, how chic! And exactly the same weave as the Prada houndstooth coat I have. You rock!" I yelp, so tickled—this is precisely the one thing I had yet to buy myself since they are hyper-expensive in Paris and tough to find, I'm guessing because French moms don't buy many of them since they don't carry their kids out and about much themselves!

"Look inside," she says excitedly as we open the zipper and un-earth all the contents from their special nooks. Zola proceeds to ex-tract items and give their full backstory or purpose. "Here, check this out: a duo of Baby Dior baby bottles fit here and here and a Bonpoint baby bib with pale blue trim goes in this pouch . . . and in this pocket, a whole array of Mustela baby creams, powders, and *savons.* Here, a set of baby brushes, combs, and a nail clipper in matching blue, and, for fun, a baby bath thermometer in the shape of a blue fish. A precious baby blanket with little beige teddy bears embroidered on it to bundle your angel. And finally, a tiny pair of handknit booties in pale blue to keep his toesies warm!" she adds with as much excitement as if all this was for her very own child.

"Oh my goodness, this is so lovely. I am so touched, thank you so, you are the best friend ever!" I say, my eyes welling with tears. I am such a sap-cryer now and this is such a thoughtful and generous gesture. We hug, toast with "Spumony," a sparkling apple juice that is our new joke of faux champagne for the two girls who once quaffed more of the real stuff than anyone in St. Germain. We take a few pics of us together, camera held at arm's length, then of my belly in profile and my chubby face full-on and laugh our way off to the resto a mere four bocks away. With the exception that we are both sober and I look like I swallowed a VW, it's all like old times and a blast.

It turned out to be a terrific night despite my initial doubts as to how I would feel to resemble a woolly mammoth and be out and about in my old element. Funnily, I forgot I was pregnant a few times and upon sighting a couple of scandalously sexy men on the stairs coming in, I went on auto into my prowl, eye-fuck mode. Absurd and laughable, since they both looked at me, then down at belly and smiled like, "Ah yes, another pregnant woman with hormones a pulsing!" Over dinner, Zola and I recapped many of our finest late-night adventures; the tales of men that got away and the ones we should've let get away sooner. (In her camp: the man who would wear white tee shirts tucked into his big white underwear with black socks. And my ex: who after a month of telling me he was separated let slip, "but we still live and sleep together—for the kids mostly!") All the while, devouring lobster salad, beet and mache salad, and the most extraordinary selection of tiny breads: poppyseed, olive walnut, and sesame toasts slathered with salted beurre. By 9:00 P.M. the crowd started to fill every banquette and the music got louder and groovier.

"Damn, I really miss going dancing, Zola. We used to go out and dance hard at least three nights a week and now, nothing. I miss that so much . . . and I miss running like mad every morning. Those endorphins were like my drug of choice. How the hell will I ever run again? As a single mother of an *enfant,* that will take some doing," I say, realizing there will be no stepping back into anything even resembling my old life.

"You will figure it out. If anyone can do it, you can. I never thought—before this pregnancy of yours—that having a child alone, by choice, was possible or even really acceptable, but you've once again dispelled one of my held-fast beliefs," she says, speaking a bit freely from having to drink the entire *boutille de vin blanc* alone. (Tidbit of a factoid: no one orders a *demi-boutille* in Paris, since it's assumed to be 1) low-class cheap of the buyer and 2) perceived as lesser quality and thus less elegant. *Quelle horreur!*)

"Really? Well, I guess that's a compliment. Thanks for saying so. Lord knows I am thrilled to have the time and situation to just devote myself to it," I reply, just noticing that the gorgeous actress Monica Bellucci and her drop-dead hot husband, Vincent Cassel, have slid into the booth next to us. How refreshing that in person she looks older and rather zaftig and not *quite* so iconic. Zola and I take that in at the same moment and nod in the silent communiqué of best friends.

"So, have you spoken to Jean-Pierre yet?" I ask, who is clearly MIA during their two-week break or dragging his feet.

"Nope. I left a message and he called back and left a message saying he was busy this weekend," she answers, clearly eager to speak about it, as I knew she would be, but she was obviously holding back so the night was more about me and my birthday. *Très* thoughtful of her.

"Zola, I know you love him dearly, and I think he is truly a great man. I haven't ever seen such a wonderful Frenchman, actually, in either of our lives. I really think you should tell him that the big ulti-matum that hangs in the air isn't so imperative. Let him decide when he is ready, he will ask you. He is so in love with you and such a ter-rific guy."

"And he was raised by a single mom!" she adds.

"Really? *Cool,* I didn't know that. How inspiring. I love to hear about amazing men who didn't have fathers in place from the get go. And Barack Obama didn't turn out half bad, right?" I add, laughing.

"Yeah, but I am Republican, so let's not go there," she replies.

"Really? You never told me that . . ." I say, semi-stunned. "But back to Jean-Pierre; you should let the big pressure ease and just get back to the love," I offer, realizing this sounds a lot like a bad song lyric.

"Kiki, you're right. Everything was perfect and I up and went and put this bomb in his lap and screwed it all up," she says wistfully.

"Believe in love. He is a jewel," I say, realizing it's so true and she found a good man. She deserves it. *We both do, but I had to go and make one!*

The night wraps with Zola so generously snagging the *l'addition* ("bill") and the two of us sauntering home, arm in arm, as women do in Europe without the absurdity of people thinking they are lesbians. In our chatter, we agree to have a midwife come to my flat on Satur-day for a private birthing class, and Zola will come over to attend and get the lowdown, to be raring to go at the birth—not that I want her to really do anything active, mind you! Triple-cheek air kiss good-bye and a hug for good measure, and off I flutter (as much as one can with fat ankles and a barrel of baby at my waist) up the stairs to my apart-ment, so content and pleased. This is the first birthday since I was, hmm, sixteen, no make that fifteen, that I didn't have a boyfriend and a big fabulous birthday extravaganza, and it was still just perfect. Had flowers delivered from my stepfather and mother (though he signs her name since she obviously can't write) and a big bouquet from David of lavender roses, a few other small arrangements from exes and my sister Lily. Got about ten text messages and e-mails, and I feel happy as a clam, even without a kiss or a romantic night. It's 9:46 P.M., and I am off to bed; time to peel myself out of this sprayed-on tight dress . . . wait, another text message is incoming:

> Kiki how is the bebe? U free for a rndvz demain? Xx, Jack

Jack? I don't know a Jack. OHMIGOD, I do. Jack of the major hotness new dad guy. Holy shit. Hmm, what to say back? What does he mean by *rendezvous*; that's so vague in France. Could be a coffee or hedonistic shag or, hell, even a dental appointment.

I climb into bed in my ridiculous flannel pajamas, slathered in *huile d'almond* and heinous pink fluffy socks my sister sent me that, despite being tacky as hell, I looove.

> bebe is great, merci. future soccer star, as kicks a lot . . . Rndvz when? Will I meet wife and child? Hope so.

I add the last bit, trying to play it neutral, since what kind of rendezvous is he getting at? It could mean sex under a bridge along the Seine or tea with the family at Angelina. In this country you never know what that word means—and they like it that way! I hit send and curse myself for not waiting until morning to 1) not look so eager and available and 2) think up something infinitely more clever. Damnit. My impatience always bites me in the ass.

I turn off the bedside light and roll over, placing a long puffy pregnancy pillow between my legs, because somehow this is infinitely more comfortable. Could be that flabby legs touching each other is ghastly and unconsciously annoying. Whatever about Jack. Ah duh, Kiki, he is a new dad and already told you, he wants to connect his wife to some other moms in the area. You are so pathetic . . . go to sleep. But just as lucid thoughts start to lure me into the arms of Morpheus, my cell phone vibrates on the windowsill. In a crack of an instant I am entirely awake and jamming at the touch keys to read the message:

Confession. I want 2 c U . . . 3.00 Café deux Magots? Don't refuse.
Xx, Jack

Jesus fucking Christ. What is this? Did Zola hire this guy to flirt with me, since I am such a sorry-ass single mess? Is this a birthday present? A joke? What the hell? Why would this guy want to see me? This is so weird *and so great.*

Attention. I have missed it more than I realized. Why the fuck is he married? Why would he, who can probably have anyone, bother with me, when I have never looked worse? Okay, I don't get this. Suddenly, I am sitting up, rail straight, sweating—literally have broken a sweat from the excitement and can hardly think as my heart pounds like a freaking techno drumbeat, throbbing in my chest.

I love that he said, "Don't refuse." So sexy, for as much as I'm always the dominant vixen with men, the "slam me up against a wall and take me" girl in me hugely prefers men à la James Bond in their authoritative voice. (Let's be clear—this doesn't mean they are the authority; I still run the show, got it?) Well, you can't do anything really scandalous at 3:00 P.M. in public—I could go. Just for my ego and curiousity. As though it were a blind study of Frenchmen's fascination with pregnant women. But to be honest, I nap then. I can't write that back to him. God! And I would look about five hundred times better under the cloak of darkness . . . what am I thinking?! I couldn't go to Deux Magots anyways, as any Parisian will tell you, you are either a life-long patron of Café du Flore *or* Deux Magots across the street and never do you betray the other. Oh fuck it, this is a riot. I have nothing to lose by texting him and just badgering him to tell me what it is he is *really after*:

Why bother mtg me? U have new baby+ wife.

I send, thinking, I could never send this blatant of a question to a Frenchman if I were really trying to be with him. This is fun. Three minutes later, SMS arrives. I instantly try to imagine the scene. Gorgeous wife and child have fallen asleep and he is sitting in a club chair, stocking feet up, book on lap face-down, and watching the fire in silence . . . *or*, I suppose, he could be standing in his bathroom, pants at ankles, masturbating in bad lighting. I prefer the former.

I guess as new dad I feel one chapter of my life closing and I saw you and that spark between us lit . . . and cannot be extinguished. R U married? Ur eyes say no.

I'm suddenly aware that I am now such a total sucker for attention and that he could become *way more* important in my quiet daily life than he should be if I allow these personal intimacies to continue. And yet, I can't *not* write him. It's beyond my control.

Mère celebitaire. Bring Ur wife and I will meet U.

I send, telling him I'm a single mother, but interestingly in French, *celebitaire* means just single, while obviously in English, it's *sans* sex—is that a *double* entendre in *double* language? *Oui.*

No. I want u. alone.

Him, French and blunt/demanding. Why is that sexy in France? If an American man wrote me all this, I wouldn't be intrigued in the slightest.

Come on. Why?

Me, losing patience and not even sure what I want him to say.

If U r this ravishing enceinte, then u must be amazing.

Him, saying precisely the shit I, or any pregnant woman, would desperately want to hear. Damn, he is good. Wow. Why is this man married?! Mother^$%er! Oh la la, I have to catch my breath; thoughts race and my gaze floats out the window onto the cobblestone street below, lit by a classic old lantern-style lamp.

Mmm. Paris at night. It could be 1790 and I could be reading love letters delivered by Jack's footman as he waits by the liveried horse-drawn cab for my written reply. *Or not.* Could just be as he says, he is a horndog of a Frenchman, not loving the emotional weight of true family life as it unfolds into reality. But of course that's it, but how weird to hit on *me. Now.* I don't think I actually want to see him. I mean really. I am so sure that someone would get the shit end of the stick if anything really happened and that would be, well, pretty much everyone—wife, child, me, and eventually Jack. But men like him always do get away with everything. I am not embarrassed to say (though maybe should be) I am loving this from my end; it's all just pure amusement and will help me pass the time with a smattering of compliments and a new distraction. That's what married men cheat for too, right? So, I send:

Bonne Nuit 4 now . . . xxx, Kiki

I sleep like a woman who has been bathed in kisses. A little adoration goes a long way these days, where months have passed without so much as holding a man's hand.

I wake in the morning smiling, feeling like it was all a dream. Vowing to refrain from any more texts. I am making a baby and that was all mad juvenile fun. That feeling fades since, not so surprisingly, a hot guy, no matter the scenario, is like a massive delicious ice cream sundae with toasted pecans and pure whipped cream—you know it's very bad for you and yet you can't stop until you get to the bottom. In short, this silly girl can't help herself: Jack and I text message about eight times a day for a week. I am fascinated, since it doesn't make any sense and I have to, for once, since I hold all the cards, just burrow into an in-depth study of a Frenchman's motivation to cheat. I ask a zillion personal questions and offer little in return.

He quickly becomes out of his head obsessed from my constant refusals to see him. A man like this—with a body built for two—is not accustomed to *not* getting his every whim and request met. It's crazy-making to discover he is so much of what I thought he was and what I would've died for in a man, and yet there is this constant flashing neon sign in my brain, HE IS PURE SHIT, TRYING TO CHEAT ON HIS NEW WIFE AND BABY! THAT'S THE LOWEST OF THE LOW, BEYOND COMPREHENSION LOW! In no time at all, it also becomes apparent that there is this delicious thrill in refusing a man who I would generally die for and who, as his punishment for being such a cad, I get to mind fuck him. And there's the bit about loving the virtually hourly attention when my social life recently bumped down to a tiny handful of faithful friends. I haven't totally lost it in all this, mind you, despite reveling and buzzing from all the attention from my new text stalker (talk about safe sex?); I did hit the pause button on all this sex-text nonsense after my big Saturday private birth class—*chez moi.*

The one-on-one tutorial on everything from nursing to water births went off quite well. Though it was rather funny to be panting out Lamaze breaths loudly at three o'clock in the afternoon, imagining the guy downstairs flipping out that I was really going into labor at home or, *more likely,* as a twisted older Frenchman, his first thought was probably I was having loud sex with the woman in my flat. The American woman, Becky Hart (how USA is that name?!), who came over to give me the half-day-long presentation was the coolest, calmest, earth-mother type. Of course, I booked an American; there was no way I was going to engage a French *sage-femme* for this hugely important lesson, since it's so clear that while Frenchwomen may be swimming in Dior *maternité,* they are also paddling in very different ideas than American mamas!

I really enjoyed the class—except the time frames of how long it can take to fully dilate; *days?!* That will be my luck. It was so magical as I held Becky's baby doll to my chest to get a sense of how to do the correct "latch-on" and to feel just at that moment my baby kick like the dickens. Wow. To envision him in my arms, in the scrumptious dimpled flesh in less than forty days; oh my god, the reality that is drawing near is so thrilling and transforming. I already feel like a very different person and am delighted to feel a growing sense of purpose. Except . . . Zola totally bailed on coming over for the meeting and had my head not been bathed in deliriously happy soon-to-be-mom thoughts, I would have been rather pissed at her. She did in fact take my advice and retreat on the hard-ass ultimatum and got her boyfriend to take her back and off they went to the northern cliffside village of Etretat for a romantic weekend, *in lieu of staying with me for the birth class. Ça va,* I guess. The whole world doesn't have to revolve around me, I'm *finally* learning. We really, each of us, are on our own and that's not something to be sad about, just to be accepted; no matter if you are single, married, or a part of a vibrant, loving family, you essentially only have yourself to find the internal means to cope, excel, and ultimately decide how to deal with everything. You have to set off on any journey knowing that. My mother, my best friend, all the men who have told me they would love me forever—sadly not really there as much as I would've thought or wished, had I held tightly to each promise. Alas, you just never know how it will shake out. In that moment, I thought of my son and felt awash in love and profound commitment to do my utmost to help him feel both independent and self-reliant—just as my mother and father had instilled in me—in tandem with the unshakable certainty that he always would know he was not truly alone. I would be there for this boy all the days I walk this planet and the days beyond that.

Amid this poignant outpouring of emotion, "*Jack la liaison dangeruse*" began a barrage of text messages and thus instantly became actually annoying. My shutting him down resulted in his "final request" to send me a handwritten letter. OK. Fine. Entertainment if nothing else for this pregnant woman whose life is getting increasingly limited to the immediate area (read, a five-block radius). I doubted he would actually send a letter anyway, since it's more than a little risky for a married man to pen something in his own, *personally traceable* hand, but he did. Yep, a long letter arrived a day later, attached with a bouquet of, get this, six dozen long-stemmed red roses, so large they wouldn't fit in the tiny French elevator of my building. Seventy-two roses is a massive bouquet and resembles something that a Kentucky Derby–winning horse might have around its neck or maybe an arrangement for a Mafia funeral. Obviously, this was getting absurd and very apparent that if I *did* actually *see* him, he would surely get over this obsession *tout de suite,* but because I wouldn't, he was over-the-top wild. *Frenchmen!*

And that letter? A lot of passion based on the few scant things he knew about me, never *trop* sexual, thankfully, but, oh, *bien sûr,* Jack puts the "sin" in sincere. It all came to a head when late the following morning, he sent a text message:

Something is waiting for you and XY at Bon Marche enfants de-partment. This afternoon. Pick it up at 4.00, Santa.

Kind of cute, calling the baby boy in my belly XY and himself Santa, just three days before Christmas. But I still have steadfastly refused him (Jack, not Santa) and don't want to pick up the *"cadeau"*; it's just nonsense. I have much bigger things to think about now for god's sakes. I ran the whole whirly gig extravaganza of it by David and he said, "Oh, Kiki, we have to go, it's just too tempting not to. Let me come with you and we will see together—if he is there, waiting to see you, we will just blow him off politely. We must check this out. Good lord, only you, Kiki, would have this kind of thing happen to you at eight months pregnant! You can notch this story alongside that jewel of when you met Matt Dillon on the subway," David adds, recollecting a tale from our college years that still makes us both collapse laughing. That caper of a scenario began with my quick exit from a bad date on the Upper East Side of NYC—by leaping into a taxi, leaving the dull as a doorstop banker dude on the street corner, only to discover I did not have sufficient funds for a taxi, so I jumped out a half block later and made my way to the subway. Crabby from poverty and the lame time with a handsome goon, I sat there all a-glowering on yet another dirty subway seat, cursing my dumb life only to look up and see the actor Matt Dillon in all his sassy beauty.

Like a gift from the gods, he said, "I like your coat," and off we went on a flirty chat, resulting in his inviting me to join him at the uber-cool club of the moment, Canal Bar. With nervousness aplenty, I agreed instantly and we set out for a night on the town, the likes of which I'd never seen. Paparazzi galore as we sauntered up—don't get much of that at college dorms—and feeling like, "Holy shit, is this really happening?" Insane to enter this private club that was packed to the rafters with the famous and beautiful, when I had been heading home to devour an entire box of Ritz crackers. The fashion designer Thierry Mugler held court at one table as Paulina Porizkova table-hopped. An intensely overwhelming crowd, in short.

Matt was meeting up with a bevy of his hipster pals, and you can bet your life a slew of the legions of young perfect models sidled up next to us in the banquette. I was trying to act cool and not so self-conscious that I was sitting there in a tailored jacket, mumsy turtleneck sweater, and dress pants when all the models were dripping in sexual allure in tiny tanktops and microminis. In truth, I felt like an old schoolmarm and was hating it. I may have made some amusing banter on the subway but now was being a bit forgotten among all the long-legged gazelles. Like the silly dimwit I was (and clearly can still sometimes be), I hatched what I thought was a clever, clever plan and excused myself to the ladies' room to begin this mini-mission. Plan: Screw the turtleneck! I am ditching this lame-o thing and reemerging to the table in just my black bra under my jacket. Very Madonna-sexy.

(Remember, this was the late eighties, kids!) But as I was executing this genius idea, my turtleneck caught on my long hair extension (I did mention this was the eighties, right?) and lo and behold, it fell right smack dab into the toilet. Damnit! As I looked down to see the once beguiling long sultry hairpiece now soaked and looking like a drowned rodent, I was fucked. That couldn't go back on my head, and now I was sporting a tiny, Woodstock from *Peanuts*-esque, pokey pigtail of one meager inch popping out of the top of my head. Like that looks sexy?! I looked frigging ridiculous. With nowhere to put the turtleneck, I chucked it into the garbage and plucked out the wet hair blob to accompany it. There went seventy bucks for the two, but what the hell could I do? I looked in the mirror feeling crazy, as dropdead gorgeous models came and went, looking at me like I must have been the sorry bathroom attendant.

Zero options, I had to head back to the table and try to pull this off as if it was so very intentional and normal. Shit, I just wanted to escape out the back door but I couldn't. Don't even know where it was. I summoned all my strength and on shaky legs made my way back to the table, where I was met by a semicircle of expressions of, "What the fuck?" I slid in next to Matt and, by way of explanation, offered to the table of mouths agape, "I was hot, so just made myself more comfortable." With a whisk of my hand in the air, as though, "Whatever." Amazingly, Matt countered with, "I like it better. But that's a pretty weird move, girl. I dig the unexpected." And all his friends laughed like lemmings and accepted me warmly back to the group despite my tiny poop of a pigtail sticking out of my head like a severed squirrel tail. More champagne was brought to the table and a divinely entertaining night kicked into high gear. Off we all went to the next club, MK, and I danced the night away with Matt and his pals. I learned that night that you gotta roll with the punches, be yourself, and take chances, and I haven't stopped since. (Oh, and also, never wear fake hair!)

And so it was that yet another pretty damn unusual adventure was laid before me. Musing over the possible laughable outcomes, David and I marched over to Bon Marché that afternoon feeling like we were being set up for a reality TV show exposé or being watched covertly by Santa a.k.a. Jack. And don't ask me if I'm being naughty or nice; my life always seems *not* to fall into the easily decipherable. Truth is, I almost felt drunk to have this little side story to distract me from the fact that my baby isn't in *the slightest way* thinking about flipping to head down to the correct birthing position. My OB-GYN looked at the sonogram and said, "He is perfectly healthy, big, and strong, but don't gorge this last month. If his belly gets any bigger, he may come out head first, then shoulders as normal but his belly could be too big and get stuck." (My internal reaction—what the fuck? Can that happen?! What a nightmare.) She followed with, "He also isn't making any progress in moving down into the birth canal, since he is pretty big and it might be a tight move. Let's not worry . . . *just yet*." Oh great, no, you won't be the one worrying will you? That would be me, plagued with insomnia of late, with increasing fears of a wild weeklong labor and, well, the other constant concern is that of any mother at this late stage—cleft palette, oxygen deprivation at birth, crib death . . . the list is as long as my arm. But there I am, somehow targeted as some silly insecure Frenchman's obsession and, well, it is a great escape from the weight of worry.

At Bon Marché, David and I take the back entrance from the *épicerie* escalator down directly into the *Enfants* department. David and I are scanning all corners and nooks for a stealthy, handsome man. None, save David, actually. I give my name to the clerk, who, I must add, looks to be about the chicest saleswoman ever, draped in Chanel and smelling of heaven. (Smell—clearly my new favorite sense.) She nods in knowing terms, asks us to wait while she goes to retrieve something from the back room.

"What do you think it is?" David asks, as he holds up a breast pump, laughing.

"Don't laugh, I just bought one of those. Oh, and I have no idea. If it's another breast pump I will feel like a cow all hooked up to a milk machine. There's a look I haven't considered!" I answer, laughing with a tinge of nerves. Why am I nervous? This is all so surreal.

The clerk returns, wheeling out the Rolls-Royce of strollers, the Stokke. The most high-design, chic, elegant, futuristic, and expensive stroller made. There are at this moment about ten in Paris and this is *"Pour vous, Madame."* Oh la la. I gotta give it to him. Killer genius gift. He isn't creepy; he didn't give me lingerie or something sexual, just this totally, unbearably cool stroller. He is as handsome as he is elegant and generous. I have to remind myself, oh yes, and he is also a cad. Right. But not my cad, phew. Still, I literally am out-of-my-mind tickled.

"No way! No . . . waaa-a-Y! This is *tooo* hilarious!" I laugh, as David and I shake our heads, checking it all out—it has a flat posh bed for a newborn and a whole other seat for a baby and another for a toddler, until age four, and a transparent rain cover for all options and a faux silver fox blanket for winter and a sun umbrella that pivots and an "underpack" for groceries.

The clerk adds, "Monsieur also thought to include a lock and cable since this is a valuable special piece. *Enfin,* here is a note from the purchaser."

I thank you for all the words and wisdom you have shared with
me . . . thru this, a complicated time of transition in my life. I know

you have your own world. I hope you and your son enjoy this and
accept it with the friendship I hope we can continue.

Xx,

Santa a.k.a. Jack

That is really, seriously generous and even if he is a rogue-rascal-scoundrel-stinky husband, I think it is a truly thoughtful gift and effort. I mean, come on, he didn't need to do any of this—I did zip-a-do for him and never even saw him, except that unforgettable first time. I feel really lucky to get this beautiful stroller to take my darling out and about in a style my single-mom budget could never afford; and it's also pretty cool that I did, frankly, get a lot out of my exchanges with Jack. Indeed, a far better understanding of the different pressure that falls on a man when a child arrives. I surely wouldn't have known—*and didn't get to know*—any of that by going through this alone and well, to be honest, thank god, it wasn't my husband who sought solace and escape. I think that must be the only man-based snafu I have side-stepped!

David and I take the massive stroller up on the elevator and out onto the streets of Paris as the night falls like a cool drape. We both just laugh all the way back to my house, since this gigantic *poussette* is so big and sha-sha that it barely fits through the mass of gawkers that flood the tiny sidewalks as they hurry to make final Christmas purchases.

"Funny thing is, Kiki, this stroller is so you . . . and he doesn't even know you," David says as we try to cram the chic beast into my tiny elevator. Once again, like all the baby furniture before it, I have to close the elevator, clod up the two flights and push "call" to get the thing into my flat. "How is this all going to work with a baby in it?" David asks, smiling.

"I will figure it out! Like everything, my *chéri!*" and we do the de rigueur double-cheek kiss good-bye.

The following days were spent quietly—sending a gracious thank-you to Jack and wedging self past the mammoth stroller each time I have to leave the apartment. Zola was off to fly back to the US for a family Christmas, but she popped by on the way to the airport. I buzz her in and plod to the door just as baby decides to test his goalie foot. Oufff. Big kick, kiddo. In fact, these little communiqués he has with me are so wonderful and I know I will miss them *even* when he is in my arms, since it's so uniquely intimate a connection and so fleeting. I pull open the door when I hear Zola's clippety steps on the tile stairs. I love this girl: always, even in the dead of winter, she wears feminine little heels.

"Sweety! How are you? I knew you'd be alone for Christmas and I thought you might like this," she announces hurriedly, holding over-head a huge red blanket satchelled into a sack.

"What? What are you up to now, girlie?" I ask, seeing once again that she has brought me some super-thoughtful and unexpected gift. We scoot back to the living room, where she places the four-foot-tall red sack on my coffee table and lets the four corners fall, revealing a small pine tree laden with a criss-cross wood stand. (Like Charlie Brown's and the way all *arbres de Noël* are sold in France. It's terribly charming and almost makes up for the horrific price. *Almost.*) The fragrant Christmas tree is just teeming with colorful ornaments and already trimmed with lights. Zola plugs in the cord while placing a silver filigree star on top.

"Check it out, it plays four songs and the lights can dance to the music . . . cheesy, yes, but adorable, *non?*" she asks, standing back, admiring her handiwork.

"Oh my god, you are so lovely. So unbelievably dear! Cannot believe your limitless thoughtfulness!" I reply, throwing my belly and self against her for a big hug. "Thank you so much, Zola! And these are for you," I say, handing her a monstrously large bag of gifts. This year, with so much gratitude for her friendship—and free time to spend shopping—I went hog wild getting her things I knew she would adore and wouldn't treat herself to—ice bucket, champagne flutes, candles, and sexy camisoles from Galeries Lafayette.

"You rock, so many gifts! I will open these when I return, better dash, Jean-Pierre is downstairs in the car, waiting to take me to the airport. I will miss you two," she says, patting my tummy. "Call you on Christmas, doll!" and off she went, leaving me and my baby to bask in the twinkling lights and have one of our private little chats accompanied by patty-cake through my tummy. I love being pregnant, life is in full bloom, which is an incredible feeling, when I think, "Wait, I am forty years old and life feels like it is just starting. That's amazing."

Christmas was quiet and charming, as I fielded calls all day and night from family and friends and passed the evening making a Christmas stocking for my son, just as my mother did for all of us "chickens," as she used to call us. Embroidering his name and tiny teddy bears all the while, hoping he will cherish this small holiday tradition with all the exuberance and thrill that I once did. It's so incredibly compelling to be on the cusp of having a child. Days seem endless and yet time is rushing by; before I know it, it's early January. (New Year's Eve spent, for first time, sleeping. I was going to say alone for the first time, but, cancel that, child in womb qualifies, and sober, though did look about the same upon waking—*bloated and tired*.)

Holy smokes, with weeks to go, my belly is so round and high, I can feel the top of his head just under my ribs. God knows where my ribs have spread to, but this kid is practically standing straight up. I literally have to catch my breath since he is crushing my lungs, and, I have to say, eating isn't much fun since food more or less stays in my throat burning for hours. Which has me instantly hating whatever I last ate and gagging at the mere thought of it. So no weight gain this last month, thank the lord.

I am getting antsy; the whole apartment is baby ready; I have read and reread every birth, breast-feeding, and pregnancy book ever published and am full-on into the stage when it all just feels cumbersome and uncomfortable. Sleeping isn't exactly a cinch, since I can't sleep on my back and literally have to slide sideways off the bed to get up, as I now have zero stomach muscles. Which all proved ridiculous-bonkers when I ran a bath today in my adored eighteenth-century bathtub. After slopping into a bubbly half-filled tub (my girth makes water displacement a mini tidal wave splashing onto the floor), I realized I could not freaking get out of my gorgeous, lion-clawed *baignoire*-sanctuary. Slippery hands + no abdominal strength = whale flailing about, legs kicking wildly trying to act as ballast. It was seriously, seriously scary. I thought, oh great, yelling *"Aidez-moi!"* aloud to have someone break down door and find me naked (I could stop there, as that's enough of a horror) with what looks like a raccoon between my legs (waxing appointment tomorrow for perfect birth scenario). I'm kidding about the raccoon. NO, really, I am.

Chapter 7

*"The soul is healed by being
with children."*

—Fyodor Dostoevsky

A week later, on the bus to the American Hospital, I realize this will
be my last doctor's appointment before the birth. I muse how, when I
first started coming for my appointments, it was scalding hot and, as
ever, no AC and I sweated like a beast, cursing this country for its back-
asswards ways; today, it's bitterly cold and this whole pregnancy is
coming to its highly anticipated end.

I have loved making these pilgrimages like adventures every
month—back to the sweetest doctor and to the land of speaking
English at the hospital. To visit the maternity ward and have my
eyes fill with tears to know that soon my baby will be there nestled
in blankets! Visit by visit, the hospital itself has become this magical

kingdom where my exciting new life unfolds. In an environment where I could feel cared for (by someone!) and be in a sanctuary of American and English language and ideas. And frankly, that's been invaluable to me on this private journey. There has been enough that's foreign, new, or both! All the while, to see my baby grow from a grain of rice to a sea horse to a reptile to now an actual chubby little baby, who sucks his thumb and looks like he's waving at me. Oh la la.

Today the doctor is backed up and, sadly, we have to rush through the appointment with a bullet-pointed punch list. Facts to deal with: my boy is breech, big time, as in frank breech. Indeed, it's the least favorable of the options, meaning he is now butt down, feet up by his ears, and I have the option to try to have him "manually manipulated" by the doctor to move him into the birth canal head down—which is done with a team in the operating room, all ready to deliver since it can result in rupturing the amniotic sac and requiring a C-section ASAP. Or I can spend all my waking hours on all fours, trying to skooch him into turning and descending while also gently trying to help him turn with gentle prodding of my belly. Oh yeah, that sounds about forty gazillion times more pleasant than the first idea.

Obviously, I choose option 2 and spend the last week before my due date trying to lure him down. Lo and behold, just when he is tilting his head and turning his shoulders, he rights himself like, "Ah *non,* I am fine, ready to go in my frogman/one-man-luge position, rocketing out of you without getting my head turned into a cone, thanks, though, Mom." And so, like the stubborn boy I was guaranteed to have, he ensured that we would need to set an appointment for a planned C-section and mommy would miss the labor of uncertain drama. It takes me all of a nanosecond to thank my lucky stars. Yes, I will always be pretty thankful for that breech stance by my boy, since, being a single mom, a zillion miles from the hospital, I wasn't that keen for the mad dash and certain ongoing pain.

With the day and time set, Zola was signed on and approved to be with me for the birth, for handholding, cheering, and taking photos, *of the baby,* not my hooch getting the "emperor's cut," as it's also known in Europe. Night before, could hardly sleep, as one would imagine. It's an amazing thing to leave your house, knowing when you return you will be bringing your child home. My bags packed for a week's stay, as I, unlike most Americans in the USA, had the luxury of staying as long as I wish at the hospital. Jean-Pierre gave Zola and me an eventful ride to the hospital in Neuilly, just outside Paris. Getting slightly lost on the way was as irksome as Jean-Pierre's casual chat about geography, weirdly enough. I was sitting in the back, hands on my belly, just wanting silence or to talk about the baby. Alas, one can't be too demanding, given I was getting massive favors from these two and they had no idea how anxious I felt.

Checked in, left my bags in my appointed room, which was really great, top floor, view of the treetops and the Seine at a distance. Switched into a not-so-heinous hospital gown (pale grey cotton tunic with mandarin collar) and went with Zola to the prep waiting room, where I had the misfortune of having some young resident botch my IV drip insertion; my hand swelled up like a football after three vicious attempts, and, finally, it hit me, wait one damn minute here, I'm paying out of pocket for this massively expensive event and I'm going to insist this idiot steps aside and goes to get me a real doctor.

That nervous meltdown complete, Zola started looking like she would faint.

"Have some water, dear. You look peaked," I say, trying to assume my mother role about thirty minutes early.

"Thanks. I am just realizing this is huge. It's kind of overwhelming," she says, slightly reeling while sitting on the edge of my bed in pre-op.

"I know. I am so excited I can't even think about any of the pain coming my way. Let's just get on with it," I say, getting up and looking out the door, trying to will the process along.

Feeling better, Zola pipes up, "I'm guessing everyone will think we are a lesbian couple and I'm the dad!" she says.

We break out laughing just as the doctor walks in to ask if I'm still wearing contact lenses, which apparently I need to take out for surgery. Hmm. Making my final bad-girl decision, I didn't abide by that request. No way am I taking out my lenses since I am bat-blind without them and they could hold up a bedpan and proclaim it my firstborn and I would not know the difference. I am *so* going to see my baby in 20/20 vision, even if I lose my sight forever after! With that, it's time to jam my hair in a bonnet, move over on the gurney, and get carted downstairs. The orderly who pushes me through the elevators and long halls strikes me as exceptionally handsome; cleverly I noted this may not be the time to ask him for his number. Would've given him a helluva good anecdote but I had other priorities, like getting further prepped to have a baby!

After the feeble IV debacle, I hit another stroke of bad luck; while I usually like multiples of anything (*deux coupes des champagne,* two Dior purses, two sets of luggage), I didn't much care for having two epidurals! *Oui, c'est vrai.* The anesthesiologist was really gentle and kind, making me feel quite relaxed as he chattered away, until after a sharp pain and what felt like a twist of a knife, he whispered ever-so-casually, "Oops. I blew that. Sorry, your tattoo distracted me. Let's give it another go . . ." No "oops," in the operating room please. NO, *non!* Focus, mister! And stop babbling on and on, dude. Maybe I can interest you in a hot cup of shut the fuck up. This meltdown kept *entirely internal,* of course, one doesn't scold man holding a gigantic needle in your spine. This much in life I *do know*.

The doctors and nurses all arrive and my legs are *hoisted* (ohmigod, it's beyond terrifying to see one's legs flopped about here and there and not feel anything—this is entirely like being paralyzed and it's a frightening feeling) onto the operating table as a drape is fixed over my belly. Zola is brought in and placed at my left, her smile is soothing as all the sudden I feel like I'm the wounded carcass in an old episode of *M*A*S*H*. Glancing at the large round light above is quickly to be avoided, since with no effort—or desire to—you can see the mirrored reflection of all that is draped and it's not for those with fragile stomachs . . . especially not for those whose stomach is being sliced into like a pork belly.

In about fifteen to twenty minutes, the activity below the drape turns from the sense someone's doing dishes in my tummy to a heightened awareness that the doctor is now elbow-deep delving into me, scooping out a baby. My baby!

"Okay . . . here he comes . . . It's a big beautiful . . . blond boy!" she says, holding him under his chubby arms as he squints in the light and cries loudly. He is covered in lanugo and kicking his little frog legs wildly. My boy! I just want to grab him but my arms are kept down with an array of IVs and he needs to have his throat cleared and get a quick wipedown. In the pregnancy plan meeting with the doctor, I had made it clear in no uncertain terms that he be brought to me ASAP and they did follow through with that, whisking him back to me, still crying and covered in pale yellow creamy goo. Believe it or not, adorable! All the while, Zola snapping away with the camera. That's right girl, don't miss a shot, I want the baby album to be a virtual flip book of every precious second and image!

"Hello my darling, it's okay, it's okay. It's momma. I love you, baby. I love you so," I chanted over and over again, as he was held to my face and I felt his warm strong breaths on my cheek . . . ahhh bliss. It does not *ever* get better than this moment.

And after all the fit I made in the doctor's office—that I get to hold him as soon as possible and let him smell my skin and nurse as every baby book dictates. In truth, as they Hoover vacuumed and stitched up whatever muckity-muck was going on below the drape, I gave oodles more kisses to his sweet cheeks, and then I was out cold for about twenty-five minutes—just as the doctor said I would be. Just as well, since he was kept busy with measurements and the like.

My luck was back and up and running, as Oscar and I made it back up to the maternity ward at the same time, and, thankfully, I felt instantly rejuvenated—good as new and just drunk with love and joy to be handed my red-faced, gummy-smiling little angel, who curled up in my arms and fell fast asleep. To finally see his dear little face and to get to utter his name aloud to him was beyond bliss. I named my son, essentially, after the Irish writer Oscar Wilde. I have just always adored the name, especially ever since I worked for Oscar de la Renta many years back. In all the 7th Avenue fashion companies where I used to work, I generally would get sick to death of the company name inside a week (as you're just besieged with the logo at every turn), but I fell more in love with "Oscar" each time I heard, saw, or said it—not to mention, Oscar Niemeyer is one of my favorite architects, so fabulous Oscars abound and I made myself yet another one!

Obviously Zola, also named for a writer, deemed it a terrific anointment for my boy as she glided about, sharing in the happiness and proclaiming him the most beautiful baby ever (though he did, actually, look an awful lot like Winston Churchill) as she sent out text messages and photos of mother and son beaming to all my chums (exes included, *bien sûr*) and family. Which instantly resulted in flowers, bouquets, and

calls pouring in from L.A., Wisconsin, Paris, and NYC—Gilbert sent
an *abonnement* ("subscription") of new bouquets each week for a year,
from Au Nom de la Rose (so generous), and Jack sent a teetering, tall
array of calla lilies, with a note, *"Félicitations, Chérie."*

Unquestionably, this was one very welcomed, healthy baby, and I
hoped his whole life would be so wonderfully celebrated. While I was
so touched by all the gestures, I truly longed for my mother to be
there. To weep with joy with me at this little miracle in my arms and
wash him in kisses. Her absence was the only sad note as Sir Oscar
cooed and smacked his lips with hunger.

After many hours together, Oscar and I didn't quite master the
perfect "latch on" as I'd hoped, but still he seemed content to place his
open palms with the tiniest perfect fingers on my chest. Of course, I
spent the whole afternoon swimming in a state of elation. Zola whisking in and out, giving us some privacy in turns with companionship. I
had hoped to hear from *cher ami* David, though I knew he was in NYC
making a presentation, but I was delighted that he had so sweetly thought
to send a big bouquet of lavender roses.

I was busy taking photos galore of Oscar, when there was a knock
on the door and Zola smiles mischievously.

"More flowers? Oh my god, we have nowhere left to put them!" I
said, loving the whole idea.

The door opens slowly and *voilà* . . . David appears all big smiles
in his YSL navy peacoat dusted with snow, "You didn't think I'd miss
this event, the arrival of your young prince!" and he sweeps in to hug
Oscar and me, as I almost cry again for the umpteenth time that day.
I am so touched he flew back to be there for me and with all the love
in the room, it was as much a family as any. David unveiled a chilled
four-pack of POP *demi boutille de champagne* with baby blue labels—so
cute. David and Zola popped two open—god, I love that sound—and

sipped away as I basked in the most delicious happiness I have ever known.

Everyone left by 9:00 P.M. and Oscar and I were finally on our own. While my doctor advised I place him in the nursery and rest— "You will need it!"—there was no way I could let this precious soul out of my sight. I waited all my life for this day, *this baby,* and I wasn't going to miss one second, one breath of this tiny angel's first day on the planet. In truth, I almost never slept during my whole hospital stay; I just held him and would doze between feedings and snuggles. I did find it terribly hard to drag the bassinette into the loo with me for quick showers and to pee as my legs were like blobby peg legs the first days. It was amazing to see I'd lost twenty-one pounds in a day (what I would give for that ability on a regular basis!) but also strange to have not really been prepared to be left with a belly that looked like mushy six-months pregnant with a nonspherical blob and an incision across my bikini line that I couldn't see, but sure as shit felt like it had been made clear through to the other side. I was so elated to be a mother that it just didn't bother me; it all felt like a tiny price to pay for being handed the treasure of my life. All that much more so when my doctor casually mentioned in one of her rounds to check on us, "This boy really is a virtual miracle. When we were patching you up, I was astounded to see your ovaries are in terrible shape, quite inflamed and out of whack. I have to make it clear, it's amazing you got pregnant and as much as I'd like to see you again," she laughed, "I don't want to see you in my office for damn sure! Seriously, do not try to get pregnant again. It would really be high risk and problematic to say the very least." I held Oscar tighter, beamed with happiness as I buried my face in his soft belly, wallowing in the joy that he, in all his miraculous glory, brought to me.

Day 3 was notable for the mammoth boobs I sprouted; known as "engorgement," your chest explodes overnight with a full milk supply. I was about 90% boobs and Oscar was like an emperor at a Roman banquet since finally we had locked into the right latch-on technique, something you never consider will be a problem—*until you try it*. It was the sole frustration I had and I kept thinking that he was rooting around like a tiny pig sniffing out a truffle and the milk is right there, why is this not working?! Worthy of note: the nursing staff was so cavalier as I asked for help, advice, *anything!* The nurse just said, "Well, you tried, I guess it's not working, I can get some formula for him."

I was like a loon, so committed to getting it right, I pronounced that a nonoption, made a big sign for his bassinette, NO FORMULA, BREAST-FED! and I immediately rang for a La Leche expert and paid this woman to come to the hospital *tout de suite* to help me! She arrived later that same day, and amazingly, inside three minutes she had us all situated (read: pinching nipple so as to resemble a straw as much as possible) and we were off and running. Words cannot express how hugely satisfying that was, since I believe so strongly in breast-feeding and would've been totally crushed not to be able to nurse my boy. Somehow these beliefs about breast-feeding and circumcising become foolproof devices in whether you will get along with other new moms or not. I liked one of the new (French—*quelle surprise?!*) mothers on the floor at first, until she said, "Oh you're breast-feeding . . . why bother? Formula is just as good and you have your freedom and your breasts back." I don't even argue with mothers like that; there is no informed person out there who can claim that formula is just as good, not to mention what a wonderful bonding experience; your body makes it for your baby, how can you deny them? Your boobs are—guess what?—made for this purpose, not for "sitting high" in some maillot poolside in St. Tropez . . . oh la la.

By the way, it's an amusing transition from day 1, where you are so

self-conscious, you try to hide your chest/nipples under scarf and blanket while nursing, to day 3, when you're so beyond it, like, Oh whatever, has anyone in this hospital *not yet* seen my boobs? I mean the
flower delivery guy has, the room service guy has, the cleaning woman
has—the entire staff has. That's more exposure in seventy-two hours
than they've had in over forty years! You just get over it so quickly that
it becomes, like so many silly self-conscious qualities, obliterated as
your baby becomes the star at center stage and you're just the happy,
humble, bowing servant to your new master.

Prebirth, I had prepaid and booked a doula, since I'd been told you
really can hardly walk, lift, or move for a week or two after a C-sec and,
well, in my general style of solo journey by choice, I quickly canceled
her commitment.

I knew the surgery and scar would hurt and it sure as hell did, a few
stabbing times during the first three days, but within four to five days,
I was mostly just fixing up my room, arranging flowers, and loving being the mom. As in, spending hours marveling over every yawn, burp,
and more or less drooling over the adorable baby's legs, toes, ears, you
name it. There was a lot of, "Hey, we both have tiny freckles in the
same place on our right foot and pinkie finger" and "He has my chin
that dimples when he smirks." Almost as fabulous was getting the best
room service of all hospitals on the planet!

Oh yeah, I was paying top euro for this whole extravaganza and,
despite the crap help with the latch on, it was so worth every *centime*,
since it was such a treat to be served meals like *filet de cabillaud crème à
l'oseille, purée de pomme de terre, fromage blanc, poire cuite aux airelles, pain
aux noix;* or the *petit déjeuner* service: *thé avec du lait, jus d'orange, assorti-
ment de pâtisseries, beurre et confiture fraise, pot de yaourt nature, compote de
pomme et fruit frais*, or dinner of *oeufs brouillés, pommes lyonnaises, épinards
en branche, Fourme d'Ambert, ananas en gondole*, and a *panier du petit pain*.

I loved all the insane feasting since I well knew, back at home, I would have little time or energy to whip up much more than soups and frozen foods from Picard that I had stocked the house with in preparation. (Not to mention, when I cook, it always ends up looking, whether I follow a recipe or not, like something from a sci-fi movie—*tasting similarly, I should add*.) I was also calling this my last gorge fest, since there were still a hefty twenty-two pounds to shed and lord knew how that was going to happen, in the dead of winter and with a new infant. Freezing weather and being commanded to abstain from exercise for six weeks cut out the running regimen I longed to get back to after nine months of slothism. Must add here that any new mother with baby-weight blobs aplenty will attest that you absolutely grow to loathe the celebs and models who have trainers, chefs, nannies, *and* the means to bounce back to their previous bodies in record time *and* be feted as though they were modern heroes. How absurd.

Frankly, I was so in the la-la land mentality: embarking on this new chapter of life, lounging in my hospital bed listening to the birds at dawn, as a wafer-thin sliver of the moonlight still peeked through the blinds, my son in my arms, a warm bundle of cooing and nuzzling—not even the fact I could've taken my saggy stomach and folded it into a giant origami whale was a downer. Indeed, with all the new babies on the floor, the joy and celebration in every room is this intoxicating force of nature, celebration of life and so clearly a rebirth for every new mother.

Thankfully, Oscar was perfectly healthy and growing well after the initial dip in weight that comes with birth. He was a darling, just magnificent . . . but as vocal with that tiny throat as he could possibly muster. Whenever I would place him in the bassinet at my bedside, out of my arms, he would shriek like a banshee, so I pretty much held him all the time. The last night I thought okay, I'd better rest or

I will just collapse, so I asked that he be put in the nursery for just the wee hours and brought to me when he woke. I felt so guilty to let him out of my sight, but I was so slap-happy-tired that the doctor *insisted* on it before she left for the evening. I think when I said to her, "I think I hear someone playing tennis," she petitioned for my sleeping *très beintôt*.

That well-laid plan lasted, honestly, all of three minutes since Oscar was already so attached that he wouldn't pipe down until back into my arms. I heard his crying all the way down the hall—even so new to me—I knew it was him. I heaved myself up in my scandalously short, pale-pink nightie (that I had bought for the hospital stay *not* taking into account that big belly and ass would hike the darn thing up to the second fold of my flabby butt, making me look like a hippo from the film *Fantasia*) and flew off to the nursery with the very first of what any mother knows is a lifelong chest-throb of concern for their child. "*Bébé, c'est moi.* It's okay, honey. So sorry. I'm here." Howling child edging on hysteria, heard my voice, opened his scrunched-up eyes, went silent, and fell asleep before I even made it back to my room.

This is so my kid. "Attention now! No, I said *now*. Thank you!"

I had spent much of my six-day hospital stay doing mom training in the nursery, where the team very seriously (as in don't try to be funny, they aren't game) teaches you how to bathe, dress, and diaper your baby. I went from semi-terror at the first class—bathe holding head, in temperature-tested water, shampoo that feather-like hair, one moisturizer for face, another for body, Q-tip applied antibiotic drops for umbilical cord, clean eyes and nose with saline-watered fresh cotton ball, don't forget the drops for eyes, six drops of vitamin D in mouth, crème for cradle cap, clip fingernails and toes so tenderly. I literally thought I would never remember all these steps, but by day 5, it's old hat. Thank god!

I was eager to get home and so left a day early. Gotta say, the American Hospital was such a smart choice. Everyone was really kind, helpful, and the facilities are top-notch. Would you believe that in Paris many of the hospitals still haven't upgraded to air-conditioning? Can you fathom giving birth in August, in 97-degree weather in a room lit with a billion hot lights? Nah, I thought not. I even met a mother there who flew in from Boston, in her last trimester, to have her baby at the hospital. And there were some royal Saudis who took over the VIP wing, men donning turbans and the women in burkas 24/7—made me think if women aren't allowed to expose their faces how the hell does a doctor help them at birth? And finally, not only did the American Hospital turn out to be far cheaper than if I had given birth in Wisconsin, but there were parting gifts galore! Like Oscar and two carts of bouquets weren't exciting enough, all mothers receive an engraved silver cup by the chic baby boutique Ovale (a shop that I could not even afford to buy a sock at) and a stash of the Ovale super-soft terry cloth pajamas that they wrap the babies in and a small sleeveless sleeping bag embroidered with the hospital name and logo. So cool. Keepsakes, much?

An hour before departure, Oscar got a final checkup, during which the physician declared him *"Splendide!"* noting it down in Oscar's *carnet de santé* (which every French child has—it's a bound booklet in which to keep all the records of a child's birth, vaccinations, every checkup, sniffle, and cold until age six—very intelligent, one point for France). I had only to pay the bill and make a grand exit. Exit not so grand—as I left my jewelry bag in my room and a bottle of Veuve (that I was so dying to drink!) in the nursery fridge. Both were "gone" when I rang for them later. Poof! I really didn't even care. Truth is, whoever stole the jewelry was going to be hideously disappointed to find out all the diamonds were faux. I'm no fool; I'm not bringing the good stuff to surgery.

After a tense ride back through Paris—where, suddenly, all the bananas-crazy traffic seemed less amusing and more like possible threats to my baby—we finally arrived back in St. Germain. As beautiful as it is, it seemed even more vivid and charming, as though it had been color retouched by the team at Disney. New motherhood does that well. David helped unload the taxi and carry the flowers and luggage back *chez moi,* since I would've surely split in half—*torso on curb, legs walking inside*—had I needed to bend at waist. I'd finally seen the scar the night before and, while a mere four inches, it was numb to the touch and looked like a red broken zipper. Sexy? *Non.* Oh, who cares?! At least I didn't have to endure arduous labor for days on end, all the while with hourly checks that felt like someone was doing a hand puppet show inside me *and* I got to avoid that episiotomy—that when you first hear about it, you're like, "Oh . . . No, you're not. Cut me where? You've got to be kidding!"

A few hours after David had left, I realized that during the whole "bringing home baby" transition, my trigger reaction to such an overwhelming, BIG event *didn't* result in my usual nervous energy running amok. Settling in with a baby to care for alone—forever—just felt natural. I think I was as relieved as everyone about this. As Zola put it later that month, "Phew. You sure have taken to motherhood with that passion you apply to everything. Thank god, girl, since I was kind of holding my breath, because you have to admit you went from the girl who enjoyed her massive freedom on a global level, as in, 'I'm done with this party. Leaving!' or 'I'm done with this guy. Leaving!' 'I don't like this career. Changing!' 'I don't like this country. Changing!' to becoming a doting, patient mom, *round the clock*," she laughed, assuming this was a big compliment.

Hmm, it did make me think. True. I have always shed skins, lovers, jobs, cities, and dinners, anything—whenever the restless intolerant Kiki took over—and now, I am just at this plateau of peace. All the drama I craved and sought—gone! And as my best childhood friend Kathy put it in a beautiful card to Oscar,

> *I have known your mother through three decades, each year bringing another adventure in her search for "The One." One day her search came to an end. Because she finally found what she was after: you. You are "The One." The One she has been waiting for, the One she has been dreaming of all these years.*

Oh gosh, I cry every time I read it. It's entirely, unequivocally true.

Chapter 8

"When I approach a child, he inspires in me two sentiments: tenderness for what he is and respect for what he may become."

—Louis Pasteur

Ahhh, the first two months of motherhood were a dream. It was perfection to be able to snuggle in these grey dark months with my precious new best friend—*and not have to expose this* après bébé *body to the sun and public.* Despite all the hype of weight loss through breast-feeding on call, as per the Attachment Parenting philosophy, the pounds were hardly pouring off. To have cellulite on your arms—which very much resembled my beloved cheese curds back in Wisconsin—was just gross. I took to hardly even looking at myself, and with only a small bathroom mirror and zero free time, it was easy to just ignore it and put weight loss on the list of things to do eventually, somewhere below trekking in Nepal but above learning Latin.

It only became truly annoying when I got a call to do a PR interview for *Jalouse* magazine for my next art show—and despite my pleas to happily submit PR photos taken prebaby or beg for a delay, they weren't having it. I was to appear for the photo shoot and interview at Café du Flore twelve days after giving birth. Holy cats, here we go. Time to just make it work as a single working mom with an extra mouth to feed. So, despite actually never being more feminine as just having given birth and put breasts to use, I *felt* I was no longer a glowing, radiant pregnant woman on the receiving end of smiles from all— now I looked like just an anonymous, amorphous blob, an asexual creature with frontal feeding devices, and here I had to get ready for this big event. Makeup felt like a ridiculous attempt in beautifying and I was so unfeminine-looking in my loose shapeless dress that I could easily be mistaken for a mid–gender reassignment patient. This bites. On the plus side (because being a "plus size" wasn't), it was a total joy to dress Oscar to the nth, since he was coming with. I quickly realized this is maybe how those bizarre Southern moms who put their kids in pageants get started. Well, yes, I am a frigging train wreck, but let me put huge effort into my child's appearance. Focus there, everyone! Christ.

In truth, the interview was super fun, with Oscar in my Baby Bjorn the whole time, since there was no valid reason in my eyes why I would not bring him. They were all cool with it, being the groovy hipsters of publishing where being a single mother is like, *whatever,* whereas the old-school establishment/aristos would have been horrified. I was interviewed with another expat, a very clever young writer, Rebecca Leffler, who within the hour exuded such intelligence and wit, she now is secure on my list of adored friends. Indeed, it was *très ironique* to be sitting next to this dewy-skinned, brunette waif, who was the vision of all that is chic, while I was full stop, *none of those,* being interviewed for *Jalouse* magazine—*jealous* I was, but playfully so. I left Flore thinking, I was that girl once, but now I have Oscar!

Oscar just instantly has become this cure-all and salve to any unanswered question or worry. The weeks were flying by, as we settled into our routine of no routine. From his birth I realized I wasn't going to be one of those mothers who set his schedule, telling him when to sleep, eat, etc. We all, no matter what age, deserve to make these choices based on need. That said, this philosophy does make it bloody difficult to attend any rendezvous, appointment, or meeting, since you don't really know if baby will be nursing, howling, sleeping, or cheerful. It became ridiculous to try to make a date with friends for *chocolat chaud* at Flore or even a walk by the Seine—with Oscar finally down for a nap and your arm pinned underneath him, knowing he will raise holy hell if you so much as cross your legs or exhale, as you watch the clock tick to the appointed hour and he still needs to have a diaper change and nip at nursing upon waking and a change of clothes and you're still wearing some spit-up-stained shirt that isn't fit for daylight or public, on and on . . . You just stop making these dates and can only hang with people that will accommodate "fly by the seat of your pants" spontaneous calls. *And* won't judge you for having forgotten that you had to abandon your makeup after lining only your top lip and arrive *comme ça,* a shadow of your former put-together self.

Interestingly, Zola had taken her relationship from the precipice of death and turned it around in three months to get that damn engagement ring she so wanted. I gotta give it to her, that's a miracle and the only story of its kind that ends with "happily ever after." So, despite her secure position as godmother, she is definitely not very available, in her flurry of Bridezilla mode. I still trundle around with her, Oscar in Baby Bjorn (decked out in a tiny snowsuit that makes him look like a tiny polar bear), looking at wedding gowns at all the boutiques, as much as I can. (Notable—You don't much see French *mamans* marching around with baby adhered to chest, I don't know if it's just not comfortable or, God forbid, *unchic* or if it's by tradition that casually pushing a posh *poussette* with one hand and a Dior bag in the other is the hard-and-fast rule.) Anyway, it's pretty wonderful to see Zola get her dream wedding organized at the same time that I am living my mom dream. She is planning on having *le grand mariage* in August, at a château outside of Paris, complete with horse-drawn carriage, fireworks over the moat, and ceremony in a fifteenth-century church. Yeah, that works. The only downside is I'm kind of unable to help with much of the planning since I have my hands full with Oscar. And, dare I say, she is semi-absent from our friendship, ordering everything from wedding dinner matchbooks to printed napkins and pencils with bells?? (One could wager there might be a tinge of jealousy on my part, that she gets the whole "French husband, château wedding, French baby, complete with relatives in place" package, while I try to figure out how to take a bath in under three minutes with a baby howling; I'm damn lucky if I get one leg shaved and can rinse the shampoo out.)

While I have come to think myself quite the master of existing on no sleep, it's no easy task to wake, I kid not, eight to ten times during the night to feed him. Not to mention, the gorgeous Natalys crib that's set up—as though for a photo shoot—hasn't so much as had Oscar's *derrière* in it for a catnap. The kid just won't even sleep two minutes alone! Which at this early stage, when he is eight pounds, is really no trouble, since I can keep him in the crook of my arm and just lean over and nurse him, but I know it's not great to let them cosleep forever as a million moms I know say, "*Bon chance,* then they *never* want to get into their own bed." A woman from the PMI (Protection Maternelle Infantile, a state-run pediatrician, nursery, and child welfare service) came to check on Oscar and me, as they do for every mother in the first three months of infancy. It's pretty cool, really, to have someone come over, ask how it's going, offer free pediatrician visits, vaccines, and advice. I couldn't gauge from chats with other new moms if this was like welfare or just a government-paid-for service, and I don't even know if you could refuse it. While the woman was really lovely, polite and gentle, when she said she herself was not yet a mother, it did kind of taint her authority. Still, as no French *mamans* do the "attachment, cosleeping" thing, she was hyper-surprised but still advised that, "to get him to sleep in his crib, you may want to try taking a soft piece of your clothing laden with your *odeur*"—that just means *smell*, no offense intended . . . I think—"and lay it near his head." That's a no-brainer and I had tried that already—no luck.

But I thought her next idea to be a priceless morsel of wisdom, and I was optimistic I was on the cusp of solving project baby, mission 269: a hot water bottle wrapped in the mom-scented tee shirt. I couldn't wait to try this and to finally get to sleep a night where I wasn't bound to lie awake paralyzed by the fear of waking the ever-lucid slumbering king. I was elated to feel a door opening on some tiny bit of freedom and realized, ah-ha, that must be why every damn *pharmacie* has loads of hot water bottles in their store windows. Always wondered who the hell still used them in this day and age. Clearly it is the secret!

That night, with a new, rectangular, 27 euro hot water bottle in its soft faux sheepskin cover at arm's reach, I set out to solve this issue with my mini miracle. After nursing Oscar for twenty minutes, his eyes grew heavy and he was almost out when the neighbor upstairs started playing the piano at the decibel level of a sonic jet reaching Mach 2! I should add that this crazy woman on the floor above is a raging alcoholic completely out of her ever-loving mind. Apparently, she used to be a renowned piano teacher and now at age eight-two she is just literally crashing her fingers on the keys à la Phantom of the Opera at least twice a day. She is both the neighbor loon and the lady who loves nothing more than to pop by for a chat. Torture. But, funny detail, to get across just how wicked stinkin' drunk she gets: when she first saw me carrying Oscar in from the hospital—after seeing me pregnant as a house for months, she blurted out, "*Mon dieu,* whose baby is that? Where did you get it?"

I was thinking, "Ah, *bonjour* . . . I was pregnant, remember? We had about thirty-nine chats in the foyer I wished I never had, and you told me once that I looked like a ripe Cavaillion melon," but I opted for saying, "He's mine . . . *bien sûr.* And I was going to apologize profusely for his occasional bouts of crying, I am sorry if it has bothered you."

"Really, a baby . . . I thought that was your cat howling," she added. Good gravy, the woman is grade A coo-coo-la. Nevertheless, she woke Oscar with that insufferable pounding and the whole damn process had to begin again after she quite possibly slid off piano stool to be devoured by her yipping shrew of a poodle. *Or so I had hoped when the noise finally stopped.*

One hour later, Oscar was coaxed back to slipping into semi-sleep, though my nipples were worse for wear (don't ask!). I thought, "Okay, here I go—I put him down ca-re-fu-lly onto my bed, just for a second and then I go heat water, fill bottle, place in crib with him," and before I could finish the sentence in my mind or make it as far as the kitchen, he was awake and shrieking for me, arms a-flailing.

Two more evenings of trying to heat bottle *first,* then nurse to sleep, then slip into his crib with now *cold* water bottle had Oscar bellowing loud enough to rattle Notre Dame's clock tower—fuck! This is so not working and obviously if I had a frigging husband or mate or *anyone* to help arrange this, it *could* work. But with my scenario, it's a nonoption. These defeating nonoption events are popping up here and there lately and are proving, despite my strong will and determination, insurmountable. I hate that. Like, try shopping any boutique or grocery store with two levels with a stroller that's as big as a tank. There is no way anyone would offer to help lift it and there is no way to collapse it and there is no way to go into the *métro* or the bus, so Oscar became mostly a Baby Bjorn kid and in the end, it's been great, since he prefers to be close—*no surprise*—and it's all Attachment Parenting theory to the max. (Still, it would've been nice not to make sometimes twice-daily trips to the store since I can only lug two bags and a baby around Paris.)

In fact, this whole Attachment Parenting philosophy became not just an idea to dabble in, as I thought it might be prebaby, but really a sensible and natural approach for us once he was born. The constant contact, reassurance, and affection definitely makes for healthy, happy babies. And while it can be slightly grueling to wake often during the night, I found it just cruel to fathom letting him cry it out. As does the idea of just leaving him alone all night (as some French *mamans* I had met adhered to); to a new baby with no rationale, it surely just feels like being abandoned *half of a full day*. And AP is unequaled for making you feel more connected to your baby while you get to know your baby so well; you can react and anticipate and soothe them so much more easily. There is no, well maybe this will work—you just *know* what works and why they are crabby or crying. And as a result, it makes you a more nurturing, patient parent who is more focused and capable to meet your baby's needs. Okay, okay, I am now stepping down from my podium as I readily admit, I really don't know what the hell makes a good mother and a happy baby. Truth is, you just fumble along, trusting your instincts.

At week six with a day before my father was to visit, I had to take Oscar for a check-up and to get an X-ray to ensure those little hip sockets that were all froglike and turned out were indeed normal (standard exam). I passed on utilizing the free local PMI in the neighborhood, as I took a look at it from the exterior last week and yeah, it does look like a welfare-esque building. Grungy, with the front door propped open and no one at the rickety reception desk circa 1865. And this is where they offer preschool and daycare! Tight security. Not! This is in one of the chicest areas of Paris, so lord only knows what the PMI looks like in the less fab areas, like in Gobelins, in the thirteenth arrondissement. (God, I love that wacky name, though; can you imagine saying, "I live in Gobelins"?)

So, I got a pediatrician's name from the Tara de Seattle mom and made an appointment for this morning. Packed Mister Master up in his smartest onesie, a pale blue velvet footy pajamas number with ivory buttons and white cotton collar. Very Lord Fauntleroy. Ten minutes before the appt, Oscar looks so scrumptious and darling— and as I have to take photos of his every breath and burp, I grab my camera, which should just be in a hip holster since I use the thing every hour, and prop him up on his bouncy seat for a photo op. Three shots, one with eyes closed, the other two perfect, as I note we both have two chins and Michelin man chubby arms. But it's adorable *on him.*

Packing him into the Baby Bjorn, after I have done a dash of makeup, put on my coat and shoes, and . . . PLLloofphh! The poor dear poops right through his diaper and all over the onesie and it's even flowed through onto my coat. Oh, god! With two minutes to go, I have to mad-dash change him; clean him, diaper, socks, a cardigan sweater; throw him into some not-so-cute cheapy fleece pants from C&A; take off my coat; clean it. We still stink—*merde*—and run out the door in crappy outfits, late and sweating. I have to throw out the whole stinking mess, wah!! Oscar's suede booties are ruined, and so I've had to jam on him some crazy-huge brown baby winter boots so that he looks more like Puss in Boots from the waist down and Humpty Dumpty from there up. Whatever.

I cruise through the busy streets, hightailing it up rue du Bac, to the pediatrician's office with a view over the Bon Marché playground. Great view and elegant office; this is why she charges 185 euros an appointment. And I'm paying out of pocket again, *comme habitude.* We have to wait for almost an hour; with a baby, this isn't easy, and I'm livid by the time we get to see the doctor, though know better than to show it. She is a stern-looking woman, about sixty years old. No-nonsense would be a nice way to describe her. Again, don't attempt humor with French professionals, it irks them and there is no recovering. So we chat about Oscar as she yanks him up to his feet to ensure he has the innate instinct to walk. Not fun for mom to watch as it looks a lot like she will drop him on his face. I explain I am a single mother and that I am at home with Oscar all the time, not using a nanny as so many French mothers do. I thought that the last bit would earn me some credit with her, since my commitment to my baby would resonate with a woman whose life work is *babies.* It didn't. She didn't care about that but did look at me with a curious if not judging expression and asked, "Well, where is the father?"

"He is not involved," I answer, thinking, "Uh-oh, she's going to slam me, isn't she?"

"*Quel dommage,* you modern American women. I don't understand it . . . Let's carry on."

Bitch. Think Nurse Ratched *en français.* I'm not loving her, but I am stuck with her and the big bill already, so I carry on and explain that I'm breast-feeding and waking pretty often and that he won't sleep without me being right there. (Yep, I'm that desperate that I will even run this by her. Trust me, when this tired you are tempted to run up to any woman on the street and beg for clues or secrets to get your baby to sleep more than twenty consecutive minutes.) You could say aghast was the reaction to my statements. "*Mon dieu,* why breast-feed? See, that is your problem. You need to detach physically. Give him formula now and let him 'find his sleep.' "

UGH!! I have heard this bullshit, "let him find his sleep" umpteen times now from French mothers; it translates to "let him cry it out." No way.

"I really believe that crying is a baby's sole means of communication. I can't do that, emotionally, it's just impossible for me to see him suffer," I reply, holding Oscar on my lap, caressing his brow.

"He's just learning to manipulate you," she retorts.

What a *crock.* He doesn't even know he has ears yet. Like he is busy *or capable* of mastering control through trial and error. As though he was plotting and scheming, looking at me: "Wretched woman didn't go for my crying bout, I shall projectile vomit and feign choking to get her over here!" I make a doubtful expression. She glares at me. Stone silent, she reaches for her address book, flips through it, and jots down a name and number on a prescription pad. Then stands, walks over to a cabinet, and pulls out four big boxes of Enfamil formula.

"Here, I advise you to call this woman," she says, handing me the note card. "She can come to your home in the evenings and train your son to sleep through the night, generally in less than three weeks. But you must allow her to do it *her way,* for she often succeeds in two weeks. You will thank me, of this I am sure. And take these boxes of formula—it is the best, tastes the most like breast milk—and start him on it immediately."

I just smile vaguely, take them, and we go to technician for the

X-ray. With all that done and confirmation that Oscar is perfect, we throw a check at the woman at the front desk and I haul ass out of there, thinking, "Fuck this country. If I were in the USA, this visit would have never been so unpleasant . . . ohhh, curses!" I intentionally left the formula boxes in the park, on a bench; let some French mom enjoy that stuff. Tossed the infant-sleeping expert's number in the *poubelle* ("garbage") and trotted off home, thinking, "I will never see that pediatrician again . . . oh great, and she was one of the few who spoke English . . . oh la la. I just wish I could call my mom, she wouldn't miss a beat, running to my defense, 'Oh, she's an idiot, Kiki, you're doing your best and Oscar's a happy baby. Everything's going to be fine.'" I feel better once home and in the safe micro-world that is my new life.

Though I don't think one can really brag about one's skills with a diaper, I do have to say, about all I'm managing expertly of late is I give good diaper and am personally, single-handedly keeping the fatso ladies jeans companies in business. Almost three months, and, while I have lost some weight, it's still next to impossible to even pull my old jeans up past my knees. I look at them, turn them around and marvel, "I was that skinny? That's ridiculous?" Why can't we all just go back to adoring Rubenesque women? I never had such curves as I'm hauling around right now. It does kind of suck that after years of having tiny boobs that went uncelebrated by my amours, now I am whopping fabulous, pouring over, full C-cup and firm like baseballs and only wee Oscar is here to whoop it up. Then again, I just don't see how new mothers even have any time or interest for a husband, since I can't fathom having a man around for quite a while. How do married women do it? When, honestly, your body, brain, and energy are shot and begging to just rest. I realized this all the more when Gilbert sent a lovely e-mail.

Ma Chère Kiki,

Would you indulge me the honor of escorting you and darling Oscar on a turn around Le Jardin du Luxembourg this Sunday afternoon at a time of your preference? I should be delighted to see the infinitely more beautiful and *ravissante* version of Kiki as a *nouvelle maman* and her young gentleman.

At your service,

Gilbert

Well, I know that sounds really gallant and lovely, doesn't it? Truth is, when you live in Paris this long, you see this is all just a Frenchman *playing* the role to the maximum, loving his own sense of skillful charm. *I think.* Or at least, I have seen this again and again, this type of courting—thoughtful invitation, waxing lyrical while being allur-ing. These men love to exercise this talent but it's a façade to a certain degree and I'm a bit wary of falling for it for the bazillionth time! And unlike Jack le Generous Married Cad, I could take Gilbert seri-ously. All that said, with not a heck of a lot to do, I considered it. Then, realized I am still a huge blob and would suffer terribly to see Gilbert's face fall as his imaginary version of me is surely far more sexy than current reality. So I sent a polite decline and he sent back a pestering,

Would a visit *chez vous* be more to your liking?

Nope. You're starting to be as annoying as a hair of unknown origin caught on my tongue. Leave me alone, I'm a chubby new mom and can't live in the uber-fab world of Paris right now. I'm busy with leak-ing boobs and wetting my pants a teensy bit, since I never did get to take those perineal uterine rejuvenation, or whatever the hell it's called, pelvic floor muscles classes. So, yes, I'm a wet mess and can hardly imagine having a conversation that's not about babies, lack of sleep, or a combo thereof. So if you're expecting me to be sexy, interesting, fashionable, and relaxed, I'm not your girl. I do "anxious-tired-monosyllabic droning" very well though!

Whatever times 347! I am over it. Men now are obstacles in the street or possible attendants to help me hold boutique doors as I lumber in with the gigantuous stroller, which does seem fairly absurd to wheel around. Yeah, sure, I am just sooo rich and lucky. I have everything any mother would desire—if you can call an overdrawn bank account (American Hospital keeps sending weird lab bills I already paid for, that's a fun project to deal with now, alone, in French, on the phone, as baby cries) and a swelling fear that I will never have a free moment again until I can put Oscar into one of the many crappy free schools, all the while surviving on baguettes, trying to pay health insurance fees for expats (looked into it, it's many thousands per person, per year—f*@k!). So, yes, the Stokke stroller is a fine mirror of my life—so coddled, opulent, and sure. Ha! It's such a farce, but I will admit, if for nothing else, I love it for the way it seems an elegant throne for king Oscar. He deserves it, even if I don't!

Meanwhile, my father came to see his grandson at month two, which was a sublime visit for us all. I had hoped to invite all my family to Paris to see and meet Oscar and come for his baptism in the early summer, but after a visit with a priest at the gorgeous seventeenth-century *église* ("church") in the seventh arrondissement, Saint Clotilde, it's becoming apparent that this isn't so easy a thing to arrange. Without giving any details other than my having a two-month-old and living around the corner, I was informed that the two parents come for an audience and interview, give testimony to their religious beliefs and knowledge and provide validity that at least one of the parents is a French-born citizen, then book a baptism many months in advance, etc., etc. An across-the-board cringe there on my end. "Where's the exit, monsieur?" That's one more mountain peak I get to only view from base camp, I guess.

Ergo, my father came as quickly as he could, and three generations *de famille* went sauntering about Paris. It's great on many levels to have family around finally and someone to gaze at Oscar with the same pure adoration I feel, and yet, breast-feeding (as it was impossible to avoid with wee Oscar lip-smacking, clamoring for them) in front of your father, regardless of thickness and shrouding under a scarf, feels odd at best. "Ignore the gobbling head under my pashmina whose lips are adhered to my boob." You get it. That was about the only time I was self-conscious about nursing, as I got so good at it, I could put Oscar in Baby Bjorn facing me, and with a loose Dries Van Noten coat over it, I could march around and shop and no one knew the wiser. Still, it was unforgettable that at our final dinner before my father's departure, dear Oscar woke (after I successfully devoured my first real meal since the haute cuisine at the American Hospital) and wriggled in the Baby Bjorn in such a way I knew he wanted to be plucked out to be social. Plopping him on my lap to face his Opa ("grandfather" in German) he looked at him, then up at me, and smiled at us both with his first intentional big gummy grin. What an unforgettable treasure to share with my father. Made all the more so precious to me as I knew my mother and I were never to enjoy any such profound moments.

After my father left, I felt a huge absence and gaping hole. It's tough to be alone all day and night with a baby, *day after day,* when there is just no family or even a structured world to be a part of. Easter arrived, and while I thought I would be just fine and content to take Oscar to service at St. Sulpice and stroll the beautiful gardens of Jardin du Luxembourg, it killed me with loneliness! Only wee Oscar got a new Easter outfit, since having to adhere to a strict budget these days gives me little "fun money" to buy new clothes *pour moi*—not to mention every meal is at home. So, while I loved putting him in his new ensemble—as my mother always bought us all charming Easter outfits every year—I myself dragged out a pale pink Alain Mounakin tweed bolero that maybe from two hundred meters looks like Chanel and some lame-ass (*literally*) fat jeans. And yet still, I ventured out for Easter Sunday with great expectations. The streets were teeming with families; gorgeous families of every age, chattering in French, pouring into cafés and bistros as big, vibrant groups full of tradition and history, and I felt, to put it succinctly, stupid.

Just like, Why are you here, in France, Kiki? You are going to raise your son with what family around? What traditions? You don't even know the French story of Easter, just that it involves some flying chocolate bells because you see them in the windows of Fauchon and Pierre Herme. Let alone how to cook a classic French holiday meal. Is this really fair to him, to be raised in *your dream,* with what looks to be a fair number of "right out of the starting block" judgments flung at the poor innocent boy? Eiii yi yi. I literally felt sick as I walked around alone, like I couldn't and didn't know how to be a mother, or a good one, *in this country.* And I couldn't reconcile the fact that I was being selfish in not having him around family: the hordes of family—cousins, aunts, uncles, and grandparents—he would have in the USA. I skipped the St. Sulpice mass, my legs ruling against dragging me to a venue where I was sure to cry and miss my mother and not feel very great about myself *as a mother.* I walked all the way to the Tour Eiffel, passing so many families, fueled only by the certainty that if I stopped I would fall down with loneliness. I vowed to, as much as possible, never burden this baby with my troubles and sure wasn't going to start now.

I came to a stop at the foot of the Tour Eiffel. Somehow the hordes of tourists nearby made me feel less alone. Dazed, I sat in a small playground and tried to nurse Oscar discreetly—as a mother looked on with a snarl as her husband looked on with a smile. Never once has a French mother at a playground ever offered me so much as a friendly glance. Then it hit me. I could leave. Go back to the USA. Why not? It's not like I have a job here or even a husband, and frankly, after eight years of hearing Frenchmen letting slip such comments as, "I think 'so and so' is really attractive but I would never really *be with* a single mother, other than briefly—How could I care about a child that isn't mine in blood?" I know Frenchmen are pretty, ah, let's say, "special" about the idea. And it's not like the grand social world I was a part of is beating down my door, begging my return. Now when I get invites to the weekly party in the Bagatelle or at Castel, I look at them as amusing. Yeah, sure I will arrive at midnight, when the fete begins. Oh la la. Even if I wanted to, there is no way it would or could happen.

So, with Zola here in physical form only and David, who will be moving back to NYC next month, I would only miss a handful of people. 'Course, I need to mull this over big time; I'm just feeling a bit sad and alone. All to be expected, somewhat, as an expat over a holiday away from family, right? And no, this is not baby blues, mind you; this is just a day and a crappy one. Hmm. But it registers that I am not loving how, *now as a mother,* I feel more of an outsider in Paris, and moreover, I am having doubts I want to be on the inside! It was definitely always my dream to live in Paris and have a *bébé.* Funny thing about dreams: when they do, by miraculous luck, come true, they tend to arrive with equal parts overwhelming confusion, a backlash of unexpected pitfalls, sprinkles of blissful elation, and all wrapped in a pretty bow with resulting effect of, "Shit, now what do I do?"

Chapter 9

"Children need models rather than critics."

—JOSEPH JOUBERT

Summer/Été

A word or two about nursing bras—I asked every hipster or even remotely cool mother where you go to get a good—or simply a not-so-ghastly—nursing bra. I found the source, the store Euroform, and while too big with baby in belly at the time to get there (even though it was in Paris!), I called and ordered three of the nicest ones, in nude, black, and white, all trimmed in lace and seemingly palatable. I'd set the bar low since I knew it wouldn't be some sexy number I would want to sport longer than necessary. Well, they arrived and other than being slightly bulletproof in texture and with a one-inch-wide strap—rather than some of the others I'd seen that looked like acrobats' apparatus—I did decide to just chuck all three of them after month two of nursing. They just feel like you're strapping into some suspension device and remind me exactly of the near trampoline-sized brassières that my great-aunt Margaret used to bend over and shimmy her enormous mammaries into. Problem solved on the cheap—I just went to H&M on boulevard Raspail, bought some cheap padded C-cup bra, and simply scooched it to the side when I nursed Oscar. A hundred times easier, cheaper, and I got to feel a tiny bit more like a girl rather then a lactating buffalo clomping around.

Speaking of baby weight, the pressure's on to lose it all in time for Zola's big wedding at the end of the summer. As a bridesmaid, the idea of having to dress up, stand in front of a sea of people, and have the masses mutter to each other, "So sad, a single mother *and* she just physically fell apart . . . Pity, she will have no luck finding a mate now." I am not kidding. Remember this is the country where the president of the Republic divorced his wife and married a supermodel . . . *after a ninety-day courtship.* Can you imagine Barack Obama dumping Michelle and getting hitched after three months to Tyra Banks?

So, I am trying to lose *kilos,* as they say; donning a tee shirt that says, "Body by Bébé" as hopefully a witty/cheesy disclaimer/explainer while taking Oscar in stroller and jogging along the path by the Seine, past the Place de la Concorde, and circling back once at Grand Palais. It's truly a glorious way to start the day, like climbing into a photo flipbook of Paris's landmarks and all the while getting cheered on by strangers yelling, *"Bravo! Bon Courage!"* (Don't think I don't get how frigging fortunate I am to have this view. I am appreciative and grateful each day for this exquisite set on which I get to play the role of my life—mom!) Oddly enough, this image of a mother running in Paris with a stroller is just totally unknown. It's akin to waving an American flag behind me and met with 50% disbelief and 50% disapproval by the legions of older women. I am coming to believe I, singularly, am giving the upper-class geriatrics contingency ample occasions to employ those scowling expressions they so love to dole out. Happy to help, as I thank you all for your handsome, sexy grandsons!

Seriously though—now, Oscar is the only male, the center and star of all my waking and nonwaking hours. Cosleeping in my tiny single bed is getting tired . . . literally! It's like sleeping next to a tornado. REM is like a distant vague memory, since Oscar still wakes five times a night. The beautiful, dreamy crib, despite providing novelty and satisfaction in the aesthetic expression department, remains totally unused.

On the upside, I did have two funny scenarios yesterday—in contrast to the sea of days of routine that are pure quiet happiness, if not terribly eventful. On my way to the baby boutique Natalys, that I am clearly addicted to, I passed by Café de Flore. As a once-celebrated patron, I now feel some absurd need to always look terribly well put together when I walk by and generally see a few friends I know. It always feels like a minor event in my day, as weird as that sounds. This time, I almost stopped dead in my tracks as my eyes fell upon a sight you would only view in Paris—a mother breast-feeding *and* smoking while quaffing a glass of *vin rouge!* I couldn't stop myself, I just hightailed over there and, shaking my head, shrieked *en français,* "You cannot be smoking and drinking while nursing?! That is so irresponsible, not to mention, criminally unhealthy for your baby!" This fat slob, who, frankly, resembled Jerry Garcia, looked at me, snorted, and went back to her conversation with the older woman sitting with her. What the fuck is that? Ohmigod, is no one else appalled? Insanity. And I am pretty damn mad she didn't seem the slightest bit intimidated or self-conscious. Oh, fuck it. I give up on you idiots.

Admittedly, I have noticed lately, with my burgeoning maternal instincts, I go on these autopilot critiques fairly often since, sadly, quite frequently I come across a mother whose baby in the stroller is totally hysterical crying while she is casually shopping, ignoring the poor baby who's so freaked out. Literally, from inside my apartment I will, at least once or twice a week, hear some little baby or child howling as though they've been left on the street, and I look out my window and a tornado of anger rises inside me as, once again, it's some mother flat-out acting as though the frantic crying of her helpless child is a nuisance to be ignored at all costs. Maddening!

And it's not just the French *mothers,* since last week, on my street, I was walking behind a man with a toddler—who I was thinking quite handsome for a microsecond—who two beats later began shouting at his son, then scooted him into a corner, and started spanking him with such ferocity, I was again compelled to read him the riot act and tell him I hoped when his son gets bigger, that he returns the favor! All this to say that, despite my thinking prebaby that Paris was an idyllic place to raise a child, it's sure as hell looking like a tough place to grow up.

I did have some pleasant chance events though—thank the lord, or I would head off home on the next flight out! Shopping for Oscar— which consists mostly of scouring for *soldes* ("sales") in every boutique and shopping at the cheapy C&A store in Montparnasse. I can't pretend the latter is any fun, as pulling clothes from massive bargain bins while fighting for that 4 euro onesie alongside a population I hadn't much hung out with before—third-world immigrants, blue collars, garbagemen, maids—is a soul killer. I am almost amazed I haven't got whiplash from the steep drop of the posh American Hospital to the French equivalent of Walmart. (I am kind of used to these extremes, though. When I lived in NYC, I remember flying in from Paris on the Concorde with my big shot boyfriend, only to quickly unpack, turn around, and take a subway to work to save money.) But now that I am in search of something *uber-French-baby* for Oscar to wear at Zola's big wedding, I must revisit the classic baby boutique and pop back into Natalys on the rue de Tournon. (*Pour moi*—nothing new to acquire, since I'm hoping to fit into an old strapless Dior cocktail dress in a dark slate blue with lace at hem so I can financially treat my boy to his first semiformal ensemble.)

Perusing the darling little beige linen knee-length jumpers embroidered with a tiny teddy bear, I see out of the corner of my eye, the supermodel (from my era) Karen Mulder, who I'd seen in the magazine *Paris Match* just a few months ago and noted that she too was having a baby, by herself—*father a secret.* I'd kind of latched on to the idea, that, "See, Kiki? You're not alone. This isn't as unheard-of as some people are making it to be." And there she was, looking very *après bébé, comme moi,* complete with muffin top—make that more like enormous brioche for me—but unlike me, in heels and makeup. I smiled at her and she smiled back. Which I've since noticed is like "mom flirting" in its manner of two moms going through the age-old dance of trying to chat, not unlike when we're scoping out a potential suitor.

Moving along, eyeing the soft play mats hanging by the register, I try to find the price. 100 euros, ouch. Oh well. When Karen appears at my side and says, "I just bought one for my daughter and she adores it. You must get one. Oh, he is darling!" she says in a voice as beautiful as she is, as she peeks in my Baby Bjorn at Oscar asleep, lips ebbing with each delicate sonorous breath. Karen and I end up leaning against some cribs and talking for quite some time, as I divulge, I am also a single mother and, obviously, an expat as well. Upon hearing that I am doing the breast-feeding/cosleeping/no-nanny path, she is taken aback, but in a very lovely way. "You are amazing! My gosh, I could never do it. I have a full-time, live-in housekeeper, *and* a nanny. I stopped breast-feeding at three months. I had to, I'm trying like hell to get back into shape and get rid of these chipmunk cheeks, big butt, and get back to work."

That works for me, a humble, real supermodel also battling the baby weight while praising *my* efforts. That's like the best shit I've heard out of anyone's mouth in months! She earns a big fat instant stamp of approval in the friend category. In fact, when she says that, I realize very few people in Paris have given me any credit for trying to do it all alone; more often they think I'm crazy to be with Oscar all day and not slide him into a *crèche* ("day care") and just go out to do what I want all day. So, she's instantly cool with me and, while not getting a single joke I made, it was rather fun to meet her.

When I finally confessed that I really can *only* afford to buy Oscar the jumper and white linen shirt to match *and not* the colorful play mat, she said, "Let me offer it to him! I will buy it as a gift for a kindred spirit. No refusals. It's my pleasure. Let's just have lunch one day soon. And you could bring Oscar over to my flat and my housekeeper can make us lunch while the children play."

Not having a load of moms who 1) had the slightest clue what it is to be a single mom or 2) are expat single moms, I thought, This is serendipity! What a treat and what a charming woman. I think I was so stunned by this turn of events, I didn't have a chance to refuse and just went with it, while thinking, Isn't this curious . . . after my thinking of her months ago as almost iconic.

Karen seemed so positively tickled to give this wonderful gift to Oscar it was quite endearing. Lo and behold, Oscar soon awakened as we were heading out of the store and back onto the noisy streets, just in time to meet his new fairy godmother.

"Where are you off to now, Kiki? Want a ride home? You shouldn't carry this huge bag with a baby too."

Okay. Sure! I soon realized why men go ape over beautiful women; you're just sort of awed-stupid and act like, "whatever you say!"

With that, she smiled and gestured to a black town car with a chauffeur sitting patiently at the wheel. She handed the Natalys bag to the driver, I gave him my address and off we went zipping through Paris, in one of the quickest friendships *sans* alcohol I have ever made. Oscar, who in truth is pretty shy and who absolutely seems to abhor Zola (sadly), instantly was goo-goo-coo-coo for Karen. Didn't hurt that when he yelped when getting cinched into a new car seat, she started singing him French lullabies that even made *me* fall half in love with her. How enchanting! Chatting away, I revealed we actually had dated the same man once, and I told her how he went on to brag to me repeatedly about having been with her. We laughed about what a fraud he was, gorgeous but a silly playboy. We discovered we both were friends with a famous writer—who I had gone out with one night and who brought Karen's ex-husband along. (The writer took us to watch an orgy—not the usual makings for a first date, mind you.)

We laughed together over our shared distaste for said man and she and I bonded like two tweens with new iPods. Exchanging cell numbers as we passed through St. Germain, vowing to get together the following *dimanche* for lunch, since she was going to be heading to St. Tropez soon, for the August holidays.

Arriving at my building, helping us to the door, Karen said, "I'm now off to the Ritz gym to burn off this *derrière*! You go, supermom! See you soon!" As I went up in the lift to my apartment, I thought, "Too funny. She may be a supermodel, but I'm a *supermom*. How much cooler is that?" Hrmph! That feeling pretty much faded instantly upon entering my tiny apartment and placing Oscar in his swing chair, one of the only places for him to sit. Supermom? Yeah sure, but she has a big apartment overlooking Jardin du Luxembourg, a driver and car, tons of money, and thus the means to take her daughter to the South of France, attend the best schools, and she doesn't have to live under a budget, wonder if she will ever get another date, etc. I cannot be sure where or when any future income will be incoming. Travel, dating, and hired help are not even in the realm of my universe; not being able to work legally in this damn country makes the whole issue of finances/ disposable income yet another daunting concern I dabble with and fling to the far reaches of my mind. Ugh! I pen a mental note—"Dear Reality, I hate you. Sincerely, Kiki."

In any case, meeting Karen was surreal, since the following Sunday came and went without a word from her. Another week and I sent her a text thanking her again for the play mat and expressing how much Oscar did, indeed, love it. She rang back instantly, "I've been going wild trying to find you. I even went to Natalys boutique and asked if they had your number. I rang our common friend and he claimed he no longer had your number. I guess somehow I lost it or entered it wrong. So glad you contacted me. Let's do that brunch this Sunday as I leave *la semaine prochaine*."

Okay. A bit wacky but fine. Her sincerity proved intact when I was simply walking by Natalys the next day and the clerk (who, I must add, was so rude and fatally pretentious to me when I made the two adventures to get the crib et al. home) came out, all smiles and waving, "Karen Mulder is trying to find you! Has she reached you?" Bananas to see how I quickly got such an upgrade by association, as to now have this bitch acting as a pseudo–social director for me. Ha! Sooo French.

But again, come Sunday, as I readied Oscar to depart for our scheduled arrival chez Karen at 1:00 P.M., busily trying to figure out how to carry a bouquet of lilies I had just got for her at Olivier Pitou on rue des Saints-Pères, with Oscar *and* a diaper bag, when Karen sent a text.

Apologies. Can't do brunch. Prblms. So sorry.rng u soon.k

And that was that. We never did see each other again, which does happen a lot in France: it's very common after the long August holidays to return and clear the slate on one's social life rather than stepping back into it.

With most everyone gone for the holidays, the next few weeks were spent having sad picnics alone in the gardens of the Tuileries and buzzing about town with baby, feeling like I was viewing a film about Paris but with no dialogue save my soundtrack of Oscar cooing away. Living in the city of love and couples smooching on every park bench used to be terribly charming. Now it all seemed like a sad in-your-face backdrop to the private adventures of Kiki and Oscar, out trying to emulate family life in Paris. Obviously becoming a mother is in itself a solo journey; you are giving so much of yourself that it's transforming and thrilling, but it's also isolating, especially when the child is hardly big enough to offer much more than burps, gurgles, and the occasional heartbreakingly dear smile.

I feel very alone. Just giving him a bath, tenderly holding him while marveling at all his beauty, that's more joy in one minute than I had in all the years in Paris as a single girl. BUT. Now my responsibility is so huge that I am plagued with every possible concern for his well-being and well-fare. I want to send him to Montessori preschool when he is three and it's like 6,000 euros a session. And it's time for more vaccines and another visit to a pediatrician.

Checkbook status—funds diminishing rapidly.

Alright then. Time to check out the once discarded notion of the

PMI and its services. A couple of the mothers, even Verania, who I met ages ago, claim it's not so welfarelike but more of a great, free benefit to living in France. Having not seen too many advantages of life in Paris of late—*except the insanely beautiful setting*—I'm game!

I notice that the squirrely nerves that I used to get when going out on a date are now strangely sparked into action when I have to take Oscar to the doctor. I, for reasons already clear, feel I have to dress *très* chic to discount the idea I'm some sorry-ass, welfare, single mom without a penny. And yet, *I'm not far from that,* but I just can't bear the weight of those judgments when I am truly doing my best. So I always take great care in prepping Oscar and myself and this time it surely didn't matter to anyone, since, despite the PMI being mere blocks from the *très elegant* Bon Marché, this was one very unchic adventure. Again, no one at the front desk, as when I'd previously scouted the building out, so I knocked on a locked door to the left and a woman in an apron opened the door, smiled, and simply gestured to a waiting room just to the right.

Despite a broken yarn mobile, small foam chairs, and a plastic box full of dirty toys, the room resembled a free AIDS clinic testing facility in Tijuana. (I'm making a guesstimate here, no firsthand experience.) I surely wasn't going to sit, nor ever take Oscar out of the Baby Bjorn and change him on the wood *table à langer* by the door that looked like it was donated from an old butcher shop. God! What the hell is this place? This is the seventh arrondissement; one would think it would be slightly pleasant, since only mothers in this area can go here.

The same dark-skinned woman, about sixty years old, clad in the apron, enters and hands me an old crunchy towel, asking me to take off Oscar's clothes to the diaper so he can be weighed and measured before we see the pediatrician. Yuck to the towel. And I scoot Oscar out of his jumper and cardigan and just hold him in my arms as he looks around, surely thinking, "Is this a bus depot? A bathroom in the *métro?*"

About a half hour later, when I am in full mental debate about whether to just dress him and leave since these French versions of "just a minute" waiting rooms are just freaking insanity, I hear the howls of an infant behind a door while the apron lady pops back in and asks that I follow her . . . to a room as big as a closet, I discover. Here, she slides out the bottom drawer from an old chest of drawers that's lined with yet another ghastly towel and a meter stick. "Please place him here, top of his head at the end, and yell out his length so I can jot it down," she says.

Check surroundings. Have I been dropped into a third-world country? What happened to the über-fab baby experiences like those at the American Hospital? Oh, right. One needs truck-loads of money to continue that. Crud.

Oscar gets weighed as well as measured for a beret. Well, they did take his cranium circumference along with noting down all the details that seem to bite me in the ass lately—single, expat, and *new issue*; no job or citizenship. Don't even bother glaring at me, lady, I will body slam you so hard. Actually, and surprisingly, she just smiled, said it's great to raise a bilingual child, and added that she was pleased he wasn't circumcised. Kind of a relief as she whisked me back to the waiting room *pour attendre le docteur*.

There were now two other mothers and kin seated there, all of whom I wouldn't have ever guessed live in this posh expensive arrondissement with their haphazard, sloppy attire, hardly attending to their screeching, messy kids. (Proof of residency in the immediate area is imperative to get an appointment and most women in this shasha neighborhood are sufficiently consumed with appearances to at least feign playing the doting *maman*.) More notable—not a friendly conversation or a smile was exchanged; everyone kept to themselves despite the close proximity and common agenda. I don't love that about the French; you can be sure *not* to drum up conversations and make friends just say, sitting at a playground watching your children play together. It's probably never happened. And that's isolating and absurd, *non?* I am the first to say, the Americans on airplane flights who just drop down next to you and tell you their life story is way too much. But we *are* friendly, engaging, and, well, downright nice. And that makes the days just a little more pleasant, with touches of human connection. Grrr. Whatever. They didn't look like very fun, happy mothers anyway!

The pediatrician finally let the poor child who was wailing go out for air and ushered me into the small box of a doctor's office. She hardly looked like a doctor but was a dead ringer for Sarkozy's first wife, with her deep tan, trim *en forme* figure, and very hipster cool clothes. No lie—she was wearing a beige suede skirt with a fringe belt and a cream silk blouse with a killer collar, Gucci for sure. What the hell? Inside two minutes we got along like a house on fire and all my worries went out the window, since she was clearly a top doctor—*normally practicing in Versailles*—but explained she offered her time here twice a week to help out. She spoke with a calm, quiet tone and with a deliberate, easy coolness about her that relayed her intelligence and experience. A mother of four children, still maybe just forty-five years old, she had all the elements about her that are symbolic in that rare perfect Frenchwoman—an elusive enigma, elegance, and knowing. In her, you see where they get their sexy reputation and why men lose their heads for them.

She handled Oscar with an authority that he even found soothing. She seemed not in the least thrown by my single mom role or choices, and, with her perfect English, she was easy to talk to about everything. She gave Oscar his vaccines so quickly he hardly noticed and only cried just after. While helping me dress and soothe him, she kindly asked if she could do anything to help me get Oscar into the *crèche* there. (As *everyone* in the country had told me, and she reiterated, it's so difficult to land a spot there, one generally gets on a list while baby is still a seahorse.)

"*C'est vrai?* I am interested in looking at the *crèche,* and if you can offer some help, I would be grateful," I found myself saying despite the fact that I really didn't want to have Oscar in *any* day care until maybe age three. *And then, half-day at most.* But, like so many things when one is a new mother in a foreign country, if the masses are telling you this is what you want to be doing or *you're just a shitty mom,* somehow you entertain the idea. She picked up her phone and rang to the staff upstairs, asking that they give me a quick tour despite the fact that I didn't have an appointment. Done. Just as I was holding out my hand to thank her, she turned and reached into a large steel cabinet and brought out four boxes of Enfamil baby formula. "You really can stop nursing now. Six months is more than enough and you need to stop all these nighttime feedings—it will age you decades!" she said with a warm smile.

Yeah, yeah, yeah. There must be some major payback to pediatricians from that baby formula company, since I cannot escape the high-intensity hard sell at any pediatrician's office. Alas, I just smiled back.

I took a few minutes in the foyer to coddle a whimpering Oscar and smooch his salty tears away. Once he was calm and well, we ascended the stairs to the floor marked CRÈCHE but stopped midpush of the buzzer when I noticed a hand-scrawled sign placed just above, INTERDIT—QUARANTINE: ENFANT AVEC LA ROUGEOLER. A kid up here has the measles?! Oscar hasn't had that vaccine yet! A stocky woman with frizzy red hair appeared at the door and swung it open as I nearly recoiled back, falling down the stairs. I was pointing to Oscar, shaking my head, saying "no measles vaccine already" in my nervous *merde* French.

She looked at me, shrugged, and claimed the sign was old and there was no danger as she ripped it off and crumpled it up, but that didn't make sense and my doubt was high—as in 99% sure she was lying. Then it occurred to me, fuck, if I piss her off, she has the ability to throw my application for a *crèche* in the *poubelle,* now and forever, and then I'd be screwed, so I'd better blow in there and make a speedy run-through just to get the gist.

Literally almost putting Oscar's head into my shirt for a bacterial filter; I followed her into her office and realized, right, I, ah, can't speak technical French very well, let alone when this flipped out about measles spores floating through the air into my baby's lungs. She plopped down behind a huge desk piled willy-nilly with papers and from her expression clearly was none too pleased to be interrupted by me for this impromptu tour-interview. I tried to ask a question in French, then gave it a go in English. It was as though I spoke Swahili, since she looked at me stone-faced, like, "No, you're *still* not making sense, lady." We staggered through the stupidest conversation I have ever been a part of, but I did get the general facts clear; that if I wanted to seek the much-desired position for Oscar to attend the *crèche,* there is no way *for me* to choose that start date, no way to say just mornings or just three days a week. If and when they deem me worthy, then I have to abide with the all-day, five-days-a-week program.

No way, indeed. I wasn't going to pursue it, regardless of the social pressure and the awareness that if I wanted any preschool plan going forward, I had no backup. I decided then and there just to let the woman assume I was interested to see how it would spin out, and so she suggested I take a peek into the playroom and then let myself out. Not terribly affable, but I was dying to exit, so bid her adieu and made a quick turn to view the playroom and escape ASAP.

HOLY SHIT! You want to see your worst nightmare realized? This was that scene: A large rectangular room, with a bit of filtered sun but otherwise as depressingly devoid of color as an insane asylum. Maybe ten ratty cribs lined the walls, all of them empty, since about nine infants were all lined up on the floor and strapped immovable into their seats—facing the same way, being completely ignored, and in various states of unrest and unhappiness. Three women (helpers) moving about talking together and picking up blankets off the floor as if this was all very normal and run of the mill to have the babies bound up and left without interaction.

I couldn't watch anymore. It was like the saddest image of day care I had ever seen in person—very much like what you'd see on TV about a Russian orphanage. I couldn't believe women, *mothers,* had come and seen this and then left their children there. Never, *never* would I understand that. Moments like that I want to run, *literally,* run hard and fast through the streets, crying home. I can't, of course, as I have dear Oscar in his pouch and I have to keep my wits together, though I want to outrun this image now burned in my mind and sob like hell for those babies. And, I guess, just cry for the desperation I feel in this city, a feeling I never ever knew or felt before here *or anywhere.*

Learning that the difference between this *crèche* and the colorful cheery Montessori preschool just three streets over (in the same neighborhood) is 6,000 euros and that would make all the difference, and yet I can't make the math/budget work to pull it off. Crazy making, after what I just saw. I have to hit pause hard on this worry or it will eat me up all my waking hours. But with a rant beckoning and one final attempt to understand it, I rang Zola, even though she is knee-deep in wedding arrangements. It only half occurs to me while dialing, that having a husband to ring at this moment would be so helpful. *I think.* Though that idea is quickly fading.

"Zola, can I have two minutes? I know you're wild-busy but I am just flipping out," I ask, almost breathless, as I plod back home.

"Gosh, sure. You okay?" she says, though I can hear her switch ears and crash through some boxes while she waits for my reply.

"Oh god, I just went to the *crèche* here in the seventh, and it was insane! The babies were all strapped into seats on the floor like prisoners! How can mothers leave their kids there?! What's with this country?!" I blurt out while passing an older woman whose head flips around in horror at my comment. I don't even care. Go to hell, lady, your country sucks.

"Really? That's crazy! Wait, maybe they were lined up to be fed lunch? That could be it. I have heard that many *crèches* are great. A lot of women I work with have their children in *crèches* and are very happy with them. Especially the ones in the suburbs," she replies.

"Hmm, maybe . . . but still. It's just not at all like the ones we know exist in the States; and it's becoming clear to me that at every step of being a mother here, I'm going to be met with these awful surprises where the constant answer is, 'Well, that's how we do it here.' Oh, shit. I am just worn out with worry. Sorry to disturb, honey. What are you doing?" I ask, knowing I'm draining her and I hate to be a drag on anyone.

"I'm stuffing lavender into organza bags for the church. Want to help? And by the way, I found someone to drive you and Oscar to the château for the wedding. A friend of Jean-Pierre. He's single."

"Lovely of you. Yes, let me chill and come over and help. On my way," I say, slightly calmer, realizing at least that "ride to château" can be checked off my list. Being one of the few singles invited to the wedding outside Paris, I was losing sleep about how to even get to the damn thing. David is in NYC again and thus can't be my gay best friend/escort and there are very few or, I guess, no other people I want to juggle for that long, with Oscar in tow. Not to mention, this all isn't exactly going to be *pas cher* ("inexpensive"). A two-day wedding at a beautiful château, a wedding gift, and the hat I still need to buy—*since Zola insists we all wear hats*—is going to chip into my Oscar money big time. Rats. Paris is so expensive, what am I doing here?

I pop in on Zola to help, and, though it's great to see her, I'm pretty sad we are palpably losing our closeness. It's heart-wrenching; she's so obsessed micro-managing this wedding that she has lost all perspective.

"We should invite more people, since it's going to be such an extravaganza, I want everyone I have ever met to see it. Every ex-boyfriend, coworker, or college friend is getting an invite! Which of the Costes brothers was it that we sat with at Castel last year, who asked us to come to St. Tropez?" she asks, possibly seriously, as she tries to search her cell phone for names.

So much for intimacy, and it reaffirms to me that if anyone *ever* wants to marry me, our wedding will be *très privé* and quiet. Frankly, I'm starting to dread this 2½ day event, since I cannot see how— with the civil ceremony at the *mairie,* the picnic on the lawn, the rehearsals, long Catholic ceremony, dinner, fireworks, toasts, DJ, and dancing—I will be able to attend, nurse Oscar, let him nap, keep him from howling, and have him with me through this obstacle course of challenges. *Just as I have so many times before, I will figure it out.*

POINTS FOR PARIS

1. Beautiful beyond words—need I say more?
2. Is, *potentially,* my dream realized—that's not easy to walk away from without a fight!
3. Idyllic in many ways but just now I can't find many reasons other than setting, friends, and great children's clothes.

Chapter 10

"Even a minor event in the life of a child is an event of that child's world and thus a world event."

—Gaston Bachelard

Two days before the wedding, I'm shuffling through St. Germain trying desperately to find a sophisticated hat to wear to this shindig. Plowing through boutiques like I'm on a scavenger hunt under a timer, since Oscar's "outing time" allows only so much of an allotment before all hell breaks loose and the boobs have to be brought out. And now that he is bigger, he isn't much for being hidden under a thin silk scarf; so he madly swipes it away, exposing his suckling me like a baby piglet to all and sundry. Ei yi yi, even French toddlers are getting an eyeful and not so surprisingly asking me or their nannies, "What dat?" Fun. Not.

Anyway, with time running out and the realization I am shopping for a *très* aristocratic item in the most expensive part of a most expensive city with a budget that would literally only be cab fare to the Right Bank, I hit on a masterful idea—I snag some delicate black feathers at 3 euros each and a half yard of black netting on the top floor of Bon Marché (the craft/fabrics section), take one of the black cups of those gigantic sculptural nursing bras, and sew up the cutest little pillbox of a chapeau complete with a mini veil. To die cute, looks perfect: 12 euros. Done. Maybe living under budget will be fun and creative. Big *maybe*.

The whole wedding affair. In short, lavish on the cheap. Really, I think they spent something like 25,000 euros (which now instantly reads to me as equal to two years at Montessori!) and got the whole schmear. It was really beautiful, well done, and most everyone had a ball. With the exception of *moi*. Even the big table of those souls with wheelchairs and no teeth got to stay later at the dinner than I did. The obvious group of American relatives was a riot. One guest devouring his *fois gras* and proclaiming it, "really tasty butter."

For me, Hectic Central. I knew from the outset it would be quite a feat of endurance, albeit in a gorgeous setting, and it was. Started out poorly, as my designated driver/setup date/friend of the groom turned out to be a total dope with dark stained teeth, heavily gelled spiky hair *that no woman could possibly find attractive,* who had the nerve to keep telling me, "Why are you tense? You should just chill." Which of course has the inverse effect of making me want to strangle him. "Just relax" was damn near the last words he'd utter on this earth! Listen, Monsieur Loathsome de Hairgel—You try to get ready for two days of formal events alone, no help with self or baby, in a non-baby-proof, sweltering hotel room, without my baby's cure-all swing chair and apply makeup while he crawls around and pulls the TV plug, only to have Zola ring me an hour ahead of the ceremony to ask if I can help get *her* ready (as I hold Oscar on my hip and lace up the back of her dress) when I haven't even had a bath yet, then on to hurriedly dressing self and baby, then following the wedding party out on twenty-minute walk uphill to tiny steaming church, all the while, carrying Oscar in arms, then on to attempting to keep a baby quiet in hot church *for an hour and a half*, then walk in high heels back from the church through the village's stone streets to the château (following the horse-drawn carriage and ensuing horse apple trail), where you have to dash up three flights of stone stairs to change own clothes, change his outfit (to a Petit Bateau cotton knit set—tired or not, this kid's going to look tops!), pump some breast milk so am able to drink champagne in the evening, got about three drops as so dehydrated from all the heat and running about, try to change baby diaper with one hand and fix makeup with other, while nursing him and carrying him everywhere—since Zola demanded I not wear the Baby Bjorn because it wasn't chic and would "look dumb in wedding photos." *Harsh.* That, in fact, may have been a *near* deathblow to our friendship. Oscar is huge now: sixteen pounds. I can't hold him all wriggling and writhing on my lap *or* while standing for over two solid days—not even a big man could. I think, given that I haven't a mate to help, she could've seen that demand was pretty over the top. *I think I will get over it, though.*

So, while the whole wedding was very pretty, picturesque beyond compare, with the ceremony in the tiny ancient church that smelled of delicious history and the sheer elegance of the château (I do so love an ornate castle with twenty-five-foot ceilings to add to one's fantasies of grandeur, however fleeting and faux), it was massively hard, and it was a pity after all that work to feel so tired that I could hardly kick back and relax at dinner. Not to mention, I was seated next to the ghastly Monsieur Loathesome de Hairgel, who I felt enraged to even glimpse across the room and now had to sit with, unable to escape his horrific cologne that must be the French version of Brut. Shouldn't anyone with French blood know a great fragrance is key? Ugh. And he went on to offer up more fun comments, "You look pretty good for having a kid."

"Pretty good," is a phrase to describe barely drinkable wine or the attractiveness of an old car half falling apart, not for a new mom who has just shed forty pounds! Listen, Frenchmen of the world: if you haven't an extravagant compliment, *ferme la bouche* ("close your mouth")! Oh, and Zola also seated me across from the most handsome single man there, Frederic, who, other than saying, "I'd love to see you breast-feeding," had very little else to say to me. Made me feel my appeal was *only possibly* that of a novelty. Not so fun for my first big party *après bébé*.

Long meal, made worse because the bread, cheese, and wine were limited to when the servers would pass and offer and they apparently got strict instructions to hide by the moat as we all were begging, "More wine! I've had like a single glass." Which is, of course, cruel, more so at a wedding and even more so *still* when I needed to drink like there was no tomorrow (though of course, there was and it was complete with a scheduled group breakfast and then, get this, a ride back to Paris with Monsieur Loathsome de Hairgel). *Après dîner,* we were all summoned to the large terrace facing onto the moat and rolling grounds as fireworks were shot into the starry night sky and couples held each other tight, engulfed in the festive celebration of love and commitment. A small pang of longing for Blake, his arm in the small of my back, as he bent over to lay a gentle kiss on Oscar's warm brow, a tender glance of shared happiness—that was hard for a moment to yearn for and realize, *ce n'est pas possible*. But life marches on and I have some newborn faith that all will be well for me and *my newborn*. A beautiful, healthy child asleep in one's arms fuels ones sense of optimism and faith in the world.

Just when the wine was starting to kick in and things were start-ing to get interesting, they wheeled out a large cake shimmering with sparklers, a miniature version of the château—which was terribly charming! I was blown away trying to imagine the hours that went into such a special wedding cake. That pleasure was brief as it turned out to be a cardboard and frosting prop used for all the weddings there and was quickly whisked away with promises that another presliced cake would be served right after. Then the DJ hit the play button on the theme from *Star Wars* (which would be my personal nightmare of musical choices; how do you say, "you're fired" in French?) at a level that would've shattered the wine glasses had they been crystal (*slam*). Oscar woke instantly, startled and scared. His little chin quivering as he whimpered from the shrieking loud "*musique.*"

That was that. Party over for Mommy. I had to beeline dash up-stairs to our hotel room, leap onto the bed, and try like the dickens to get him to sleep despite the fact that disco circa 1984 was blaring as loud as an AC/DC concert and with *no AC* there was no way to shut the windows and get some relief. The music went until 3:00 A.M. and then drunken yelling in the courtyard until 5:00 A.M. I didn't know I could be crabby in a beautiful château, but apparently it's possible. Just as the rowdy guests were all going back to their rooms and silence finally fell, Oscar woke to start the day. Enough said. Though I am sure if one at-tended *avec un amour et sans bébé,* it probably was pretty lovely.

Chapter 11

> *"The training of children is a profession, where we must know how to waste time in order to save it."*
>
> —Jean-Jacques Rousseau

Paris in September . . . the time of year when Paris is more magical than one can almost endure. The warm sunny afternoons, strolling by the Seine as gentle breezes sweep off the waves just enough to cool your skin to a temperature that makes you, well, want to have sex all afternoon.

Mais, ma vie: I'm dragging a child's easel from street side—someone's garbage—back home the five blocks with Oscar strapped to my chest and kicking and screaming, sweat running down my temple (*très sexy, n'est-ce pas?*), and my cell phone begins to ring. With this rare incoming call event now occurring a scant two to three times a day lately, I actually

place the easel down on one foot and lean it on hip while scrambling for
the phone. Could be one of my fabulous ex-boyfriends calling to say he is
out-of-his-mind distraught I somehow got away and now wants me back
at all costs. Surely that is the call, I tell myself, as I finally scavenge my
cell from the bottom of the diaper bag, dragging it out with a nursing
pad stuck to its face. Ripping it off frantically to see just which sexy
Frenchman is on a mission to get me back.

F*@k. Just Gilbert. Poof. Another dashed fantasy. I let him leave a
message, as I heave the easel onto my shoulder and proceed as the latest
version of my appearing a vagabond mother lugging large cumbersome
objects through elegant St. Germain with baby adhered to self. Once
home, I slide the easel under my bed alongside the children's cardboard
castle I got Oscar a week ago at The Conran Shop—*on sale for 20
euros*—it was such a steal that I was compelled to call Zola and get the
concurred opinion that I needed to get it. Even though she was on her
honeymoon in India, she took the time to green light it. She says she
was bored with India—how does one ever get bored in a place as lavish
and compelling as that?!

I finally listen to Gilbert's message as I unleash Oscar from the
Baby Bjorn and place him on his beloved play mat to bat about the
purple giraffe.

Bonjour Kiki . . . Comment ça va? Tout va bien? *I still have that*
cadeau *for Oscar and am hoping to see you* très bientôt. *Let me
know when you are free. Or perhaps you could join me for a
cocktail party this* vendredi soir. *It's at 20h on* Place des États-
Unis, *just send word and we can arrange it.* Gros bisous, chérie.

Almost tempting to see him. The company of any man would be welcome these days. Monsieur Right can enter stage left anytime now.

Alas, I know it's not Gilbert. I think he's after me *only* because I won't see him. Frenchmen loooove that shit. This all reminds me of when I once showed the faintest interest in a Frenchman and his instant reaction: A couple years back, while I was happily hobnobbing at the *très* elegant Prix de Flore fete for writers at my beloved Café de Flore, I had spent a good hour locking eyes with a to-die-for sexy *homme français,* and when he finally approached me and asked what my plans were for the rest of the evening, I offered up, "My friends and I are headed to Castel, would you like to join us?" thinking that a casual normal invite, in no way improper. His stunning reply, "I am not your dog and going to chase after you!" Hell-o! What the hell? Way to wig, dude. Alas, it's a lesson hard learned—play it cool with these men and, better yet, turn your back on them and they will come running. Beyond absurd, *non?* But back to the Gilbert invite—it's not exactly like I can just get a babysitter out of the blue and leave Oscar for hours to go out gallivanting. I know he would lose it with a stranger since he is a clingy little monkey these days. So, poor Gilbert. Denied again.

Anyway, I have a meeting early Saturday morning at an *immobilier* ("real estate office") just off rue du Bac, since I am totally obligated to find a new apartment *tout de suite*. This quaint flat is just getting ridiculous; with the oodles more time spent at home and the acquiring of hordes of new toys and accessories for Oscar, the walls are closing in and there is hardly any space for Monsieur à Quatre Pattes ("on all fours") to crawl.

Not to mention, the tiles are patina-ed seventeenth-century terracotta—*Jolie? Bien sûr.* Good for an infant's bobbing heavy head, fleshy elbows and knees? *Pas du tout.* The last time I did this apartment-search shenanigans was eight years ago and it was such a production, I ended up having to pay two years' rent in cash to get this apartment. This time I think I am quite prepared though we shall see; when it comes to anything involving a contract or business in France, there is always some crazy trip wire.

After a long, dull Friday night, where I often thought, Crapper. I could be at a cocktail party in the presence of real men . . . or at least *French* men *and* people who don't wear diapers and spit up. Ratsfinkle. Soon I have to get some kind of sitter or help so I can have a scrimpet of grown-up fun. Right. One thing at a time. First: The new apartment must be found, seized, and decorated!

As I trundle off that Saturday morning to the real estate office, with a small dossier of ID and financial documents under my arm, Oscar strapped to my chest, I am a flurry of nerves. Oh, here goes yet another massively important meeting *en français* and, while I have "dating French" down (or maybe not, obviously!), I stink at bureaucratic French. I entertain myself decorating fantastical apartments in my mind as I cross boulevard St. Germain. The castle from the Conran Shop will go in Oscar's room to the right of his daybed, and I will handpaint French coats of arms emblems along the circumference of the moldings . . . tra la la.

Alas, the big meeting goes like this: In the narrow, one-room office, the proprietor is seated at the back and I instantly surmise her to be classically the type of woman who generally hates me on sight. Still, I walk in all smiles and friendly. Error: that's never a hit with Frenchwomen, and I'm meeting one who could not be more French *or more bizarre looking*. For starters, she is wearing a wig resembling that 1970s TV show, Mrs. Brady style. And she is dressed as though she were 1) going for lunch beachside in Ibiza, thinking she is about thirty years younger than she is, and 2) is wearing a sick amount of very obvious huge faux diamonds. Who's impressed? I always find this accessory outlay mystifying: *if those were real diamonds, lady, you could buy the Louvre so you wouldn't be doing this shit job, would you? Is anyone buying that they are real?*

No surprise that she doesn't stand up as I approach, merely offers a limp handshake. I take a seat, though it's not even offered, and begin my routine of rattling on in semicoherent Franglais. My spiel of seeking *à trois pièces* ("three-room apartment"), preferably in the seventh arrondissement, *lumineux* ("sunny"), *avec une cuisine équipée* ("kitchen with appliances") and an *ascenseur* (elevator), in *un immeuble ancien* ("an older building"—I mean what's the point of living in Paris if you live in one of the modern Lego block buildings?), and either *poutres apparentes* ("exposed beams," as I have now) or *moulures* ("moldings") or *cheminée* (I think that's obvious) would be great. Budget: 2,000 euros per month. And that's assuming I'm fine with eating only ramen noodles and apples for the rest of my life, as 2,000 euros is almost $3,000 with the current exchange rate. Oh, and insert in all that my shushing Oscar a few times with kisses to the head and a couple nervous tics like tucking my hair behind my ears.

Her instant response: "Well, you must already know it is extremely difficult for a single woman with a child to ever rent in France as laws strictly forbid a landlord from evicting a mother and child, *hélas,* you will categorically be anyone's last choice. Frankly, no one would want to put themselves in the position of taking you on, not getting the rent, and getting stuck with tenants and no income."

Gulp.

"And to that end, as an expat with no employer or husband with a formidable income, you really have no hope of securing an apartment by *legal means*. I am sorry, but it would be an enormous waste of your time and mine. Thank you. *Bon après-midi.*" And she stood up, establishing it was now time for me to gather the array of bank documents, art gallery recommendations, and magazine articles (I'd brought them to prove my worth) and get the hell out of her office. I jam it all in the diaper bag and go to shake her hand good-bye, but she has already turned to work on the computer and make a phone call.

Goddamnit! This is bonkers—bullshit! In the USA, I have an 810 credit rating since I have never carried credit card debt or paid even a gas bill late, but here I am like a pariah who, I might add, is getting judged, glared at, and dismissed right and left. Until I got pregnant I was, *or at least was made to feel like,* the belle of the ball, invited to everything and given *carte blanche* at restos, clubs, art events . . . everywhere! I got whisked to the front of the long queue at La Grande Roue (the enormous Ferris wheel set in Place de la Concorde), waved in at Baron, sat in the VIP area of every hipster joint, and now I am as popular as gum stuck to the bottom of your shoe. I think Osama bin Laden would be a few notches ahead of me on the desirable tenant list.

For the time being, I am just going to have to put word out there—among my friends—that I am looking for a new flat and hope for some miracle. Oscar's first Halloween is coming and I am going to throw myself into this long-awaited exciting project with a vengeance. This Halloween business is loaded with history and self-inflicted pressure, since my mother was always so extraordinary at making Halloween fantastical and memorable. All us kids are still bowled over at her talents; making all our costumes every year, hosting a big party for all our friends, decorating the house and yard with such invention and staging that it was transformed into a spooky forest. And she did it with such an artistic hand; nothing was ever store bought. In a word, she executed Halloween with the same mentality she brought to every holiday: it was always, *"Elaborate!"* She would gather ideas, unusual objects, accessories, and fabrics all year. Making sketches and models of armatures for clever totem poles, knights on horses, robots with flashing lights, and cloven-hoofed wood fairies. All five of us kids were guaranteed winners of best costume at school, year after year. Teach-

ers would come to my mother to ask her for help with any and everything artistic, so she became the artist who gave our school handmade
puppets and a puppet theater, donated palatial *elaborate*ly decorated
gingerbread houses at Christmas, designed sets for the plays, painted
the murals, etc. Obviously, for so many years I have ached to have a
child that I could amuse with just some of the creativity I learned at her
side. And now Halloween is here. Poop that I'm in Paris. (Did I just say
that?)

Halloween is butchered here in France. They don't get it at all,
though of course they have freshly adopted this holiday, as they have
Valentine's Day, to bring in revenue. My expat friends and I all laugh
at how ridiculous it is to see the huge yellow gourds sold at Monoprix
for carving, as though they are pumpkins. There's no candy corn, no
trick-or-treating, so it's a freaking gift that my new mom friend, Tara
de Seattle, has kindly invited us to her apartment for a real Halloween
party.

In the week before the big day, I toyed with making Oscar into a
tiny Putti (cupid) and struck out to the craft store Creation, in the
sous-sol ("basement") of the Carrousel du Louvre to get supplies. I
used to turn up my nose at this mini-mall beneath the Louvre; it just
seemed so vulgar. But now, with limited walking range, I am kind of
digging it. And there is a charming children's boutique there that's
just packed to the rafters with *Le Petit Prince* trinkets and Babar um-
brellas and toys. For some unknown reason, when I am in that darling
shop, I am buying up lunch boxes and plates for Oscar like he is four
years old and I am rich. Neither is true. At Creations I pile pipe cleaners, bags of white feathers, a hot glue gun (you know you're really
a mom when you buy one of these), fabric felt, and fabric paint tubes.
At checkout, 56 euros—Garf! My money system has been recalibrated to, well, that's like two boxes of diapers or one pair of kids'

shoes! (BTW—You have to take out a mortgage to get a kid shoes in France. *And we all know I would be denied one, merci.* They are like 50 to 60 euros for toddler's tennis shoes that can be worn all of two weeks.)

I take home my loot, and with Oscar taking a rare nap of more than thirty minutes, I leap into action to whip up this cupid costume. The idea is little wings made with a structure of cardboard covered with feathers, attached like a backpack over shoulders and tied with a white satin ribbon and a halo of pipe cleaners edging an organza disk with fairy dust, all over a white onesie trimmed with ribbons. Thirty-nine minutes in holy hell! I haven't been this frustrated or such a monumental failure at something since seventh grade math. The wings looked like furry albino ears, four attempts at recuts and finally a bit like wings, but just so flimsy, "loving hands at home" that it looked less like a cupid and more like a fallen angel hitting on bad times or roadkill of a swan. I couldn't believe it just wasn't coming together and every idea and attempt to rectify it just made it more pathetic. Fook that idea. Damnit, that was expensive, too, but what's really killing me is I waited decades to do this kind of stuff, always been pretty damn creatively skilled, and now somehow I am crap at it. I am a lousy, shitty mom. That's apparent now.

Took a day to chill after that meltdown, but really, as a new mom, when you botch some major project or idea, since your identity and worth is so wrapped up in this, you just are coldcocked.

Plan B: With two days to go before the big party, I opt to go as a cowgirl and Oscar as a baby cow. All this is inspired by 1) I'm from a state famous for cows, 2) I have no money left for costumes, and 3) Oscar will look precious and I won't look half as stupid as I would if I went as a giant purple gum drop or something. My costume is a cinch, just stuff I have already; check shirt, bandana, jeans, boots, hat, cowboy belt, and jean jacket. Save the hat and bandana, this could be an ensemble I wear any old day, to be honest. Oscar's is the small white union suit that I've painted dark grey cow spots on, with his cashmere grey bonnet (that I am willing to ruin by affixing black felt cow ears) and matching booties with faux hooves, all polished off with a tiny white rubber glove on his belly as mini udders. Darling as all get-out and so cheap—phew, I'm saved.

The afternoon of the Halloween party, I am trying to steer my young calf to nap early so we can attend at least a fraction of this party that I have prepared more for than any other. Miraculously, he accommodates, but I, nerves a-plenty (which should be my middle name), made an error in judgment I haven't made in ages. With fluttery anxiety based on nothing worthy of such concern, I snuck a nip of cold *vin blanc,* unconsciously recalling that I used to be quite the riot/raconteur with a bit of vino in the old belly. After not drinking for so long, I didn't realize that one glass would have the effect of two, which had the effect of making me think, "I'm not feeling a thing (a-duh), I can have another." So, by departure time, I was *feeling no pain,* as they say, trotted out the three blocks over to Tara de Seattle's apartment on rue du Bac (it overlooks the little park with the mossy lichen-covered sculpture of Chateaubriand that I so adore). Oscar was a perfect little sweety, just smiling and kicking his little hooves like mad while strapped in the Baby Bjorn, facing out to the masses. It was one of the cutest things you could ever hope to see and I couldn't believe people we would pass wouldn't just ooh and ahh over him (*"as they would in the States" is implied BIG TIME HERE*).

Right. Paris. The only reaction was to me, in my big-ass cowboy hat and lasso at hip, and it was more like expressions of, "Hmm, how curious . . . Why ever would someone wear such a hat?" Clearly the older generation still hadn't been informed that the state had adopted Halloween, as they were clueless. Consequently, I've worn skirts of ten inches in length and felt more comfortable.

Upon arrival and pushing the door code, it hit me: I'm two sheets to the wind, what a mess. Oh wait, maybe it will be great; clever stories will just ooze out of my mouth. Ooze? That's a wacky word choice. Oh fuck, I'm drunk and dumb. Aces. My one big outing/event and I am snokkered. Suddenly buzzed inside, I realize I didn't even check which *étage* ("floor") they are listed on. So, there I am; I'm buzzed in and *buzzed* and standing in the lobby while they await me on some floor in seconds and I'm not even sure where to go. Oh, so dumb. I wait a few minutes thinking surely they will yell down the stairs for me. Nope, this isn't a frat party, Kiki. Thankfully, in another five minutes a few other guests arrive and I follow along, sworn to silence.

Streaming (read, *staggering*) up the red-carpeted staircase to the *deuxième étage* with another couple, I realize the parents are gorgeous and French and this building is smashing and I'm getting more smashed. We are all greeted at the door by Tara, who much to my relief is decked in a witch costume, albeit one of those nylon "Made in China" numbers with handkerchief hem and felt hat.

"Welcome! Happy Halloween! *Entrez!*" she says with great enthusiasm. Which after hearing so many tepid and tempered French utterings of late, is a delight to my ears. Intonation and enthusiasm; lovely, what a treat! She scampers off to the kitchen to check on the baked Brie in filo and sends us to her husband to be set with drinks. Jesus! Her husband, Perry, *is as Jack the cad was*—yet another specimen of perfection. This time the American version. Tall, dark, and movie-star attractive, dressed in pale grey cashmere V-neck with a white tee underneath and a slouchy pair of jeans.

Perry asks me, "A glass of wine, Kiki?"

Eeks. There's a bad idea. "I will gladly take a pop or Evian, if you have it?" I reply, thinking, "I will take *you* . . . God damnit, you are lovely to look at and because I already know you are a doting father, a loving husband, and a terribly brilliant man, I am duly bowled over. Hmmm." Tara didn't seem like the kind of woman who could snag such a feast of a man. Bravo, girl!

"Ahh, an American. No one says 'pop'! And this must be the famous Oscar," he says, caressing Oscar's cheek tenderly. "Let me go get Sam and then the two of them can play in the salon. Want to come to the bedroom?" he asks, handing me a Coke Light and gesturing to the hall.

Drunk trigger response: Oh, yeah but I think your wife would be so mad. Semiconscious realization: he means *to get his son*. Sure. I will take what I can get.

And with Oscar on hip, I turn to follow Perry, passing through the long hall with luscious parquet floors, when it suddenly dawns on me, this is one fabulous huge apartment. I should've anticipated that as this whole street is known for the luxe (or, as the French say, *raffinés*) apartments with ceilings fifteen, sometimes twenty, feet high, since they were the private homes of the highest level of the aristocracy of France in the seventeenth and eighteenth centuries. The entire apartment is flooded with light, as vast windows fill the entire width facing south onto the park and gardens below. The *grand salon* ("living room") is three times the size of my whole apartment, with big white Catherine Memmi couches placed next to Jean Nouvel coffee tables laden with Giacometti lamps. A huge Basquiat painting faces a cross and the word "Exodus" on one wall while a quadrant of Cindy Sherman photographs span another. Killer cool. Not to mention, the whole apartment is filled with every imaginable Halloween decoration ever made—life-size skeletons are speaking, fake tombstones pave the foyer, holographic mirrors with ghosts and ghouls reflect back as legions of spiders, some furry, some rubber, some small and serving as napkin holders, gobs of cobwebs in every corner, witches, cats, and real carved pumpkins are placed throughout with great flair. The formal dining room table is overflowing with Halloween novelties, wax skull candles and spider rings as well as crystal dishes of candy corn, gummy worms in Oreo "dirt," cupcakes with fake fangs that bite back, pumpkin cookies, bowls of mini candy bars and shiny black licorice jelly beans, all along the periphery to be within reach of small fingers. The center of the table is laden with a vast array of cheeses, tarts, brioche, tiny quiche, salmon tea sandwiches, and asparagus and shrimp hors d'oeuvres.

"Tara went all out on the festive decorations, didn't she?" comments Perry.

"It's astonishing. Where on earth did she find it all? I couldn't even find a single pumpkin to carve," I reply, thinking, Well obviously to carve, Kiki, you are just downright fascinating. Keep up the "state the obvious" retorts, that's always scintillating!

"She ordered it all online, of course"—he smiles, as a silent acknowledgement of "online" being his domain—"and we literally had shipments arriving every day for the last month!" Perry explains, clearly impressed with his wife executing her vision so wonderfully.

I nod in agreement. Christ. Must be nice to have it ALL. I was going with the current mantra, "You can have it all but not *at the same time*." But apparently no one here has to chant that round the clock, *comme moi.*

I meet a few other arrivals of whom only the children are wearing costumes. *And crummy, plastic, store-bought ones at that.* Growing up in our house, those were to be scowled at with the same appalled expression reserved for fake flowers, lawn art, fake shutters, snow mobiles, and hunters. I clearly have inherited my mother's discerning eye if not her talents!

Not quite able to hold a real conversation *yet* (read, inching toward sober), I smile, hand Oscar a rubber spider, and take in the scene. Divine home and, for once, pretty much exactly as I would do the décor, which makes it all the more unfair that I don't just live here! And it hardly lessens my envy/awe that Tara has told me they are renting and don't own this awesome abode, since they are not sure how long they will stay in Paris with Perry's job often taking the family round the globe. Wasn't I supposed to have that life? Or at least this apartment? Or at least a man like that? Tall glass French doors lead one room to another, in addition to the generous hall lit with Chihuly blown-glass chandeliers. I happen to have met the renowned designer Dale Chihuly a few times and try to make conversation as I trail along with Perry.

"I adore your Chihuly. He is a character isn't he? With that eye patch he would be a great pirate at the party today," exits my mouth. Despite it sounding *a lot* more clever in my mind, this is a lame thing to say, since the dear man lost his eye blowing glass.

Perry half laughs and says, "Yeah, he was our neighbor in Seattle and we are quite fond of him."

Right. That sounds a lot more like a grown-up, sober and smart. I vow to shush and mostly observe until I can be sure not to be a sloshy blathering mess. Because if I utter the phrase "at the end of the day" one more time, I should be shot. Really though, can we please call for a worldwide moratorium on this incessantly tiresome line that latches on to your vocabulary like a bad lyric from some cheesy pop song. (By the way, when you start using the phrase "pop song" you do realize you're a certified geezer.)

Turning at the end of the hall to walk the length of yet another *couloir,* we finally arrive at Sam's bedroom. Which turns out to be almost exactly like the one I have decorated in my mind for Oscar, complete with marble fireplace and a huge oversized recliner to sit and nurse him in, rather than the wood-back chair I use now, acquired for 8 euros at a flea market.

Sam is attended to by a chubby sweet nanny of unknown origin; she literally slips away without a word, allowing Perry to get Sam into his lion Halloween costume. I smile as I watch them—it's dear to see a father being such a gentle and yet strong presence to a young boy. And I realize since becoming a mother, I haven't seen many, if any, fathers with their sons in such an intimate and sweet exchange. And it charms and kills me, equally. I may be a wildly loving and attentive mother, but boys do need male role models and I know I have to find this for my dear precious boy. When? Where?

Sam takes his father's hand, says, *"Bonjour"* to Oscar and me, and we all make our way back to the *salon* as guests can be heard arriving and bustling about. The rest of the party is really relaxed and cool, all the guests are interesting and hyper-successful smart people. Since I spend a lot of time with people in the art, design, and antique fields, I rarely meet savvy business minds. And while they are less eccentric, it was terrific to see just a mass of real people who don't need to be the center of attention or put on airs. Need it be said? Very few were French and all were quite polite and kind.

While it was a very pleasant afternoon, dare I say that I felt strange to be the only single parent. And again that gnawing feeling that, *as in any big city,* either you are loaded and living large with every conceivable want, need, and whim or you are scraping by on a shoestring. To put it (I was going to say "in layman's terms," but even thinking "lay" and "man" reminds me I am so not getting either!) succinctly: living the latter is starting to suck, since I know the same amount of money it takes to keep my head barely above water here would set us afloat on the sea of luxury back home. The inescapable lingering question hangs in the air—Poor in Paris or wealthy in Wisconsin? Has it really come to this?

POINTS AGAINST PARIS

1. Tiny apartment living situation—even if I were *twice* as wealthy.
2. No yards for kids, thus no tree houses, which curiously I am fixating on for my child.
3. Language barriers galore!
4. Apartments never have fire exits, security gates, smoke alarms, and are probably laden with centuries of lead paint.
5. No family.
6. No idea how to really do this all *en français*!

Chapter 12

*"The best way to make children good
is to make them happy."*
—Oscar Wilde

It's official. I am too loopy-confused about whether to stay in Paris, owing to what I call a "lactation lobotomy"—the inability to focus due to mental faculties heavily drained from constant breast-feeding—so I am reaching out into cyberspace for answers. With baby to breast, typing with one hand, I log on again to that expat mothers site, Message Moms (US- and UK-born mothers raising kids in France). Hmm. Let's see what sage wisdom my compatriots have for me, since I cannot struggle with whether I should stay and raise Oscar here—is this moving back to Wisconsin just a mental escape hatch? This question haunts my waking hours, and, with sleeping hours being few and hard to come by, it's safe to say I'm dealing with this 24/7. I type:

Dear Expat Moms de France,

If you would indulge me, what would you say are the joys/pleasures/advantages/moments that you find raising your child in France that make it vastly superior to your homeland? Would you please be so kind as to chime in and complete the following sentence: I am thrilled to live in and raise my child in France when . . .

Here are their poignant and revealing answers, all of them true:

- My 4-year-old son says no Mommy, it's not Picasso, it's Picas-O, making the distinct accent.
- I make a quick dinner for my daughter and she asks me if it's the *premier plat*.
- I am giving my children snails for dinner and they adore them!!
- My 9-year-old son asks if he can have a snack and comes out of the fridge with cheese and olives.
- My 4-year-old son brings home his school workbook and I see that he has done a re-creation of a Matisse.
- The boulangère takes an extra five minutes to wrap up my pastry selection in a box with a bow and their logo sticker DESPITE there being a long line of customers waiting to be served.
- I breast-feed in the park and it initiates an absorbing discussion between a 4-year-old leaning over to watch and his nanny, all completely as though I weren't even there!
- I visit the butcher, the cheese shop, the wine shop, the bakery, the market—just to do the shopping—and have conversations with all the vendors. I've turned into a cook since being here!
- My kids ask to eat green salad!!
- Having a glass of champagne without needing to be celebrating something!!

- I realized I wouldn't dare leave the house in tennis shoes or a sweatshirt.
- The waiters leave you alone and don't come back 50 million times to try to refill my glass, ask me how everything is, or if I am still "working on it."
- I can get about ten errands done by just walking around the block and never having to get into a car.
- I buy lily of the valley on every street corner on May 1st.
- Having French grandparents over for Xmas: fois-gras, oysters & champagne on Xmas Eve.
- Taking all afternoon over a meal instead of an hour or so in a restaurant.
- Stuck to choose wine in a restaurant, you can ask the waiter for his/her advice and be considered not stupid but flattering their experience and knowledge AND feel confident that it'll be drinkable.
- My daughter asks which café we shall go to for *apéro*.
- I learned there is a charity to send poor people on vacation.
- Your kid's field trip is to Versailles and your 4-year-old knows who Louis XIV is.
- You learn you can make your guests cook their own food (raclette or fondue) and they still bring you flowers and wine!
- You discover you can invite people over for an aperitif and that's all and they don't expect a five-course meal!!
- A man greets you with charmingly flirty *"enchantée"* on the simple pleasure of walking past one another.
- You fill a prescription and exit the pharmacy with a bag full of medications that cost you nothing.
- A fire truck rushes your 2-year-old to the emergency room because his hand was stuck in a door for twenty minutes; and you and

your son get to ride the fire truck (which completely helps allevi-
ate his pain!).

- Your 5-year-old daughter begs her father for "strong stinky
cheese," Époisses in particular, for her snack.
- Your daughter exclaims during *Ratatouille,* "We live there!"
- Every time you see the Eiffel Tower sparkling it gives you shivers.
- You've scoped out five or six bakeries, all within four minutes of
your place, and figured out which one makes the best baguettes,
which has the best croissants, which one has the best madeleines,
and which one has the best *gâteaux,* and so on.
- You go to the fruit seller and you are asked whether it's to be
eaten today or tomorrow.
- My daughter says "*oh la la*" when she drops something.
- You go to the butchers & you're told exactly how to cook the meat
you've bought (what temperature, how long, best-yet recipe,
etc.—not your usual roast which you just stick in the oven).
- My son eats some fruit off a stall at a market and the vendor
smiles and gives him more with a "*Bon appetit!*"
- You go to a pharmacy and they will patch your child up when he
has had a bad fall and therefore a nasty cut on his knee or patch
up your big brother who cut his finger on his razor while packing to leave for the airport—free of charge!!
- My son recounts the tale of *Pierre et le loup.*
- A meal lasts five hours and nobody thinks it strange that we then
start preparing for the next one.
- The meat is better dressed than you are.
- You don't consider going out of the house without at least lipstick and a matching bag.
- You're standing at the school gates with a host of other care-
givers in complete silence, no gossiping, no nothing.

- The shop assistants offer to gift wrap your purchases, even when it's not Christmas.
- Buying a bottle of wine, the wine merchant asks you what you plan to eat with it.
- Buying a baguette at your local baker's & the shop assistant asks if you prefer "*très cuite ou pas trop cuite?*"
- You commute to work via the *voie expresse* on the Seine, and, with silvery winter sunlight glinting off the water, you watch the working barges chug down the river past the Conciergerie, Pont Neuf, Île Saint Louis, etc., instead of watching the road.
- You walk into your grocery store at Christmas time and there is an entire aisle devoted to lovely boxes of delicious chocolates.
- People count with their fingers using the thumb as "one" (and thus your child doesn't show you that he's 3 years old with the same three fingers you use).
- After years of hearing as a child that it's nice manners to keep your hands in your lap on your napkin at the dinner table, you hear your (French) spouse teaching your children to keep their hands on the table.
- You realize all doctors still make house calls.
- You're considered courageous for breast-feeding longer than, say, a month.
- Your toddler doesn't have school on Wednesdays.
- In a presentation sponsored by a public sector institution, the refreshment includes oysters and champagne!
- You do your grocery shopping in an open market down the road twice a week. And when in that same open market, there's a veggie stand that carries five different types of radish and a *traiteur* that prepares *fromage de tête* and *tête de veau*.

- Window shopping becomes a pleasure for the eyes . . . no matter what neighborhood you are in.
- The perfectly coiffed chic young woman ahead of you in line wearing high-heeled shoes, a tight little skirt, and equally tight top on her trim little body, turns around and is older than your grandmother. I still get fooled after ten years here.
- Even over 40 with a wedding band, most men you don't know will address you as "mademoiselle" just for the charm or *possibilities* of it.
- A real beater of a car pulls up and the driver who gets out is dressed to kill and as chic as can be.
- Mayonnaise is actually a homemade sauce.
- You have a whole repertoire of phrases to use that don't require *"tu"* or *"vous,"* for the occasions you don't know which form to use.
- Coffee at breakfast time is served in a cereal bowl (or at least that's what you initially thought it was).
- Breakfast for children seems to have chocolate on everything.
- You're braving the Christmas crowds head down to the wind and you happen to look up and see . . . the Opéra de Paris down the street beautifully lit, glinting golden in the lights.
- Your infant has a cold, the medical advice given is to squirt sea water up his/her nose, then suck out the resulting goo with a plastic pipe.
- Your child has a temperature, he's given a suppository; when you have a sore throat, you take a suppository; when your contractions start, you take a suppository; when you have blocked sinuses, you take a suppository.

Oh la la, I gotta take a month here and think.

Chapter 13

"There never was a child so lovely, but his mother was glad to get him asleep."

—RALPH WALDO EMERSON

I was just getting into full swing of scolding Zola (*she went and got an eye job and she's not even forty!*) when a path to follow was laid before me.

As for the Zola stunt, she knew I thought plastic surgery was a bonkers thing to do, so she didn't even tell me in advance; just rang one afternoon saying she was home from work.

I said, "Terrific, I'll stop by."

She was compelled to admit, "Kiki, I know you think I am crazy but I got my eyes done, so if you come by, I have to stay in bed, one eye is dripping blood."

"What?! That's madness. You look younger than anyone and, oh god . . . Girl, is this because Jean-Pierre is seven years younger? Come on, I notice you're getting hyper-obsessed with your weight, appearance, dressing more trendy. You even told me you sleep in your makeup every night. You can't live forever with that much anxiety about how you look," I remind her. Clearly, I am as great at doling out advice as I am terrible at taking it when it comes to self-consciousness.

"I know. I know. Come over but I am wearing sunglasses, as it's pretty gross to see right now."

"That's it, that is positively crazy, girl. I'm there in five minutes," I say, clutching Oscar more closely in the Baby Bjorn, picking up the pace on rue Jacob. My cell phone rings.

Sure it's Zola ringing me back to tell me not to come, I answer and say, "I'm coming, girl, there's no stopping me. Alright, just tell me, can I bring you anything, you stinker?"

"Kiki, it's Tony. I have to speak to you about your mother. Are you at home?" My stepfather, back in Wisconsin, asks, cutting to the chase.

"What's going on? I can be home in five minutes but just tell me. What happened?" I ask, feeling the blood drain from my limbs as they plod on by some miracle.

"Well, your mother's not well. She had an attack and we are all in the cardiac ICU. Because of her diminished state, the doctors suggested I call you. She is in a coma right now and they are trying to stabilize her. Are you okay, Kiki?" he asks with a voice I've never heard from him. It's absolutely terrifying to hear this horrible news *and* the pain and desperation in his voice.

Everything in sight stops like someone hit the master switch on my life. Then some internal device kicks in and reactivates, so you don't just drop dead. Sounds are muffled but amplified and all I can see is the streaming blur of movements as though the shutter speed of my eyes is stuck on open frame. A breath replaces the silent sustained gasp.

We speak about the particulars of my getting back to Wisconsin ASAP, and then I just hear my own voice saying over and over, "No, no, no, we can't lose her . . . not now . . . no . . ." Once back in our apartment, Oscar generously falls asleep within minutes as I sit in that initial paralyzed shock.

Then on to a frenzy of manic energy: I make several phone calls, to arrange flights, to my sister and brothers, and again to Tony, asking for more news. Her heart rate is in defib (unsteady) and she is still unconscious. Family is en route from all over the States. I want frantically to hug someone and there's no one. With a 5:00 A.M. flight home, I must let Oscar be spared this raw emotional energy. I am up all the night pacing in the living room, waiting for any news and packing. I open my closet and just slide onto the floor—to pack thinking you are going to very likely need a black dress for your mother's funeral is horrifying, surreal, insane. And the toughest thing is you want more than anything, in this panic nightmare where you feel a desperation like a lost child, to call one person—*your mother*.

EN ROUTE TO WISCONSIN

I adore my perfect son for sleeping and nursing on the plane like an angel. People even approach me at baggage claim to say, "I saw you come on with your baby and thought, 'oh god' and then he was so good. To see you two sleeping was sweet." I can only manage to smile weakly and say a quiet, "Thanks." I am proud of my boy but can only think of keeping him calm and getting to my mother's bedside.

She is in ICU still, opened her eyes but without recognition and closed them. Tony picks us up at the airport. After a long hug where we almost have to hold each other up, we speed straight to the hospital to see my momma bear. She's in the biggest room in the ICU since she has the most apparatus attached to her. Amazingly, lying there, she still looks beautiful with her high cheekbones and elegant nose; she always looks stunning. With her hair now all grey, long and in a braid, she somehow, even with all the tubes and wires, still looks like a queen. There is a regalness to her that in spite of everything is so powerful.

Days pass. Her heart rate stabilizes then defibs again. All the children are there, not in shifts but as a team, "Team Susie," we call ourselves. It occurs to me as everyone takes turns entertaining Oscar in their own unique playful way how divine it would be for him to get this much family time, *all the time.* And how much my mother would be so pleased to see us all, "her chickens," together, laughing, as we always did, just talking endlessly about her, our own lives, and playing with Oscar as days turn to nights. The doctor who we name Dr. Deadpan, because he is such a downer and unpleasant, claims she won't leave the hospital. Crushing.

Day 3, while I'm caressing her arm, she suddenly opens her eyes and looks at me with a big smile—which turns to a laugh! I am astounded. Am I dreaming?! This can't be. She seems like her old self, *before Alzheimer's,* as she is giggling and looking at me with total connection and an expression of, "There you are, Baby Bear! Oh, how I've missed you. What a great surprise!" I look at Tony, the only other person in the room at the moment, and he and I are both overjoyed and stupefied. With his exceptional generosity, he steps back, takes Oscar in his arms and says, "You can have this time with her," smiling, knowing I am so honored and thrilled, as I'm already sitting on the bed, leaning over her, stroking her cheeks. "Momma," holding her face in my palms.

I speak to her excitedly and with tears in my eyes to feel for the first time in years a conversation. We are having a conversation. Though she isn't able to speak, her eyes dance and she seems to follow my every word and answer me. After maybe a half hour, she grows a bit tired and slowly fades. I tell her, "It's okay, Momma, sleep a little." And she slips back into a nap. I leap, literally skipping down the halls to Tony, Oscar, and my brother to tell them of this incredible experience. We are all just shaking our heads in awe and Andy runs back to her room.

The excitement fades as weeks pass and she doesn't open her eyes again. A month. Nothing. Just fed, propped up, eyes closed, sleep, coughing, turned every two hours to avoid bed sores. And this is the woman who raced me up Palatine Hill when we went to Rome together when I was twenty-five. The woman who would juggle five kids, an art career, and a marriage and was president of the art guild, all while being chic, witty, well read, passionate, thoughtful, and a glorious treasured friend to so many. Now, the silent form that has her great mom smell, those long pretty hands, and the shoulders that we all cried on and embraced so many times.

We have to make the horrible, painful decision to move her to an assisted living home since even round-the-clock nurses couldn't keep her at home now. To see her clothes, her high heels, and cool purses from her heyday still hanging in her closet is like being skinned alive. Your head never wraps around the idea that she won't "wake up." You look at her and you just want to crawl inside her and be wherever she is in there.

She would loathe all this more than words can express. *And that's what's worse than losing her.* This invasive vicious disease is robbing her of the enormous dignity she so grandly deserves.

After being so close to family all these weeks, surrounded by the great support network and loving souls, returning to France to raise

Oscar seemed ridiculous. With little in Paris—save the great architecture, an increasing tension, and disconnect with Zola and a smattering of friends—I return only to bid my adieus and have my apartment packed and shipped.

I feel strangely excited to leave. Like I have finally given myself permission to say, "Enough." I have lived this dream to beyond my wildest fantasies, but now with Oscar I have nothing to prove to anyone. I have lived it *all* here and in NYC . . . the whole deal. Drama? Had it in spades. Passion? Glam, etc. More than my share. Now, Kiki, just go be a good mother in a place where not everything is a struggle, not every event is alone without family. Where you know how to do it and, more importantly, can!

The movers arrive at 7:00 A.M. Yipes. Five huge black guys and a zillion boxes. I have to stay in the apartment all day to occasionally answer questions and assign labels. The shriekingly loud masking tape and the accompanying earsplitting packing has Oscar crying. Good god, where to go with my baby? We literally end up sitting on a folded-over futon on the tiny bathroom floor with the door shut to extinguish some of the noise. Nursing, drinking Evian, and nibbling sandwiches from the boulangerie and playing with a few toys, trapped there until almost 8:00 P.M., when they are finally done packing 129 boxes, 38 of them books. Christ. It may seem like an enforced hell to spend a day in a loo with a baby and yet, somehow, Oscar was cool and we managed. That seemed significant to note. Almost symbolic.

That last night in Paris, with nothing more than luggage, spare linens, and that futon, Oscar crawled around the empty apartment giggling and laughing endlessly at how the acoustics carried his voice now. He reminded me that, "Look, there is nothing here, just you and your baby and life is great." I looked around at my apartment that has seen so many love affairs, paintings created, tears shed, champagne, laughter, baguettes, and candles flickering, and I knew it was the right thing to do, time to move to the next chapter of life.

NINE THINGS YOU NEVER THOUGHT YOU'D DO AS A NEW MOM

1. Need to abandon writing every e-mail after two sentences because of child howling in feigned neglect or crawling up back of legs dragging pants to knees.

2. Blowing off daily bath and hair washing as time only warrants child is bathed, coiffed, and perfectly manicured down to those little toenails that grow like wild fire.

3. Somehow unconsciously slide from making those pureed veggies every day to serving mister picky eater pants Kraft mac and cheese in the microwavable fast packs. Good god, I vowed never to be too tired to be such a subpar mom. And alas, I have even been known to zap a Lean Cuisine and plop it onto his highchair tray with a fork jammed in it.

4. Let oneself and one's appearance go to such an extent that one is mistaken for a) homeless, b) the father, and c) the grandmother!

5. Spending far more money and time choosing child's outfit than one's own, resulting in child decked out in a Dior silk-wool beret, Petit Bateau sweater set with suede trim in cocoa, Bonpoint corduroy overalls with embroidered reindeer, and Robeez with appliquéd acorns—while mother is clad in spit-stained, pilled acrylic turtleneck from clearance sale and stretch maternity leggings pulled *back out* of "for charity box."

6. Actually derive great sense of self-esteem from merely remembering to pack Neosporin, Purell, and snacks in diaper bag.

7. Spend so much of your daily life wiping! My hands are like an elephant's knee, since I spend literally hours wiping: baby butt, nose, floor laden with crumbs of Gerber cookies, juice box drippings. I find myself wishing I had an extra arm, hell, even a monkey tail, so I can simultaneously serve my master lunch and answer the phone while picking Play-Doh out of my hair and wiping chocolate handprints from the wall. To be frank, if this whole child-rearing system of evolution were truly advanced, mothers would spring a third arm for the duration or at least be able to detach breasts at will while baby nurses so that you can hustle off to the bathroom to mop up the floor after a bath-toy-flinging extravaganza.

8. More often than not, you feel like you're in a "Beat the Clock" contest when you have any need to go to the bathroom. I swear to god, I can pee and wash my hands and be out of the bathroom in under fifteen seconds now. Not really a talent I was shooting for in life but, hey, it's not like I am getting the time to tackle learning Italian right now.

9. You find yourself saying things to your child like, "Please don't jam the string cheese in your ear, and let Mommy finish scrubbing the floor . . . if you let me finish, I will give you a chocolate." Moments like these are just a nightmare of all that we once vowed against—bribery and begging submissively weren't in the game plan.

Chapter 14

"There is no finer investment for any community than putting milk into babies."

—Winston Churchill

After a sweet good-bye to Zola, where we vowed not to cry (for her sake—I hope the fact one of her eyes still looks wonky isn't because her tear ducts are butchered, what a botched job that was, the poor girl) and hugged like koala bears, the taxi sped Oscar and me along the Seine, passing the Louvre and the Conciegerie and miraculously I didn't cry. I always thought if I ever left Paris I would sob like mad and possibly collapse with sadness. Nope. I'm finding monumental events in life never seem to be as bad as you've feared. *It's always the things you don't anticipate that knock you on your ass.*

I have returned to my hometown, Lake Geneva, Wisconsin. Picture-perfect snowy wonderland. People cross-country ski to work and winter sports are as popular here as shopping is in Paris. It's so family oriented and community minded that I am constantly taken aback at people's kindness and smiles at the ready. What a refreshing and welcome change.

Impatient as ever, I set off to buy a house *tout de suite,* since I think it's about time at forty years old to stop paying rent for god's sake and build some equity! Even house hunting is an adventure in hometown charm as home owners leave trays of fresh cookies and thermoses of cocoa and cider for you as you trounce through their homes.

I knew I wanted to live in Shorewood Hills, *the* place to live for yuppie (does anyone use that moniker anymore?) families and is just the most beautiful, child-friendly area in town. The neighborhood is strictly limited to post-modern homes of the Mies Van der Rohe style all situated around a nature conservancy, lush forests, rolling hills, and ponds, embracing the lake's edge. What more could a kid want?

I bought the first house I saw, totally thrilling as my father claimed it was too expensive and big—and so, of course, I had to have it. My mother would be ecstatic on all fronts. I am finally a homeowner and a mom and while it seems ridiculous, I am so excited about it all. A two-car garage and I don't even have a car. For a woman who has lived within four small walls for far too long, it rocks to now have four bedrooms, a painting studio, and a mortgage that is less than I was paying for my tiny Paris rental apartment.

It's cool for a change to feel I'm doing the "right things" and there is a certain sense of accomplishment in making this leap of faith and assuming the role of a grown-up—*enfin*—life and health insurance, the all-important 529 college fund, and the whole "I've left behind living a dream life and am embracing real life." I write to all my friends back in Paris that I have moved home, for how long I don't know, but it feels right, *right now*. Many are aghast: "Is Wisconsin near South Dakota?" "Why are you doing this? You don't have to discard your whole life just because you're a mother now!" Not so shockingly, some people don't even write me back, as out of sight, out of town is out of their lives, and more to that point, moving to Wisconsin is officially nowhere to those elitists. Fine.

Surprisingly, Gilbert writes a sweet e-mail that he is "deeply saddened," since he believes he fell a "little bit in love with me." Very charming of him. I'm touched, since Frenchmen love to hold all the cards and rarely show their hand. Alas, I think American men are considerably better at accepting women with children and, frankly, are a helluva lot more genuine and honest, if not as literary or sophisticated, on the whole.

First month

Setting up house is a riot. So nice to have space and actually put linens in—wow—a *linen closet* instead of wrapped in garbage bags and kept under my bed. It's great fun to see my life unpacked; like facets of oneself get to be exposed to the sun again. With each box, I feel more of the pieces of me, my life, fit back into their niches. Oscar's loving it, too; crawling has evolved to walking, and one of my greatest pleasures is to look into his nursery and have it be exactly as I dreamt it up. We are having a blast with our new quiet life; simply plopped on the kitchen floor (you find you spend hours on the floor as a new parent) smelling various tins of French Mariage Frères tea and with each one I remember the last time I drank it in Paris. Not missing it, just reveling it. For now.

As we were setting up his huge playroom on the lower floor, I took out some vibrant green acrylic paint and just painted "Oscar Is King" on the wall, laughing like a hyena; he just looked at me like, "You can do that?" I remember vividly how my mother gave us all free rein to create and express ourselves as children—taking whatever we wanted in the kitchen cabinets and mixing it all together; "cooking" up some vile but wildly entertaining concoction. Or how she and my father gave each of us our own plot to garden with whatever we wished and of course—very cool to me—the permission to wear whatever we felt like was our mood and spirit. She nurtured our innate choices and gave us all the belief that what we felt was of value, unique and meaningful. That is exactly what I want for Oscar—you can do, be, create, live any dream and idea.

Confession: In the midst of all this celebrating and happiness, I was blindsided to find myself literally almost weeping while unpacking my ex-NYC/Paris diva clothes. Bear with me, ridiculous metaphor incomin' here—it was as if a cowboy, who always wanted to be a cowboy and finally became one, all the sudden put his hat, horse, and saddle to pasture. *I'm fixating on cowboys a lot lately, weird.* In other words, it was like bidding adieu to dear old friends. Each purse and dress was laden with memories of late nights and stolen kisses under lamplights on the breathtaking bridges of Paris. The white embroidered Chloe slipdress from the crazy chic Diner Blanc party in front of Notre Dame, the taupe one-shouldered chiffon gown I wore to my dear friend Fabian's birthday party at the French embassy, and my treasured pair of Louboutins that have trounced the finest cobblestones of Paris. Oh, maybe I'm exaggerating a bit there, trying to romanticize the images of old Brassaï and Helmut Newton photos. In truth, there were enough foolish events and stagger-down drunk scenarios ending in solo bed spins . . . or *not always solo,* I'm embarrassed to say. Like the time I made a big play for some playboy and once in the throes of passion, I realized this was all a very bad idea, leapt up, threw back on my black crepe dress, and marched out, feigning a spontaneous illness. Back out on the streets of Paris, I felt terribly relieved and pleased with self to have made a quick getaway before he knew what hit him, when I glanced down. Standing at a taxi stand among a good dozen late-night hipsters, my dress was entirely inside out. Oh, Jesus, a hard moment to pull off with grace when one's optic-white shoulder pads are boomeranging out and the care label is waving in the wind. Oops!

The real gig now is, when will I ever get a chance to wear an evening gown again? Heels, even? Or carry that Dior saddlebag purse (as a nod to my former shallow self, I am compelled to say it was a gift and from a limited edition of 100, which added to my level of joy exponentially and, yes, that is the definition of quintessential shallow materialism that I coveted like life itself three years ago). But where do I fit in here? Two days ago, I wore a long-sleeved black shirt to lunch that said, "Chanel No. 5" and a woman at the next table asked me if I worked for the local Channel 5 TV station.

Cringe.

I guess I should've seen the signs when house hunting—I was rather taken aback to see every house had a plasma big-screen TV in the living room and not a single bookshelf, save the entertainment center's collection of *TV Guide,* the odd Bible, and *Scrapbooking Made Easy* next to the DVD collections. Oh, and all the walk-in closets were laughably just tee shirts and sweatshirts on hangers and nary a heel or nonsneaker. I know this sounds very judgmental *and it is.* These are people who are wonderfully community and civic minded, excellent parents, and honorable hardworking souls; but the truth is, I'm just a different breed and, as one boyfriend of mine said, "You're not like everyone *or for everyone*." Which obviously isn't a compliment either. Alas, the defense rests.

Month 2: Full-blast winter in 3-D!

Snowboots—I am so sick of wearing sensible, no-chance-of-falling-while-carrying-baby, flat MOM boots. I vowed long ago never to wear a shoe with the sole of a Monster truck tread, trimmed with fake fur, and here I am sporting a boot that has all the sex appeal of road kill.

Enduring the month with the most snowfall on record (forty inches) warrants these ugly beasts of a shoe and other fugly cold-weather fare. Hey, I wouldn't condemn this bundled-up winter look if the local options weren't either Green Bay Packers puff coats or those goddamn "sleeping bag" chin-to-ankle quilted coats, in which you look and feel like you're walking around wearing a futon.

Fun. I did receive two bouquets of "welcome to the neighborhood" flowers on my doorstep. With accompanying letters and maps of fun kid-friendly places and activities. That was super charming and helped me not feel so lonely and isolated. It reminded me that one does this kind of thing in the real world, as my mother would make huge Bundt cakes drizzled with dark chocolate for new neighbors—how 1970s and how lovely of her!

Funny. That after eight years of not owning or even seeing one, I have a TV again and this is exactly like being dropped onto another planet. To see the old famous TV personalities I knew—Mary Hart and Bryant Gumbel look *exactly* the same, which is more than eerie. But Joan Rivers and the nothing what-the-hell-is-she-famous-for Lily Rinna are fucking freakish looking. Are there not limits to plastic surgeons' willingness to take cash?!

Adventure. I eagerly braved the hip-deep snow to get to my first and longed-for new mothers group, luckily just a block beyond Shorewood Hills, within walking distance, as I still have no car (more on that later). Fair warning—I'm well aware that what follows is going to appear very snarky, but as a born-and-bred Wisconsinite, I think I can criticize this state with authority . . . well, maybe not authority per se, but with permission granted from experience and familiarity. It's not like I am some snob blue blood that is appalled by life here. It's more that I adored my childhood and the people who live here, but that doesn't mean I am able to live here without making the occasional neighborhood critique.

After a bit of unexpected ice sailing through the snow, I arrive to the meeting with Oscar all dressed in his best French (Bonpoint—a gift from an ex) snowsuit, riding high like a sultan in that Stokke stroller, and me in a Mongolian lamb jacket and some warm Helmut Lang leather pants. I was all excited with the hope of meeting similar hipster moms and making a circle of kids for Oscar's summer playdates. I could envision it perfectly: The kids all playing in the sand box with its adorable striped canopy I already ordered from Pottery Barn Kids, while I make the moms margaritas served in the great bottle green glasses I got online from Williams-Sonoma. Very *Desperate Housewives* of me—part Bree Van de Kamp and part Susan the clumsy single mom.

Ooph! Foiled again, as upon pushing open the front door, I see the attendees are a motley group of hippie, hard-core eco-friendly, home birth, grow your own yams for baby food in gardens with compost from their diapers, greasy-haired, Birkenstocks with hemp hand-knit socks, tree-hugging mothers with their spawn clad in tie-dyed onesies. Too harsh?

Oh, I think not. These women have never seen the inside of a hair salon or met a carob cookie they didn't like. In short, many were dead ringers for Jabba the Hut or Cheech and Chong. Needless to say, I wasn't the biggest hit of the meeting, my opening line during the round-robin introductions—"I just moved here from Paris"—was met by the sound of crickets. Ah, lovely, I was as welcome in this group as a can of aerosol hairspray. (Wasn't terribly surprising that all attendees weren't from Shorewood Hills but were from surrounding small towns.)

I made an attempt at conversation, asking, "Can anyone suggest a babysitter or nanny service? I'd like to try getting back to running again a couple hours a week," which was met with looks spanning from, "Exercising? Why bother?" to "If you think it imperative to leave your child with a stranger perhaps you should place your child in daycare and leave the child rearing to people who enjoy it."

Gulp. Huh? I love my baby, love being a mom. Man, am I not blending in here. Which surely became apparent when the following chat came about:

Mother with whisker beard, thighs like ham hocks, and blue-veined boob with nipple the size of a plate hanging out of her tie-dye shirt to the extreme disinterest of her baby, who resembled a small primate, "Well, I was lucky, the staff at the hospital didn't mind at all that I brought a Crock-Pot and simmered my baby's afterbirth into stew the night he was born." Attendees snicker in a murmured scoff at the appalling notion that Whisker Mom didn't have child at home with midwife in her own bath, *like the rest of the pack.*

Mother wearing prairie skirt of dishcloth fragments while sporting toe socks with fake-leather Birkenstocks announces, "*I* have to say, I was tickled pink to be able to make a fresh omelette from my afterbirth and share it with the other children. We all rejoiced in the addition to the clan."

Insert my gag reflex stifled only by the sheer horror of being asked to leave and there was no way I wanted to miss what was coming next on this line of thought! *Clan? Afterbirth omelette?* What in god's name are you people thinking? I'm curious, are *you* the kind of kook-a-la parents that will tell your kids to eat their own scabs and snot as it's part of the cycle of life? Yikers, I cannot raise my son in a town where this is what his neighbor friends are up to. Hey, I'm all for a good compost pile, vegetarianism, noncircumcising, and limiting preservatives in kids' snacks, but what the hell, ladies?

To start with, I am rather astounded that you all found men who want to sleep with you, since I can't find a sexy aspect in a one of you earthy crunch goblins. Moreover, in this day and age, are you, Toe Socks Mom, not doing your child a massive disservice by raising him eons away from the modern world. (She and clan live in a teepee in Pee-waukee. That's a helluva lot of *e*'s, no?) All I know is if I fit in anywhere as a new mom, it apparently is in a parallel universe unknown to mankind. Yikes.

NOTABLE REALIZATIONS OF LIFE AS NEW MOM

- You find yourself feeling lonely, yet you're never alone.
- You find yourself feeling bored, yet you've never been more busy.
- You find yourself getting excited to finger paint (or play tea party or play dolls or read a children's book, etc.) and are seriously miffed when your child is dead set against it and wanders off to play something else. "Get back here this instant and have fun with Mommy!"
- You know you're really into parenting when you are more wildly excited about the newest tricked-out Matchbox car than your child is.
- Life is short, yes, but the days drag.

As a new maman *your whole life is now about*

- Cleaning sippy cups and baby bottles with scalding water—have you ever had such dry hands in your life? Mine are like a nineteenth-century blacksmith's at best.
- You are able to hurriedly reel out your ready stock of snack bags of Cheerios and Goldfish crackers for a screaming child as though it's from a tool belt . . . which ain't a bad idea, actually.
- You always have Purell germ-killing gel at the ready, generally in tandem with the scolding-tone *"NO!"* when child reaches to grab gum off the sidewalk and put in mouth.
- Diapers and wipes accompany every outing as faithfully as you once checked your lipstick, which is now replaced with chapstick because who the hell has time to look in the mirror. I swear I see my own face three times a day now—which is more than enough these days—wake and put in contacts, then once in afternoon to check if you really exist and to look into your own eyes and say to self, "C'mon it's 3:00 P.M., you can make it until bedtime," and then taking contacts out in mid-collapse at bedtime.

Chapter 15

*"I must take issue with the term
'a mere child,' for it has been my
invariable experience that the company
of a mere child is infinitely preferable
to that of a mere adult."*

—Fran Lebowitz

I don't know what the hell got into me, but I chopped off all my hair yesterday and dyed it "chestnut," which really looks more like blond that someone lightly spray painted "Crayola Brown." I somehow came to think that maybe the long blond hair is a bit too sha-sha/big city and *that's why* I'm as welcome with the locals as day-old dirty diapers left in the sun. By the way, you know you're far too into motherhood when all your similes have to do with kids' stuff.

Somebody save me . . . from myself! I mean, really, who butchers their hair to such a degree in the name of finding friends? It was all a stupid exercise in homogeny. And truth be told, I am now a frigging dead ringer for the house-mouse anonymous chick who does the Glad snack bag ads, where she shakes a bag of peas with all the enthusiasm of having won the lottery. This is not a good look and one forgets that looking as shitty as possible doesn't do wonders for the mood.

Now as a crabby, forgettable suburban housefrau, I'm really struggling with my identity. Clever, clever gal. Something about breast-feeding gives you that Momnesia-lactose lobotomy, and you are only able to think of things in a surface way. If I'd thought about it a second, I would've realized that the home hairdo fiasco was exactly what I used to do in high school and college—when I was trying to find my identity. Am I back in that place? Dear god. Frankly, I convinced myself that I could seamlessly adapt *back* to my mother tongue and culture. As my childhood BFF Kathy put it when I recently begged, "How could you let me come back here? The place we so desperately wanted to escape?" she replied, "You were hell-bent on it and, after knowing you thirty years, I know there is no arguing with you, just best to step aside and support your adventure."

Crap! I will admittedly slam the living daylights out of my hometown and in doing so, I very well may get blackballed here with the local chapter of the Junior League; I am okay with that. Because now, firmly back in America's Dairyland, reverse culture shock is hittin' hard, as I find my social options are either the local "Troll Beer Fest" or "The Quilters' Convention"! (Google them, I am not making this up).

It occurred to me the other day I haven't seen a single man who looks remotely like someone I would be interested in. Which makes me wonder if I should even try to start to date. I have neither felt nor exhibited any interest, but recently my father and his wife invited me to their country club BBQ——*I'm thinking with an eye for me to meet a possible mate.* I thought, why not.

I can answer that well *now.* First off: they were serving lemonade *or* coffee! No alcohol?! Never a good start to an evening out. Next brutal observation—it was just a long buffet of soft food . . . since it was Geezer Central! No single men here save widowers, all of whom last dated in the Roosevelt administration, surely. I'm relatively certain many of the attendees sported hairpieces and dentures. Neither a huge turn-on, right? With the median age hovering around eighty, this group made an AARP conference look like a Cub Scout meeting. I ate my potato salad, coleslaw, and fish fry and went home.

Moreover, when I think of dating in general, I'm just not excited about it. A neighbor mom tells me she and her husband often drop forty bucks on a babysitter for their Saturday night date and end up at Target buying garden hoses next to other couples out on "date nights." I am sure if I were still in Paris, the lure of a possible aperitif with a man at Plaza Athénée would have me saddlin' up to any XY specimen. 'Nough said.

It's not exactly like I'm bouncing around town at night anyway. My outings are limited to day and must be arranged to Master Oscar's nap schedule. It changes every day, as his mood and the weather dictate, which I am generally fine with but today I have stolen some time to shop, thinking it might be nice to get some "me time," since I haven't had any in . . . two years!

Shopping options are scarce and I end up at the local mall, West Lake, where I, *even at age fifteen,* knew the venue to be subpar-suburban-trash outlet (and smirked while prancing the catwalk in local fashion show). So, wait one fucking minute—*what the hell time warp has hap-*

pened that now I'm here *again*?! Dropped off by my dad—just like at age twelve, and all those elitist hopes and dreams of "I will show you all and get the hell out of here" are nullified by the fact I am right back here and it's even lamer than it was then. I try to chill and say, "Well, at least I can buy something here whereas in Paris I was too *limited* in funds." Ironically at age twelve, I *was* definitely the girl who shopped at The Limited and thought it was akin to Dior, since I was a middle school fashionista. And now? I'm not a Lane Bryant client (thank the lord) but obviously am no longer a tiny-hipped, trend-hound, Contempo Casuals girl. Ann Taylor is out, as a coatdress or a gabardine suit isn't my gig and reminds me it's rather nice to *not* be working at a credit union in accounting—my worst fear of life. That leaves Sears and JC Penney, oh, shoot me now. Better still, fly me back to Paris this instant and make this all a bad dream.

Clearly, exchanging a membership at the Ritz Club in Paris for Famous Footwear's discount reward card is not an easy transition and I double-dare anyone to step off the cobblestone streets of Paris onto the asphalt driveway of cheese land suburbia and not get the bends. Pausing at the cash machine at the mall, a little buzz-cut creep-o of a five-year-old boy comes up to my precious Oscar (clad ever so Euro charmingly in his Peter Pan collar linen shirt and jumper, with his soft blond curls). This toad of a kid—in Sponge Bob Square Pants muscle tee shirt (a style of shirt that should be illegal for *any human, any age*) and cheesy nylon Spider-Man trunklike shorts (another look awful on all mammals) blurts out to me, "That's one ugly girl." I could've smacked the hick-lette. Puh-lease. He is a *boy,* a darling little chap, whose outfit costs more than you will make in a month as an adult. Oup. Pretentious alert! Shit, that snob lives on when I feel offended or disappointed, and what a mouth she has. Truth is, I don't know what I am doing and until I can get my footing on this whole project, anyone, I mean anyone, who criticizes me or Oscar is going to get clobbered!

After wandering the mall aimlessly for an hour, passing the chubby kids scarfing down at the food court, I spot an H&M. Hurrah. Terribly cute Euro clothes on the cheap—I guess that's who I am now. Okay. It doesn't feel so cheesy, I tell myself, since they also have a store on boulevard Raspail in Paris! I felt positively elated to drop $121 and bring home three pairs of low-waisted jeans, a pair of white high tops for Oscar, and, for each of us, classic French maritime horizontal blue-and-white stripe long-sleeved tees. Came home thinking that wasn't so bad. Maybe it isn't so tragic to live here, I just have to get the right perspective and then all these constant comparisons with Paris will fade . . . *I hope.*

Spoke to Zola after I put Oscar down for his afternoon nap and it only makes me miss Paris more. The weather is always better there and there is always something exciting to report, like this great art exhibit or that groovy new resto. Not to mention, I miss my partner in crime: as single girl expats, we forged a bond that was phenomenally close. And now she reports she is gleefully three months pregnant and it would be so fun to share this time with her, not to mention our children would be wonderful little chums together. A part of me finds it amazing she didn't tell me like two and a half months ago, but I guess that speaks that she's 1) focused on her husband as *le* best friend and 2) she has oodles more patience in waiting out the dicey first three months than I did. I really wish I could be there to see her little Buddha belly grow and offer her some of the tremendous generosity of spirit she gave to me while I was enduring those final months of pregnancy. The pros and cons of living here just keep battling it out . . . how frustrating.

. . .

Later that evening, I had the greatest experience. Few and far between are the moments that you feel like your pre-mom free-spirited self. I mean, *really* feel it, and, not so surprisingly, sometimes it's just putting on a pretty dress you last wore as carefree seductress with not a worry about child-proofing cabinets nor a thought to too much plastic in your baby's life. And other times it's hearing a song that you once loved so madly and came to be almost a soundtrack to that chapter of your life.

So, after making dinner of tortellini with cream sauce that Oscar balked at (and begged instead for his fave turkey hot dogs), it seemed like just another night in the realm of our routine: one cartoon, a bath, bedtime story, and night-night with Mr. Bear in his arms. While I'm mindlessly cleaning the dishes, Oscar scampers over and hands me a CD he grabbed from the collection. "Pay, pay!" (which translates to "play this NOW"), he yells, followed by a demand for "a num a num" (M&M).

What, am I raising a dictator? Is this how Mussolini's mother felt? Are these the signs of my having created a young Stalin? Oh la la! I said to my tired self until I noticed the CD and a smile came over my face. Coldplay, album *X&Y*—I used to love that CD, listened to it in Paris for what seemed like a year solid. I haven't heard it since. Hmmm.

I handed Oscar three M&Ms while putting on the CD, hit track 7, and we went to play in the living room by the fireplace—of course, turned on during dinner as per Oscar's demand once his tiny *derrière* hits the highchair every night, "Fire!" The song began and with the first few beats, I felt flooded with memories and back in that place I was at when this song was my companion as much as anyone was. The lyrics rolling off my tongue as if they were my own: "How long before I get in? . . ."

Listening to it again, I literally felt all the same senses, the wind coming through the open windows in my apartment by the Seine, the lights from the Bateaux Mouches dancing off the buildings as it passes. The way my low-slung jeans skim my hips and the longing, the physical ache of not finding the right man and having a child yet. All that love I felt had nowhere to go, no destination, and in a life that felt so glamorous and yet so empty. There was too much freedom and not enough being responsible and connected to a bigger picture.

I remembered once, when living there, complaining to my father I hadn't been on a vacation for a year, and he replied, "Your whole life is a vacation. You live in Paris." I smiled gently to myself thinking, So true and now I have this, looking down at Oscar as he climbed up onto the chaise and slid down on his belly, grinning from ear to ear. As the song went on, I was overcome with a tinge of missing that self and all her naïveté. I swept up Oscar into my arms and held him close to do one of our little waltzes. His warm chocolaty breath on my face, as the lyric, *"If you never try, then you'll never know"* echoes around me. I suddenly realized in a very deep place, "Ah . . . I *tried*! And now I have what I wanted so much, *so desperately*—this boy!" And Oscar and I whirled about, his tiny hands around my neck, my consciousness finally tangibly grasping that the empty place that literally plagued my life was now gloriously filled. I felt a completeness that I certainly understood since he was born, but in this private dance, just mother and son, with this music, I went to a new place. A place of awareness that with all the disquiet, doubts, and worry in my life, this little boy is my dream *realized,* and he is even more divinely wonderful than my wildest dreams. I think most every mother has an experience like this, where you feel that intense reality that you are *finally* a mother. No one is on the same journey you are on, and it is all magic.

MUCH TO MY DISMAY, THINGS I'VE DISCOVERED ABOUT LIFE IN WISCONSIN

1. It is a place where people still decorate their homes with "$39 and Under!" oil paintings, care of the local "Starving Artists Art Fair" at the Holiday Inn. Picking *art,* and I use that word loosely, is based on size need, as in "We need something, anything fifty inches by thirty inches, to put above the couch in the den. Oh, and in royal blue, to match the pillows we got at Pier 1."

2. I have also noticed a high degree of preframed posters from World Market and a smattering of Patrick Nagel pink-and-black drawings circa 1982, as well as a massive fondness for the ubiquitous Gustav Klimt's *The Kiss* hanging above many a Heat-N-Glo electric fireplace.

3. Life here is giving me an understanding of what I imagine it must feel like to be so inherently discontent in one's reality that it's akin to what it must feel like to be a woman trapped in a man's body.

4. Winter here is like living in the Overlook Hotel from the film *The Shining*—that crazy-making, torturous isolation that makes one go stark raving mad and I'm mere days from starting to scrawl in crayon a hundred pages of "All work and no play makes a Kiki a dull girl."

5. People make Jell-O desserts like "puddin' in a cloud" and serve weiner wraps, seven-layer dip, and deviled eggs at cocktail parties.

6. Ads on TV for dinner at Pizza Hut pitch the sale as "Three pounds of pasta for $12.99!" I cannot get over the idea that a meal's appeal is supposed to be in the ghastly huge quantity

rather than in the quality. That's like the old, "buy one suit, get one free" at the local Big and Tall men's store. Listen, people—*two of shit is shit.*

7. When loading up on cheap crap at the monster Target or Walmart superstores, you do take note that a lot of the children clearly from the surrounding small towns look like goats or druids.

8. Log-rolling is an actual career.

9. No fine food to be had—anywhere. I miss French cuisine madly. That you could go into any family-run *brasserie* or *bistro du coin* ("corner bistro") and be sure you would get a homemade savory meal from the ever-changing list of specials dictated by seasonal treasures of the freshest ingredients, like white asparagus bathed in a lemon-dill cream paired with grilled fresh salmon in a mornay sauce. Here, you can bet your ass it's some out-of-a-can/defrosted something concocted out of mostly chemicals and flavor additives, preprepared so that it resembles the photo from the slick menu of some global chain. Garf! I will say, if you are in the market for burritos as big as your head, pizzas with seven different meats on top and a cheese-filled crust, or deep-fried anything, this is your paradise. And the local sushi is such a joke, with its faux crab and tasteless plastic seaweed, I call it "pseudo-shi," as it appears to be more of a fridge magnet than an edible item.

10. When asking the manager at the local liquor store which is the best chardonnay they stock, he offered, "This one here, is more guzzle-able."

11. Many conversations between locals wrap up with, "*I'm tellin' ya, dare.*"

Chapter 16

"If children grew up according to early indications, we should have nothing but geniuses."

—Johann Wolfgang Von Goethe

I am mortified to admit . . .

1. I know what a "Shamwow" is *and considered buying one.*

2. While I once used to be annoyed (in Paris) by the local *boulangerie*'s subpar baguettes and would defiantly walk an additional eight blocks to get the infinitely finer baguettes on rue du Bac, now I happily munch down generic Oreos without a care for calories or quality. Lovely!

3. While I once quaffed fine Chassagne Montrachet with a

discerning nose for the bouquet, I now slurp-guzzle Walmart's box-o-wine with abandon. Chic!

4. I used to view *The Flight of the Bumblebee* from a box seat at Opéra de Paris—now I pathetically "track" a stray sock's movement down the gutters on the street on my block.

5(a). Horrors—one day the highlight of the day was my father coming over to scrub down the boat trailer he left in my garage for storage.

5(b). The highlight of another day was the mad scramble with the neighbor kids to fish frogs and salamanders out of the sewer drain at the bottom of our street. There I was the only adult among six kids, lying on my belly in the pouring rain, head pressed to the asphalt, with a butterfly net in hand, hauling up amphibians to the giddy children holding buckets for our finds. In truth, this was terrific fun and Oscar was tickled silly with awe. I thought, "Not bad for an ex-diva," and I honestly had a ball.

6. The hideous slogan "Supersize Me" has somehow attached itself to my ass. I have, against all willpower, succumbed to gaining almost ten pounds and now am giving the local mallrat tarty-tween girls a run for their money in the way-too-tight jeans department. I just can't allow myself to buy the next size up; that's a defeat my shaky self-image cannot survive, so I'm crammed into my old jeans and am barely able to bend at the waist without feeling like I'm giving myself the Heimlich maneuver.

7. I am now a neighborhood busybody. For lack of anything better to do while I watch Oscar crayon up the walls and crawl up and down the stairs like Sir Oscar Hilary one hundred times a day, I am observing my neighbors' every movement like a loon. Man, am I giving Grace Kelly in *Rear Window* a real run for the money—

without being nearly as glam, I should add. There is nothing to do here, no human activity to be seen aside from the odd person walking a dog and the mass exodus in the morning of office workers off to jobs. I am horrified to seriously be taking mental note that the older couple across the street got a new rug and there I am, glued to window trying to see what style it is with the same interest I once read the front page of *Le Figaro*. Though, when the ice cream truck makes its lazy tour of the neighborhood, somehow all the charm is reinstated by the magnetic pull of kids streaming out of houses, cash in hand, running as though their lives depended on it toward the truck. It's all terribly Norman Rockwell–esque sweet. (That is, if you don't look at the driver—some Goth kid with piercings in every possible fold of his flesh.)

8. I am doing the ultimate in suburban self-warfare—home hair color! Once upon a time I had balayage highlights and a *coup* at the shi-shi Christian's salon by the Place Vendôme, often sitting next to Vanessa Paradis (married to Johnny Depp) while I nibbled at tea sandwiches with a piping hot cup of Mariage Frères tea in hand. Now, when able to even get to a Walgreens, I am quickly grabbing any old box of some Clairol blond *something-or-other* while my child wails to get out of shopping cart, only to take said box home, and pour directly onto head (so much for the enclosed "highlights painting brush") during my child's scant nap time from 10:00 until 11:00 A.M., racing against time as child wakes and demands to be held while I have sopping wet hair and "color gloves" on as bleaching agent drips onto my brows and neck, resulting in terrifying the youngster from his initial mere demanding whine into an all-out howl. I think these two enormously different hair color experiences (posh Paris salon vs.

Wisconsin bathroom) qualify as the two quintessential pillars of the spectrum of my life.

9. I will also admit that *occasionally* my giving Oscar his daily baths are more about using up a good half hour than about hygiene. Hey, it's insanely hard to entertain a one-and-a-half-year-old kid with the attention span of a gnat for eighteen hours a day when one has had no break, had almost no sleep, and is just shot with boredom. As the mom, it's mission control—social agenda and activity headquarters over here. As the sole recreation director, I'm in charge of getting through the long days, and that means filling every second with fun things to do, eat, paint, play with, and see. All the while, ensuring diapers are changed, hands clean, and (in theory) there is a lot of learning along the way. It's like a shuttle run of toy to toy, cleaning up along the way, and prepping for the next activity between being the cook and then kitchen maid; leaping instantly into "butt-wipe manager" and "keep-out-of-danger-supervisor"; along the way nursemaid, wet nurse, and nurse. I'm lucky if my overconfident wild man of eighteen months with no depth perception escapes a day without at least two minor injuries. It's such a massive task it makes one wonder why would anyone want to be a nursery school teacher for a dozen kids *that aren't yours*? It's my own son and sometimes, I have to admit, by 8:00 P.M., I'm like, "Shut up already with that nonsensical chatter and stream of demands, chucking of toys to all four corners and repeating, 'Train? Momma, I heard it . . . you heard it? Train!'" *And* I am mad crazy, falling down silly in love with my son.

10. I am going to lay it out for you and you may think I am bonkers—*like you don't already*. I still don't have a Wisconsin driver's license. The backstory here is that at sixteen, and I kid you

not, on the very day I got my license, in the first two hours, I was taking my pal Lily Slattery downtown to shop and generally prance about with pride. Halfway there I got hit by a motorcycle who crashed through my windshield and landed on my lap. In short, no one was hurt, since we were both going like 7 mph, but I wasn't too keen to get behind the wheel again of what I have long since referred to as "those killing machines." And then at age seventeen, I moved to Tokyo, then NYC, and then Paris, so the need to drive never came up. I thought when I planned to move home, "Oh hell, I have lived everywhere, had a baby, there is nothing I can't do!" and yet I am stalling and keep finding excuses not to go for the damn road test again. With a baby, it's easy to rationalize, "I'm not able to take classes. Or is it even safe for me to drive my precious cargo with so little experience?!" No one is buying it and I'm so embarrassed to say I'm taking this stay-at-home-mom thing to the nth, putting the *stay* into its literal meaning.

Therefore, my being at the isolation level of what you could seriously call house arrest, I'm in need of asking for a ride from family for any errand that's not in walking distance. (Not to mention, in the deep winter, when it's cold to the bone, I can rule out any walking and have found myself stuck at home, out of toilet paper, and having to use Spider Man napkins for the loo. Poor Spidey surely has had better adventures.) Even when weather permits, that walking distance is limited to the kids' park, the grocery store, Starbucks, a macrobiotic restaurant for children (neighborhood reviews include, "Who wants a buckwheat cookie or beansprout smoothie?"!). I'm pretty screwed. Wait, I'm forgetting, there *is* a café in Shorewood Hills. That needs to be clarified—knowing of this sha-sha neighborhood when I was still in Paris *and so excited to move back,* I conjured up all kinds of optimistic images of this café, though I had never actually been there. Like a complete idiot, in my mind I imagined a pseudo French café with a bevy of fascinating *habitués,* where one could hang out and meet people. (Read, men. Ergo, future father to Oscar and marvelous husband to me.) Little did I know then, just behind this café is an upscale geriatric assisted-living facility with a thousand white-haired geezer residents. So, much to my disappointment, the café is entirely not cool and groovy but packed with only the "uber-retired," who hobble over there in wheelchairs or with canes and walkers. Café de Flore this is not . . . *by a long shot.*

No. 483. Idealized vision sputtering out. But on the upside, I never considered there would be a neighborhood Fourth of July parade and party for Shorewood Hills kids, and it was simply adorable. There I was decorating Oscar's stroller with crepe paper, American flags-a-plenty, neon stars, and sparklers with memories of my mother's skills channeling through me and into a spectacular celebration of America the Great! While it seemed cheesy at the get-go to follow along with the other two hundred parents and kids on decorated bikes, trikes, and strollers, trailing behind a slew of fire trucks blaring their sirens down the hill, it was outrageously cute. Oscar had a blast feasting on popsicles, checking out the "girls," and "driving" the fire truck, though the hired clowns scared the wits out of everyone, as they always seem to do. (Fun Fourth of July parade—add another point for Wisconsin. Does that make half a dozen yet? Paris has . . . fifty thousand or so?)

11. With not a lot of people to chat with in my daily life, I am getting increasingly closer to being one of those desperate souls

that you could summarize by saying, "She was one of those people at Costco who make a beeline for the Dixie cup of free samples of granola" *and would actually wait in line for them and chat up the clerk.*

12(a). Frankly, since I have become a mother, I have turned into some self-appointed global children's welfare advocate. As in Paris, I continue here! I just cannot bear to see any child cry, be sad or ignored, or—*the ultimate nightmare*—get smacked. I just march right up there every time and try to make it all better. Read, stick my nose in where it's not wanted and generally scowl or scold the parent. Which did not go well recently when, at the mall, I saw a teenage black mom, screaming at her baby to shut up while her other toddler was standing in the seat sobbing and about to crash his skull four feet down to the floor. After one of my tirades, I usually get a flustered, embarrassed reaction to my pointing out the obvious ("he should be buckled in"), but this time I was on the receiving end of, "Get the hell away from us, bitch, or I will fuck you up. Who do you fucking think you are? The fucking Pope?!" as she came tearing toward me with her friend of the same age and size of two hippos, I might add. This time it was I who was flustered and seriously scared shit-/speechless as I hustled off and hid in the Hallmark store. (Good move, right? Seems like nothing bad could happen to you in such a goody-two-shoes shoppe!) And then recently, when we were at the zoo and I caught sight of a mom (that I must add had a tattoo that I could not believe, spread all across her back: an homage to Hostess Twinkies. Yes, Twinkie the Kid riding on a horse-drawn carriage with six-inch-high cactus and a full posse) yelling at her kid, "Shut up, already. You ain't gettin' no fuck-ing candy!" I just silently shook my head and bit my tongue. I tend to edit myself a little more now in the interest of personal safety.

12(b). On the flip side of this global children's welfare ambassador role, I have to admit to now full-on loathing Angelina Jolie. The entire globe (including the UN) thinks Angelina Jolie is the reincarnation of Mother Theresa. As she spends hours on set, filming movie after movie, appearing so unreasonably glamorous weeks after delivering twins, and really—is she not at every film premiere? She has four nannys! How hands-on is a mom like that? Don't women like this skew our perceptions of motherhood and pregnancy? If we must applaud a mother for doing important work in a global stage, can we not tip our hats to someone like Christiane Amanpour? Her work is honest, selfless, and profoundly relevant. Which reminds me of a massive error I made about six months ago, when, after meeting up with a darling little girl and her Spanish nanny at the neighborhood playground for the billionth time, I finally asked the nanny, "Just what does her mother do that she is absolutely never with her own daughter, *not even on weekends?*" I threw it out there like a gauntlet of loaded judgment. Nanny replied, "She is the leader of the scientific team at the University of Wisconsin Biotech, working to find a cure for AIDS." Me, eating crow, big fat fleets of crow—"Oh, okay, that's, ah, legitimate . . . good . . . important work." Lordy! Never again will I assume I know what the hell a woman's motivation is for working, *not working* . . . having a dozen kids, *having none.*

13. I am breast-feeding—still! We are down to only once a day, for naps—but nevertheless. While I know it's best for Oscar in about ten million ways, I am getting a little sore now, thank you, and this kid is committed to it with an obsessive passion. I am very

proud that I've stuck to this whole idea, but I would very much like to have a word with Dr. Sears, who coined this whole At-tachment Parenting scheme and philosophy. I'm anxiously awaiting the *DE-tachment* edition of your book so I can get back to something resembling a life, mister!

14. I have become a dullard. With Oscar as my primary co-conver-sationalist, I feel like I'm living in the film *Rainman* over here as I find myself saying, "It's a lovely . . . lovely day," and Oscar parrots back, "lovely day," then I say, "What a clever boy . . . clever, clever boy," and he chirps, "Clever boy," and on and on like this all day. Oh, we are a couple of Algonquin Round Table regulars with our fascinating banter. Mensa card revoked.

15. Horrible, painful admission—I succumbed to signing up for an online dating service. But come on, talk about "coitus interruptus"—I haven't so much as been kissed by a man in almost two, ohmigod, *three years.* And I will admit that, for prebaby Kiki, three weeks *sans amour* used to be a trial. I think I am officially a born-again virgin. This wasn't on my wish list. Not by a long shot.

Speaking of "long," after so many man-free days and nights, and not so much as a peck on the cheek, I *long* for the nights of being split in half like cordwood by some sexy man with a hard body. How's that for crass? I don't even get much chance to *think* of men and it's not like I am seeing all kinds of hotties in this town that make me wild with desire, but occasionally I will glimpse someone like Jude Law in a film on TV or far more evocative; recently, paging through *Vogue,* I got blindsided by an unexpected waft of men's fragrance from a perfume strip. It hit me, damn, I miss that warm utterly masculine scent like a missing limb. I miss that divine pleasure of waking from bed and your boyfriend has showered, dressed, and left for work and his fragrance still hangs in the air dizzying you with its sensuality.

I think it's safe to say you know you're ready to date again when you see ducks coupled off paddling away in a pond and you find yourself jealous and almost irked by such blatant displays of intimacy. Occasionally on my outings, I have glimpsed a few Monet Men, as I call them—men who look great from a distance but up close are a real mess. And even those are few and far between, so I have come to terms with the fact that, unless the UPS man or the garbageman are going to ask me out, I am not going to meet Mr. Right, let alone meet *any* man in my little world. Thus, I have hit rock bottom. To clarify, I have gone down further, hit it, and turned it over, climbed beneath, and burrowed self ten feet lower. All because in about five minutes I'm going to wake up and be seventy years old and an old spinster: I have signed up for eHarmony.

Yep, I fell for the TV ads and the smattering of stories of success that float through the grapevine, and there I am, answering questions online like, "Would you describe yourself as easygoing?" Oh, that would be a big frigging *non* and no one would even use *me* and *easygoing* in the same sentence. I am well aware that I am rather a complicated girl. I simultaneously believe life is what you make it *and* I am also a fatalist that thinks everything happens for a reason. Which I guess suggests I want to cover all the bases. And I admit I am a very complicated girl when it comes to men. (*Par example*—I can simultaneously say I tend to like men who are somewhat metrosexual in their taste and presentation, as I surely prefer a man who *manscapes* a tad, and yet part of me thinks it kind of queer and too self-conscious.

It's a tenuous balance and very few American men get, *or care to,* hit that note.)

Questionnaires are funny things since you inherently want to present this super-fab version of yourself but you know to do so, you'd have to lie a smidge and then you'd be matched with a good-hearted deli worker in Ohio and that's just a waste of time. So I was honest and went for it, thinking, wow this could be amazing to find someone who knew all my issues and eccentricities and still loved me, hell, *celebrated* or was even looking for that?! But I am here to say after a good three-month go of it and $130 I could've spent on my son's college fund, I got matched with absolutely, absurdly, ridiculously wrong men. *Not to overstate it.* I really think it's like astrology fanatics—where the kind of people who want to believe and buy into it, *do so* and think, "this fifty-year-old man from Detroit who is just out on probation doesn't seem 'on paper' to be my type but the experts at eHarmony think he is, so he must be the ONE," and they go full speed ahead.

Each morning I admittedly raced to the computer to see the flood of what I hoped to be a sea of potentially fabulous mates, and I was crushed day after day. And I was paying for this staggering agony of crushed hopes—that's what really killed me. After painstakingly listing my interests as opera, literature, European history, painting, fashion and interiors, and travel, I was matched with men so completely off the mark it was like the whole system was being revealed as actually a random statistical roulette based on zip-a-do. Case in point, I was matched to a bevy of men like a plumbing contractor in Alabama with what I call a "meat or fish" hairstyle (as in, short on top and long in back, suggesting he can't decide a simple idea like "meat or fish"), a sixty-year-old mathematician in Virginia, and a troll in Alaska who makes Stephen Hawking look like Brad Pitt and whose "favorites" list was *five math theorems and, I swear to god, "high colonics."* Now there is a dream date! Actually, most of my so-called Perfect Match Men were apparently living in Alberta, Canada. Almost always mid-fifties and bald (which, actually, can be very sexy, like in actor Jason Statham— *he kills me*). Though *my* batch-o-eHarmony baldys were always sporting some 1980s black mock turtleneck under a mustard yellow suit coat and gelled hair à la gelmet. Time warp much, gentlemen? AND then you'd read their careers, and god strike me down if I'm lying: one was a chewing gum distributor and another a truck driver who actually wrote under "occupation" "truck driver of truck *that I own.*" Oh, well, you *own* it, that's the clincher! Sold! Sign me up for this tycoon. And another man who took his profile picture—crooked and off center—in the mirror of what appeared to be a restaurant toilet. (Married much?)

But it was all worth it when I finally found a man whose photo was seriously handsome and with a personality profile of equal appeal. He was listed as an architect, divorced father of three little boys, and living in London. Which isn't a drawback as much as a possible way outta here! He even, to my huge surprise, wrote me instantly asking for a "fast-track" communiqué—where you skip the standard questions and just e-mail freely. I was in heaven. He was funny and so charming, asking all the right questions and sending me goodnight kisses, which if you are as insanely deprived of some as I am, you fall hook, line, and sinker for, like a tween for *High School Musical.* Well, of course, I wrote this "Jamie in London" back, thinking my letter the end all of wit, elusive sassiness, and intrigue, though with Oscar crawling up the back of my pajamas pulling them to ankles as I typed and the neighbor's husband waving hello as he glimpsed the whole gory scene, it may not have been all that.

I started to worry since three or four days went by, then two weeks. I was, to be frank, crushed that apparently my letter was a dud and, furthermore, I couldn't believe how quickly I had hung my hopes on this tiny scrimpet of hope and attention. Had I been out of the flirting/dating market so long so as to not even be able to appeal to a man with words? Then I received a note from eHarmony:

> Dear eHarmony Friend,
>
> Making your eHarmony experience safe and successful is important to us. As a past or present user, we want to inform you that eHarmony has taken action to remove one of your matches, Jamie from London, from the eHarmony.com service. This decision was made in accordance with our terms and conditions.
>
> Consistent with our privacy policy, we do not disclose the specific reasons for this person's removal. eHarmony.com disclaims any responsibility or liability with respect to any continued involvement between you and any person whose account is closed by eHarmony.com. Please visit the links below for further information on our privacy policy and to obtain safety tips on corresponding with matches.

Like clockwork a day later, I got some phony direct e-mail—supposedly from a bank in Zurich—claiming I had a secret deposit to the tune of 100,000 euros in my name and I just needed to wire 200 euros immediately to the attached location for "processing charges." I was seeing my dear, beloved "Jamie," *cyber scammer* Jamie, at work. Wahhh!!! I had to laugh, since it just seemed so apropos, *so me*, that the single man I found myself actually interested in turned out to be a conjured-up nonreality. My Mister Right doesn't exist. Great.

I love this story for the amazing slap-in-your face reality of that tired line people use when all goes to hell: "If it looks too good to be true, it is." Needless to say, I wanted to get so drunk I could've woken up spooning a squirrel in a field and it would have been understandable. Fine. It's all rationalized after a day's mulling. I mean really? How could I date with a child on my hip and a boob in his mouth 24/7? Not to mention, this is not the body I want to offer up to anyone who wasn't created *in* it. Plus, lord knows, I've lost all social skills, though I have vowed and stuck to never chatting about stool movements or even weaning issues (in public), but can I even carry on an adult conversation anymore that is vaguely interesting, let alone witty?

AM I EXPECTED TO?

1. Stay awake after 8:00 P.M.
2. And be attractive in the slightest way, meaning dolling up in any makeup or accessories that aren't diaper bags or sippy-cup oriented.
3. And speak about things in any depth, subjects that segue into others, *and* be a good listener without zoning out wondering if my child is okay and calling out for me with a sense of abandonment? If any of those are required, I can't make it. Doubt I could pull off *any* of the three requirements since haven't a clue how to converse in grown-up world anymore. What did I use to talk about until the wee hours with such ferocity and what the hell was it about me that men ever found beguiling, let alone appealing?
4. The offer of an invite to do something, *anything*, non—baby oriented is just, I will say it, *kind of scary*. The rigors and routine of our daily life, with all its schedules, while sometimes boring

to the bone, are comfortable, predictable, and reliable. The massive risk taker in me is silenced by the fact that, as a single mother, I can't do anything to risk losing control—like drink copious amounts and dance on the tables—since I have to be in top form to perform motherly role at his majesty's chosen wake-up hour.

5. I'm starting to evolve, make that *devolve,* into midwestern speak with the long *o's*, à la Marge Gunderson in the film *Fargo*. If anyone ever hears me utter a phrase as midwestern as "It's a real crowd pleaser" in regard to, say, making Chex Mix by the bucket for a Super Bowl party, you have my permission to shoot me lock, stock, and smoking barrel! In my singular possible public daily outing, I venture off to the Piggly Wiggly grocery store to, god help me, chat up the octogenarian lady who serves up free samples on her foldout cardboard lectern while bellowing, "The latest from Nabisco, everyone! The pretzel cracker!" But I did have to howl in laughter at the park the other day when I heard one kid criticize another by ranting, "Your mother does collage!" as the ultimate in cuts. Needless to say, I liked the kid instantly.

6. Need it be said? Bon Marché, Vuitton, and Galeries Lafayette have been sorrily replaced with Target, Walmart, Home Depot, and garage sales. (Which, frankly, are gold mines in my 'hood, where people are just like, "Oh, this two-story jungle gym structure with climbing wall, two slides, and swings retailed at $2,000, but you know what? We are done with it . . . just get it out of the yard and it's yours." Whereas in Paris, every kids' toy or bookstore is total highway robbery. Oscar's xylophone was 38 euros=$50. Ouch.) Another point for suburbia: a size 6 at Target is actually like a size 12 in Europe. I do enjoy this

charade with my new postpregnancy body all a-movin' around like Jell-O. I swear when I make a rapid turn chasing after Oscar, my backside swings around moments after like a boat trailer careening wildly.

7. I'm totally sold on being/dressing comfortable now—still wearing maternity underwear since they are so frigging comfy. Love flat shoes. No makeup is cinch and cuts out twenty minutes of application and cleansing each day that I can now use to scrub the juice-box carpet stains. Every now and then, I see a photo of prebaby Kiki and I don't even recognize the woman I once was, wearing heels, thongs, short skirts. Let me say it before anyone else, I was venturing into the tart arena and, while it's a tiny thing to note, I am so glad to be a mother now since I was just losing it there with my "I'm careening into forty, single, and really need male attention fast and furious over here, waking too many a morning with 'The Wrath of Grapes' (hungover)." I mean really, what was I thinking on my thirty-eighth birthday? While celebrating with friends at Castel, I happened upon a drop-dead twenty-two-year-old Frenchman, Florent, who was also celebrating his birthday. So with my neurons swimming in champagne and dared by *mes amies,* I decided a proper birthday self-treat would be this youngster. *Oui,* while many women may have opted for a new purse, I snagged this sexy young pup and dragged him home. On one hand, I can see how women can become "cougars," since the sheer notion he was in any way game was insanely complimentary but, truth be said, what young men have to offer is not worth all the trouble of undressing. It was like having sex with a totem pole. Dude, you can move your arms and stop the expression of shock and awe. In retrospect, it felt a lot like playing tennis alone against a

backboard. Not worth breaking a sweat. That's what I get for indulging in the men who frequent nightclubs. Duh! No wonder I was attracting playboy piglets and married men. Cancel that, at eight months pregnant to the hilt and wearing a long muumuu and marching around a grocery store, I still was inexplicably chased by married men, like that ridiculously sexy rogue-cad Jack of the extreme generosity. Alright, then, that theory holds no weight as Frenchmen often need only their minds to set sail in seduction.

FURTHER DIATRIBE ON FRENCHMEN, AS SEEN AFRESH
BY POST-PARIS KIKI . . .

Married Frenchmen are, well, very often just dogs. I have to say, I found it just excruciatingly sad to see all the married expat women's posts last August on that Message Moms site. There were dozens of wives with children at home, complaining how, by tradition, in France they went to the country with the kids for August holidays and would call their own home and some woman would answer.

Or they would write about how their husbands would be MIA for days on end. Or how the husbands would claim they had to work the weekends that were previously planned visits to see wife/kids and hubby from hell would steal off to the South of France with some new young beauty.

I know this happens, since I have been on the receiving end of many a Frenchman's power-packed-seduction-attack in August, since I love to be in the city when it's virtually deserted. It's almost laughably funny to see the influx of men out and about, looking to charm and seduce in equal measure.

Obviously, reading all these expat wives' sad and desperate tales of

"Should I worry?" when it was so clear they were being cheated on was both appalling and heartwrenching. I am sure on some level, it also fed my desire to leave Paris, as I, like these women, was not raised to accept this in a husband and would be devastated to the core by such news. Damn, it's good to not be in the firing line of all that nonsense anymore!

IT'S ALL WORTH IT WHEN . . .

1. The simple pleasure of seeing your child gobble up a cookie, especially one you made with or for him/her.

2. When you get one of those deep-squeeze hugs unexpectedly or those snuggly bear embraces to your neck.

3. When you first hear your child say, "Mom" or "Momma"—it feels like a place inside you is filled that nothing else and no one ever could. A magic badge of honor and eternal gift no one can ever take from you and never diminishes.

4. When you spend a whole day and night thick as thieves, communicating beautifully and in sync. Especially when you thought, "Oh Christ, a rainy day, this is going to be (choose your favorite) endless/a grind/hell/sheer hell/unbearable hell."

5. Anytime—day or night, nap or asleep in the car—when you see them sleep. Oscar once fell asleep midnibble, eating a cookie, and it teetered on his dry lip as his little breaths dusted light crumbs to his lap in the sun. I shall never forget the pure charm of this precious image.

6. When they wake you with sweet voices and tender kisses—for the life of me, it's astonishing how much I thought waking before dawn would be insufferable and when I hear him say, "nose"

and tap me on the nose to wake me, it somehow is a delight. Lucky for him, as if a boyfriend did that I would be instant Grendel and swipe his hand off in a swoop without so much as lifting an eyelid, while growling in morning-breath fumes.

7. The pure and untainted comments that your children offer up, like Oscar with his, "no hairs falling" critique when I wear my hair loose, his way of telling me he isn't a fan of my hair down. Come to think of it, that's very French of him. More charming maybe: "Grandpa's fun . . . like candy." (Needless to say, for a toddler, this level of adoration is unsurpassed.)

8. The delicious pleasure of seeing your child laugh with side-splitting abandon. It's true—their happiness=your happiness.

Chapter 17

"Do not confine your children to your own learning, for they were born in another time."

—CHINESE PROVERB

Fall into winter & Noël, strike that; Christmas . . .

I'm still trying here! Autumn has arrived to Wisconsin and it's as picturesque as those quintessential Ansel Adams black-and-white photos. The dazzling dappling of the array of treetops is breathtaking, with all the oranges, scarlet reds, cognac browns, and warm yellows. It adds a depth and richness that conjures up that classic American image of cozy homes with white picket fences and the smell of burning leaves at sunset. Indeed, the enchanting fragrance of dry leaves, cool dew on morning grass, fresh breezes, and a certain crispness in the air that is as soothing as any elixir I have experienced (Cristal champagne and Guerlain Insolence *parfum* included). It's always been my favorite season and, as much as I bitch and moan about being here, it's truly lovely. With a meteor shower last night that had everyone out in their yards, children on laps or lying on their backs, oohing and aahing watching nature's fireworks, it was really sweet to feel a sense of community and to know you don't get this experience in big cities where the delis and street lights fill the night sky. (One more point for the Midwest.)

Just as I was tallying a hash mark in the "plus" column, I got another sideswipe of the life I'd left behind. Was on a search for a black jacket to wear this morning and casually went to my guest bedroom closet to unearth something decent as my actual closet is now all mom clothes (shapeless cotton pieces as sexy as a car mechanic's jumpsuit). Opening that closet is akin to stepping back in time and though I know not to do so unless I am "in a good place," I wasn't quite ready to be swept back to an event that frankly was astonishing. Rifling through the abandoned evening gowns, as an array of hats leered at me from the top shelf and my collection of sublime heels kicked at me from the floor, I stumbled across a dark chocolate beaded Armani corset and was stopped dead by the memory of last time I wore it. In Paris.

Three years ago, there was an event in Paris that most people probably didn't hear about. The most extravagant and expensive wedding in history. No, *really*. The father of the bride, billionaire steel magnate Lakshmi Mittal, spent a rumored 55 million euros (80 million dollars) on the most elaborate five-day wedding, which sent Paris spinning with its opulence and splendor. And Paris knows a thing or two about extravagance, right? By way of my Big Shot Ex in NYC (who happened to be a financial advisor to Mr. Mitall), I got to attend this lavish affair. Insane, I know! I believe twelve hundred people received the five-kilo, silver-plattered invitation of twenty pages describing the various venues and functions of this almost weeklong fete beyond compare. No expense was spared for the nuptials of the young Indian couple, Vanisha and Amit. Twelve Boeing jets were hired to fly in guests from India, and all six hundred rooms of the posh Hotel Le Grand InterContinental were booked for guests. Celebrations and parties night after night, held in the magnificent home of Louis XIV; the Palace of Versailles; the seventeenth-century architectural masterpiece of the king's Minister, Vaux-le-Vicomte, set on an estate just outside Paris (where an entire Hindu temple was built for the evening and the bridegroom arrived by chariot while the bride swept in with a red velvet canopy, held overhead by bridesmaids); a dinner held in the Tuileries (closed for the soiree and complete with Bengal tigers brought in for "ambiance"—*I often opt for scented candles, thanks*).

To me, the most staggering locale was the complete reconstruction of an entire immense palace in the Parc de Saint-Cloud, created over many months for just a single evening's festivities. All this as the stage and setting for an extravagant show of Bollywood stars and a concert by Kylie Minogue, topped off with a dinner of one hundred twenty different dishes and a magnificent fireworks show with the Eiffel Tower as a backdrop.

It all started with a call from my ex, who tossed out the invitation to join him as his guest as casually as if this were a matinee showing of *Driving Miss Daisy*. I remember telling him, "Fantastic, I can wear that Jean Paul Gaultier couture dress I got for that wedding we went to in Venice" (as my inner voice mused, "Right . . . life with this man was always so damn glamorous and to even say those kinds of phrases out loud doesn't even enter my mind let alone fall out of my mouth anymore, as the lifestyle of a struggling artist in Paris is about free champagne at art vernissages and the rare purchase of new shoes from cheap-o boutique Etam).

His reply: "Absolutely not. Go buy something exquisite and new, I will pay you back for whatever you need. But, Kiki, you need to look exceptional . . . perfect."

Which would seem to any woman like a freaking dream come true and it is if you don't know what that really implies. As my ex is the definitive master of all that is aesthetic elegance, it frankly is a massive request loaded with pressure—if I get this wrong I will be in the dog house (my words) while he would comment, "That's not suitable" and shake his head with shaming disappointment. To get a hint of the pressure laid on me, consider that before dating me, he dated Princess Diana. Imagine what a cheese ball I felt like in the early days—"Well, Princess Diana wouldn't have her cat's litter box in her clothes closet," etc. I loved this man like no other, but his rigid obsession that every damn detail of life must be the utmost, the rarest beauty, the best, was in the first years together fascinating and educational, but it became irritating to set the table for dinner at his country house and have him tell me, "This is all wrong," sweeping it all aside and redoing it as though we were going to be photographing it for French *Elle Décor.* That got grating and add in that he never wanted to have children, so after five years, I had to exit. Paris seemed the ideal place to find a new life and that I did.

Let's be serious, it was truly a riot, to fly in and out of boutiques all over Paris, acquiring a vast array of Indian-themed gowns, spectacular accessories like immense hand-beaded scarves, jeweled strappy heels from Louboutin and Michel Perry and matching purses that were limited editions of Ungaro and McQueen, all the while knowing that on my own I couldn't even afford the taxi ride to boutiques on rue du Fauborg St. Honoré. My life—always a study in contrasts!

By the third night of the festivities I was feeling, hmm, I guess how Siena Miller must feel everyday—glam and fab. Readying myself for the arrival of my ex, I was positive I had hit on the most exceptional ensemble I had ever created, and for a few hours had a tiny understanding of how these "ladies who lunch" socialites must live all the time—a whole day structured around the presentation of oneself at a posh event. It's so involving, narcissistic, and shallow but, ridiculously enough, with all the prep work, there is no time to think of the poor starving souls that are plagued by natural disaster and disease. Absurd, but you see how their micro worlds don't allow it; there is just no freaking time between swanning off to the salon and the manicurists arriving *chez vous*! Ghastly.

A half hour before my date's arrival, with the greatest care, I slid into the espresso brown beaded corset with its delicate three-eighth-inch straps of tiny beads and its quietly elegant transparent crystal embroidery. I felt an instant, mad, passionate love for this piece the second I laid my eyes on it. It was the epitome of sophistication and pure, unadulterated feminine beauty. In every woman's mind there are certain fantasy clothes that somehow embody that quintessential aura of what she always dreamed of as the key to eternal joy, whether it be a shoe or dress that you would die to possess, thinking that would be utter perfection. This corset was that piece. And, I think, will always be. Paired it with a cocoa Indian pashmina scarf, wrapped snugly at my hip and secured with an antique Indian tiger's eye brooch as a modern take on an evening skirt. Pulled my hair back into a sleek long braid and slipped on a pair of regal chandelier earrings of tiny red coral beads that were just long enough to skim my bronzed shoulders gleaming with a fresh light tan (snagged while eating a 3 euro baguette for lunch in the sun of Jardin du Luxembourg) and glimmering with a sheer spray of Clarins body oil.

I let my cat, Verdi, bat at the long ribbons of my lace-up heels, as I put my Lancôme compact, cell phone, and lipstick in my tiny Indian embroidered clutch. "Okay, that's enough, angel, I have to put on these beauties and you can't slice them into smithereens," I chided, as I slid on the heels, lacing them just so they climbed up my ankles a scant three inches to ensure they weren't too sexy, as my ex hates too blatant sexy. This is a man who thinks any exposed cleavage is déclassé and women are sexiest in a one-piece maillot (over a bikini). In a word—classicist.

With a quick spritz of that Guerlain Insolence *parfum* and a dash of cinnamon lipstick (fook, my lipstick is Maybelline, how cheesy . . . *C'est la vie*, it is what it is), I am ready. Wish I could take a camera, but that's not done, as my Big Shot Ex would say, and he would be mortified. But come on, unquestionably I won't be attending any shindig this sha-sha ever again and it would be amazing to have photos (maybe, Kiki, if you weren't saying words like "shindig" you would fly on a higher stratosphere). My silly self-chatter kicks in as I realize I am nervous. It's been a long time since I have done these big-deal affairs and this is all a different caliber of, well, everything; I don't run with a crowd these days that has several "suites" of jewels to wear every night and while I adore the necklace I'm wearing that I made of huge red coral branches (I found for sale for a mere 17 euros on that trip to Vienna with my dad four years ago at a flea market and just had to have) and maybe the handmade clasp of *faux* silver I got at the craft store is screamingly cheap, but I strung it myself and it's a dead ringer for the Yves Saint Laurent one that's all the rage this season, so there. I think I have a very creative and interesting outfit on and feel like a million bucks.

Bzzz! My ex has arrived downstairs and is at the door in a blink, as Verdi leaps into action as door greeter. I sweep open the door and wish instantly I had thought to change the music from my adored Coldplay to Mozart. I am out of practice on all that prep work; lighting Dyptique *figue* candles and setting the right lighting, etc. . . . all that goes with receiving my ex *chez moi*. I smile since he looks just dashing in his Savile Row suit, John Lobb custom shoes, and Kenzo tie—impeccable to the nth.

His face falls. "Oh, Kiki . . . what are you wearing? Too, too sexy. The skirt's too short and couldn't you have chosen something simple? That won't do at all," he says, scowling as he hands me a bottle of chilled Cristal for us to have a *coupe* before we set out for the thirty-minute drive to Saint-Cloud.

I am shocked, crestfallen, and mad (not about the champagne, that's all good). Sad to feel he could be so blatantly, instantly rude and make me feel as though I am standing here in Kmart brand garters and a pink boa and little else. "You are not serious. This is Armani, how do you argue with Armani?" I say, with self-assurance trying to mask my crushed confidence (AND remembering back that when I first met him eight years ago, he wasn't the best dresser, I am the one that introduced him to the elegance of Yohji Yamamoto and Dries Van Noten).

"No, no . . . that skirt is just all wrong."

"Fine. Open the champagne and I will go fix it, but the rest stays," I say semi-acquiescing and, frankly, steaming mad. Cursing under my breath as I trot to my bedroom to tell myself, "God, am I glad I am not dating this man anymore. Ruthless of him to make me feel so bad. I swear since we split he is getting unbearable pretentious and grand." I swap the scarf skirt for, ha, another scarf, albeit a longer version that will fall at mid-calf and be essentially the same look with some additional length. I come back to the living room and he looks at me and huffs, sits down, and takes a sip of champagne. We make forced small talk about the night ahead with a tone that could be effectively labeled "undelightful."

What a prick. I look amazing. I never looked this good when I was with him. It's an outfit with style and inimitable thought, since it's not an off-the-rack, designer look head-to-toe, and that's what personal style is you shitfuck-nitwit. I was the design-school-educated fashion designer, so bugger off, meany-pants. More to the point—and then I will stop—I was brokenhearted that this man, who used to think I was the most amazing woman ever and who has always treated me with almost worshipful adoration, was now being so harsh, ridiculous, and nonloving. It's a skirt, for fuck's sake.

I will admit that early on in our love story, when he first fell in love with me, the mere notion that this iconic figure was head over heels for me gave me validation and confidence that carried me on my way. He was supremely romantic and the most thoughtful, loving man I had ever been with. For god's sake, each morning he used to take out the cardboard paper that his dry-cleaned shirts were folded around and make me an india ink watercolor painting complete with a spontaneously written amorous poem, leaving it propped up by my bedside for me to awaken to. And that is just but one of the many creative and lovely gestures he would make in any given day. Thus all through my days and nights, throughout this journey to Paris solo, to start an art career, etc., he had fed me a lifelong gift to feel special and confident and to just be comfortable in my own skin. *And now* it felt like it was all being rescinded—because of an outfit he didn't care for. To me, the outfit was like a symbol of who I am now and not who I was then; back when he would choose my gowns for big events since I knew he loved to (control freak) and, hell, he was paying for them, so no hardship for me to let him. Now, this odd reaction by him somehow turned my world on its ear and negated the rosy recollections I had held of that love and acceptance.

"We'd better go soon. No chance you will opt for another sartorial option? I would even prefer to see you in the Gaultier gown you mentioned at the outset," he begs, while standing up and leaving his champagne flute on the table where Verdi will surely knock it to the floor inside three minutes. (This man has never done a dish and hasn't the slightest notion of taking it to the sink out of courtesy. Once, when I asked him to help me hang a new chandelier at my apartment in NYC, he refused even that basic a physical task: "Kiki, there are people for that. I can hire someone to do it." I digress. Time to go.)

"Nope, I love what I am wearing and there you go," I reply, with a miffed air. There is no way I am shunning the "me I have become" for the "me he wants to control." I kiss Verdi good-bye and we make our way to the chauffeured car, setting off for the palace in Saint-Cloud. It's annoying how divine a chauffeured car feels after so many years holding onto petri dish subway poles, swaying viciously at the turns. This, I can't pretend I don't miss.

"The woman I was dating . . . ," he begins.

"The married woman with little kids?" I interject with loads of judgment, though I frankly don't care.

"Yes, well, she and I split a week ago and I invited you to come to these events as I knew she would catch wind of it and——." He pauses as he stares at Place de la Concorde. "——to put it succinctly, the strategy worked. She heard you were here, she rang me, and we spent the day with one another. We are together again and she will be there tonight. I just thought you should know, as I so hoped we could all spend the evening having a pleasant time but she will be the woman on my arm," he says as though I will just nod and find that wonderful fun news.

"*Charmant*," I reply curtly, thinking this is full stop crappy as I thought this was one of our "carpe diem" adventures, the name we give to our random bi-annual love fests of meeting up. No-sir-ee, I am a pawn in the game and have been played like a chip that's now worthless but stuck in his pocket like a piece of lint he will discard at the earliest possible moment. We drive on in silence as I struggle to find some mental place (does one even exist?) where I can be cool with being a hanger-on as the lovebirds swoon in my midst and make me feel like toilet paper stuck to their custom calf-soled shoes.

We arrive to the venue, where the majestic reconstructed palace holds court just in the distance, nestled in the woods. Security teams surround the car, asking for presentation of invitations and identities. I smile to myself, remembering the last time I was subject to such an experience of sitting in a chauffeured car, in evening wear and getting carded—with the same man at my side, off to a dinner at Bill Gates's house (another financial client of Big Shot Ex's). Hilarious. Security? I don't even have a concierge to move the massive pile of Pages Jaunes telephone books that are stacked high in my building lobby like a wall in the Alamo.

Okay, Kiki, time to pull off the "completely at ease" expression that seems unfathomable to fake but is so damn necessary since I am not letting anything squelch the thrill of attending this grand fete, even if I am going to be an appendage to a cozy couple, one half of whom I once loved more than life itself. My ex and I descend the long red velvet carpet path that winds up to the vast terrace bustling with as many bejeweled guests as white tuxedoed waiters. We pass a dozen Rolls-Royce Corniches splayed out like piles of heaping bank notes, taking special notice of the gleaming silver one for the wedding couple that has set mouths agape all over Paris for a week. We climb to the lavish terrace; the view is sublime. Men in turbans with regal white beards, formal Nehru jackets, and faces lined with life and mystery speak in quiet tones with one another as beautiful Indian women in breathtaking beaded saris, laden with enormous rubies and emeralds, move with grace and poise. Need it be said, I feel like a piece of big white Wonder Bread despite my attempts at Indian-influenced elegance.

Literally, the entire length of the two-hundred-foot terrace is set with one enormous square crystal vessel after another (I was going to say as big as buckets, but how inelegant is that?), eight inches deep and overflowing with shimmering grey Beluga caviar as hundreds of mother-of-pearl spoons and demi-plates await the casual indulgence of pure delicious decadence. A team of perhaps fifty handsome waiters pass silently throughout, offering some of the twenty-three hundred bottles of Dom Perignon champagne as the most extraordinary floral arrangements (of ten thousand specially jetted-in blooms from India) embrace the guests as much as do the life-size ice sculptures of famous artistic vignettes like Rodin's passionate masterpiece, *The Kiss*. A series of massive ornate French doors open onto the interior, richly deco-rated as if for a sultan's feast for a thousand. Indeed, the whole scene is something your eye can't really adjust to—it's so fantastical, sumptu-ous, and otherworldly that one's mental faculties are just not up to fil-ing and processing such extravagance. (Where do we put this? Next to that ghastly image I have of witnessing a homeless man in NYC defecat-ing on the front steps of the Met and wiping his ass with a Kentucky Fried Chicken bag? Oh, I think, *non*.)

We drink champagne—well, I drink like it's the last beverage I will be offered before my being taken in shackles off to the Con-ciergerie à la Marie Antoinette. Inside of ten minutes, I feel a bit more relaxed since it is positively fascinating to see everything, everyone, all the amazing details that have been conjured and executed with "sky's the limit" grandeur. It would be fun to be the wedding planner and ask, "And the budget is what figure, Monsieur Mittal?" "No bud-get. Money is of no importance."

Christ.

Lovely men and women dressed to the nines, with expressions of delight, roam and come by to chat. (Many compliment my necklace and unique attire! See, you major poop, it IS a cool look.) The main subject at hand—the supreme astonishment at the opulence as well as a universal intrigue at how we all came to be invited to such an affair. One woman simply because she was the family's personal shopper at Cartier and another because she was a curator at the Louvre, when all the sudden my date—make that "escort" in a vague sense—veers off and into the arms of his grand amour, leaving me alone in the crowd. With his back to me, now standing about fifteen feet away, he is speaking to the girlfriend. She, who I have never met or seen before, is eyeing me up and down as they speak, and she looks how I feel—pissed and semi-crazed. I kind of love that. In her classic black strapless gown and dripping diamond necklace, her golden hair unquestionably upswept by some chic salonist, she is positively looking emotionally undone. Perhaps he didn't warn her I would appear *ce soir*. Whatever the exchange, she is livid, giving me the rudest sneer. This is my entrée to be the cool-headed woman who can just fuck with her a tiny bit. Listen, I am getting the shit end of the stick here, since I clearly am as unwelcome by my ex as by his girlfriend and they both wish I would just disappear, so you two, grin and bear it, because you'll soon be just fine as a couple, back to your extravagant lifestyles where this kind of a soiree is the norm, and I will be home alone, reading a paperback with my cat and a bottle of Orangina on the windowsill.

My ex turns to glance at me while his social X-ray (hiss hiss) girlfriend snorts at him, and I simply smile at them, as if oblivious to the storm brewing. I take myself over to make a polite act of self-introduction, despite the fact that I'm as welcome as shit on a stick at their tête-à-tête. Trying to glide over there, without letting on that this is all a charade of calm contentment, is no mean feat. Miraculously, I am the epitome of self-restraint, surely channeling my mother's spirit as she would relish this kind of a face-off. Madame X-Ray Girlfriend can hardly utter a reply to my *"enchantée,"* let alone make any pleasant small talk, as she quickly turns to my ex (as though I have already walked away) and mutters in French, though she is as American as I am, "This cannot be happening. Either she leaves or I do."

And with that, I am stunned to be made aware that I can, literally, be dismissed. I don't want to go. Even though I am feeling this massive loss of love and acceptance from my favorite man ever, I am eager to endure, to stay, to make this night something that I can salvage for my sense of strength and for the sheer experience of being here. He steps back at my side and, with a hand on my arm, leads me back to one of the many ornately set tables. I am so tickled, thinking, "Finally, he has come to his senses since the girlfriend is behaving like a twelve-year-old girl without a scrimpet of that elegance he so adores and insists on. I win, thanks to her blatant immature rudeness spurred by a hostile takeover of jealousy. She will have to endure. Ha!"

"Kiki, we are leaving. You and I. My girlfriend is terribly uncomfortable with you here and, frankly, this isn't as smooth an evening as I had hoped," he states matter-of-factly, as the guests start to make their way to the grand ballroom (stadium size) for Kylie's concert.

"No way, you are seriously going to do this? We have been here maybe forty-five minutes," I say, thinking this is next to impossible that I thought I was seizing some control and I am being shown what a farce that notion was. "I can't believe this. You invited me and I spent a lot of time preparing for this night and, of course, was really looking forward to it. And I don't want to leave, can't we at least stay for the dinner?" (and the five hundred bottles of Mouton Rothschild

1986 that I could drink all by my own self right about now), I say, incredulous.

"I have the decency, of course, to escort you home, but, no, we are not staying," he replies curtly, making his way to the terrace, assuming I will follow like an automaton. I stand for a few seconds and realize I have no option—it's not like I can sidle up to a bunch of strangers and sit at an unassigned seat, asking people for a lift back to Paris at night's end as though we were all at a rave. Fook! I am screwed. No plan B or way to argue it out. I chose to muster some dignity and take myself off the premises with a shred of class. (Read, not making a scene or coming to fisticuffs with fuck-wit ex though I could box his lights out I am so mad.) I consider telling him I will take the chauffeured car home solo so as to just be done with him and his shitty company but then think, "No, make it hard for him. Let him go back the half-hour ride to Paris with you, allowing Madame X-Ray to sit and stew about what we are up to and then let the bastard go back to his bag-of-bones bitch." I mean if she really knew how to handle our meeting, she would've acted with sophistication, as though seeing me was as much a nonevent as seeing the postman. Her big fuss made me feel like I was a worthy opponent and threat and thereby, in effect, gave me the power. Even if she can make me disappear, she still looks like the insecure ninny. I guess, only to me and, well, that matters a lot.

As we, ex and I, not so much hand-in-hand as "fury and disappointment intermingling," leave the palace, dark clouds have arrived—and not just to my mood. The sky unleashes a downpour as lightning crashes over the spectacular view of the Tour Eiffel. With my makeup running, and my ex all but running to get the hell out of there, I look back over my shoulder at the scene on the terrace as servants have simply left everything to stand the trials of nature. My final glimpse of the party is of buckets of rain pelting the extraordinary bouquets to a pulp and diluting hundreds of glasses of champagne, as sculptures and silk brocade swags tip and teeter with moisture and I spot the dozens of heaping crystal bowls of Beluga being drowned to oblivion. For some inexplicable reason, this atrocity, the idea that certainly $100,000 worth of caviar is just being left to be ruined, seems so vulgar. Why is no one madly dashing to and fro trying to save it? And it occurs to me such a reaction would look like low-class panic and, in this world, that is just not done. And moreover, in this world, it simply doesn't matter. There is always more luxury, more opulence to be found. In effect, that is how my Big Shot Ex has made me feel: like Beluga left in the rain. It doesn't matter since there is more Beluga inside waiting for him when he dumps me at my doorstep. Yep, F. Scott Fitzgerald was right; the rich aren't like you and me . . . They are infinitely more rude.

What a night that was. I came home from the silent drive back to my flat with my ex sitting there in the car, acting like I was—horrors—a fired staff member who needed to be deposited at a distant locale. Truth be told, it must've sucked for him to have set this strategy all up, indeed, get back his desired girlfriend and still have me to bring to the big affair. There was no way we were all going to walk away unscathed.

Once home and simmered down, I looked in the mirror, put thoughts of my ex on hold, and embraced my ongoing life theme of carpe diem. Despite my being tossed aside like old shoes that have had their day, this night cannot end in flames, so I called up my amour at the time, a drop-dead sexy and geniusly talented (read what you want into that) twenty-nine-year-old Italian boy, and he dashed over to help me polish off the Cristal left by my ex and kiss away the wounds— also, left by my ex. *And, he looooved my outfit, merci.* Ladies, there is always an antidote to the injuries made by a man you once loved. In a word: Italians.

Now, back in my new little Wisconsin life of a suburban mom, I shake that vivid memory off quickly as I am reminded of what made it possible to leave that lifestyle I once knew so well—the French phrase *"Mieux vaut être seul que mal accompagné"* ("It is better to be alone than in bad company"). And when you're SO not loving and respecting your companion, it doesn't matter where the hell you are, whether you're eating caviar washed down with Dom in a palace or fried eggs in a diner. Because I have been sad in some insanely luxurious settings in my day, I know all too well no purse, view, cuvée, or feast can take away the emptiness.

Et voilà, another supremely intense "Oh, I long for the good old days" flashback rationalized to reality from its regal perch. Easy to embrace life à la Wisconsin at the moment, with the array of family holidays ahead that are loaded with so much history, love, and memories: Halloween, Thanksgiving, and Christmas. I get to do them the USA way, full-blast and with loved ones. Hurrah! The trio that had made me feel so lonely in Paris, making me just ache to be back home with family. Ahhh. There is a continuous sense of pleasure in being here and being able to give Oscar as many of those cherished and magical experiences as I possibly can, even if, now and then, that "missing Paris bug" does at times appear like an annoying mosquito in the dark. I bat it away and it reappears later, buzzing more loudly. But for now, thankfully, as though that bloodsucking creature was away (possibly vacationing in St. Barths), when Halloween rolled around it all couldn't have been more wonderful and perfect.

Having never had a house to decorate before, I just went hog wild with the festive decorations, hastily carved pumpkins on every step, candlelit paper bags along the walkway, cobwebs spanning the front deck, a Halloween "scary howls" CD playing, huge spiders suspended from the windows, graveyard of skeletons in the yard, and would you believe this was all rather low-key compared to the rest of Shorewood Hills residents. I gotta give it to them; all my neighbors are whizzes at festivities. Every yard, house, and terrace was decked to the nines, and for as much as it's a commercial holiday, it was soooo very cool to see, and to live there. For once, my hopes were exceeded and surpassed. "Awesome," as Oscar would say.

Since we would be out ourselves (doing the ding-dong candy bit) and not be home to greet trick-or-treaters, I left a heaping basket of every candy bar imaginable with a sign, HELP YOURSELF. I remember, well, that was always the most thrilling sign and bounty to happen upon as a kid, and who would I be if not the house with all the candy? It all was flawless, as I made Oscar's little crab costume, complete with stuffed claws, spinnerets, and hood with wobbly antennae. After carving a small pumpkin together that we grew in our garden, at around 6:00 P.M. I got Oscar into his getup—I think I took 387 photos of him in it as he immediately got up and ran off to ride his fire truck around the house. Cutest thing ever—him driving his "fire truck" in full crustacean gear. Hilarious! As he scooted about, I treated self to an ample amount of champagne, as I miss it madly and don't find many occasions to imbibe. (Have considered toasting to Oscar's incoming teeth, but that's a bit of stretch.) Truth is, I was a teensy bit nervous again to be in the USA, really doing it all full-on and taking Oscar out trick-or-treating, which in advance felt a little weird as a single mother. (Note to self: Halloween seems to trigger drinking copious amounts of alcohol. Don't drink and drive, even a Red Wagon.) It's just that I knew everyone else would be in full-blown family mode and it's slightly hard to carry a small crab around alone door-to-door. Luckily, my super-cool neighbors Jessica and David and their brood of four kids let us trail around with them and it was instantly ridiculous fun and very chill. Dear Oscar started out terribly confused as to why the streets were all buzzing with little princesses and Pokémons but quickly took to the free candy aspect and was one happy little crab.

It felt great to cross that hurdle/holiday and we flew through Thanksgiving *en famille* with flying colors. The snow fell and, god, is it charming to see the delight and awe on your child's face. These are the moments that you long for when you're pregnant and, even with all the beautiful visions you conjure in your mind, it's infinitely more touching and dear than you could fathom (and fuels one through the days when your child is a decidedly stinky, stubborn *actual* crab).

With Christmas approaching and having acquired only enough new "friends" that I could count them on one hand, I was pretty pleased to be invited to a neighborhood Christmas party. The singular single man in Shorewood Hills rolled out the carpet for his annual Christmas party. Since he was a successful businessman (owned three sports bars, yuck!), unmarried, and lived within a stone's throw, there was chatter I should be set up with him. After spotting him on three separate occasions, each time sporting a Packers baseball cap and with a bimbo on his arm (think bad perm à la the flat, one-color blond variety, in faux pearls, tight mom shorts, and platform sandals—ugh, I realize that sounds like me sans perm, sheesh, give me another year here and maybe I will be sittin' in perm rods, too—horrors). Anyway, I put the quick kibosh on that "date the Sports Bar King" plan. Still, a party *chez lui* sounded like something more fun than watching the neighborhood dogs—out for a poop—slip down the hill on ice, paws a-scrambling (official low point to one's cerebral amusement).

Three feet of snow outside to wade through to the party and a

"Bring something festive to pass" request ensured I wasn't going to be making that profiterole pyramid ensconced in whisper-thin caramel branches I always wanted to create (and surely never will). So, frosted and decorated gingerbread men and women, stars, and Xmas trees were our task. Not so easy to pull off, mind you, with a toddler dying to open the oven, scoop handfuls of frosting into hair while gobbling sprinkles aplenty, but we pulled it off masterfully, *considering*.

You know what's really hard? Carrying mini-Michelin man Oscar, also known as Sir Cries a Lot, in his snowsuit through the snow three blocks as he writhes wildly, while transporting a teetering tray of cookies—while snowflakes melted my mascara and snow got in my boots. I arrived almost throwing Oscar into the massive pile of eight billion coats and shoes splayed all over hall—like Mount Everest, god, something else to scale to even *enter* the party. No time or way to dodge the immense crowd to fix the (very weepy raccoon) eye makeup, had to lurch right in with hellos and meetings instantly. God, just give me some wine! That was slow in coming and was warm in a plastic cup. I had to stand with Oscar on hip, since if I put him down he would be trampled in the mass crush of kids and adults all jostling to the buffet table; it was a mob scene. For a blip of a second it reminded me of my old club days in NYC: the stampede lines for open bar. Alas, the comparisons end there, since, as a single NYC clubber, I spent more time and thought getting ready than the entire population at this fiesta. One word—sweatshirts. There was only one sweatshirt that ever had any sexiness, that one-shoulder number from the film *Flashdance* and that, like the attire of this crowd, should be sealed in a time capsule forever.

And no wonder I got an invite, as he seemingly invited all five hundred residents of Shorewood Hills. Hey, if you have a two-thousand-square-foot house, don't ask that we all come and find our four cubic square feet. Even had we stood like totem poles on each other's shoulders or splayed out horizontally, like Chinese acrobats, it would have been packed to the rafters. In my world, being trapped in suburbia, in elbow-to-elbow sweatshirt-land with warm bad wine in a plastic cup was akin to enduring waterboarding in Guantánamo: *I would've told any lie to get outta there ASAP.* The food was good in a sort of "to hell with my hips" way, and the people were nice, but it's a wacky evening when the most memorable event was the following (and please forgive the grossness of it): someone's used mini-pad somehow found itself on the living room floor and resulted in all of the guests sitting there like theater in the round, circling this disgusting thing while trying to act oblivious—even to the climax, when the dog raced through and made a quick scamper by and sniff of it. It was all so absurd in its ridiculousness, like a bad episode of *Family Guy* or some dumb Adam Sandler prank, yet it evoked not the slightest reaction from the crowd. I tried to wait it out to some conclusion, but it just sat there for forever. Okay, twenty minutes, but Oscar had hit the wall—he'd had all he could endure of the crowd and begged to be "home!" so we shipped out. Frankly, the certain horrendous awkwardness of the panty-liner retrieval surely must've been the high point of said party, so I was rather miffed to have to miss that.

That minor disappointment passed quickly as Christmas was just amazing! Christmas decorations—lights, reindeer, sleighs, wreaths bigger than Volkswagens, life-size snowmen, elves, and Santas galore—ubiquitous in every yard in Shorewood Hills and it was a treat to get our first truly, glorious Xmas tree at home. Of course, I tried to channel my parents' Christmas traditions, since my parents were masters of ceremonies and creating true magic: real candles on the tree, our every wish materialized, hiring Santas to appear Christmas Eve, faking the sound of reindeers on the roof, thousands of opulent tiny white lights ("always white, colored lights are garish") in all the trees in the yard, beef bourguignonne and lime sherbet in cranberry juice "cocktails" for Christmas dinner. I will never forget as a young budding ballerina the Christmas my mother and father placed a sparkling tutu (she handmade for me) in the treetops, as if it just fell from Santa's sleigh. If I had doubts about Santa's existence, they vanished instantly. What a priceless memory.

Thus, it was divine to re-create the traditions of decorating the fireplace mantels with pine boughs, holly, candles, and some of my mother's glass ornaments while drinking hot cocoa and listening to Kiri Te Kanawa's Christmas arias. It was heaven to finally be dressing our tree with an array of the hand-blown ornaments I had collected over my many years in Paris. Each year I lived there, I would saunter through the posh shop Bon Marché, lingering for hours on the top floor, in awe of the breathtaking Christmas trees and opulent décor. Just standing in ecstasy, reveling in the lights and astonishingly beautiful, towering, twelve-foot firs sprinkled with small glass crowns, delicate globes, cascades of sparkling lights and hand-blown doves, thinking, "*Mon dieu,* if god has a Christmas tree it surely looks like this." After much internal debate as to actual need versus budget, I would chuck that all out the window and happily splurge on a single ornament each year, always a delicate glass piece. The previous year, a perfect flawless fleur-de-lis, as big as your hand, so lovely it struck me as just the epitome of elegance.

This year, tree now trimmed to within an inch of its life with all my precious finds, Oscar, so enchanted with this shimmering spectacle that when Mommy stepped back to grab the camera to document, her dear boy on tip toes, cheeks aglow with fascination, raced in and pulled on the tiny sleigh and, somehow, pulled the entire tree over, sending fragile glass shattering into shards *all over* the parquet wood floor. My recent efforts to utter "butterscotch" instead of swearing went the way of the glass and more of a "faaauucckk!" was unleashed. After the innate, lightning-quick retrieval of Oscar from harm's way and instant injury check (none), full-blast fury was given free rein. Instantly mourning—all the years it took to get these most prized possessions, all the hopes of having them for years and generations, all the money, and the fact that in all my years in France, these were, strangely, among my most special and personal acquisitions—gone! Despite my hopes of always maintaining a happy face for Oscar, I fell apart with sadness and disappointment and cried for a good five minutes. I was just so sad to *not* be able to stop this personal meltdown and also to *have to* manage Oscar. At that moment, with so much to clean—water from the tree stand, mixing with tree needles, and glass everywhere—and my need to cry, I wanted, if not a husband, someone, *anyone* to clean it all up so I didn't have to see each treasured piece destroyed *or* to hold Oscar. But to have to both, when I felt such an inexplicable loss, was hell. It was one of those moments when you have to juggle it all and it's crushing you. I'm sure whether or not you're a single mom, these are experiences you never forget and slide into your mental files under "incidents I could've lived without." I pulled myself together soon after and held Oscar extra tight the rest of the evening, realizing my terribly good fortune that he was unhurt and safe again, in my arms. Children have a way of shattering things in an instant, one of them being overvaluing material possessions!

On the upside of late, *enfin,* Oscar naps soundly and for hours at a time. (Whereas, as a baby he would wake howling if you so much as passed through his room in stocking feet and yet still sleep through a crashing thunderstorm at night. Another rhetorical "Why??")

A naptime routine is huge to a new mom. I cannot overstate the value of a teensy bit of freedom to execute *sexy* tasks uninterrupted, like folding laundry, cleaning toilets, and returning e-mails. Oh la la. Seriously, I am elated to discover that I can now sneak off during his morning nap and take a bath. This is a rare and real luxury for a mom to bathe in silence—not to be pelted with incoming toys or demands like "Where is fire truck, come find, Momma!" Good lord, just to lie back in a steaming bath, fragrant with bath oils—heaven! I remember before I got pregnant reading an interview in *Vogue* with Gwyneth Paltrow, who claimed her passion as a new mother was baths, and I was like, "Yeah, right, like a bath beats going to the Oscars dripping in diamonds and couture!" Now, I totally get her bath obsession since it *is* like self-renewal—though I'm kind of doubting we have much else in common, since I'd bet she's not signing up for rain checks on the jumbo pack of Huggies at Costco.

ADMISSION: I WAS CAUGHT FAKING IT BY THE MAN IN MY LIFE

No, it's not what you think and I'm as disappointed as you, as that would make for a very fine anecdote. But I still am amazed to see how intensely the cause-and-result comes to the fore when, for instance, you're not such a happy-happy mom. Whoa nelly, instantly your child can sense the slightest hint of insincerity in a forced faux smile or a joyless gaze.

As I cheerlessly made Oscar an omelette the other morning (after he savagely refused the full menu offered and served up in succession—yogurt and raisins, then toast with jelly, then cereal) in the style of a tired short-order cook at IHOP, I feigned a pleasant face while serving the monster demanding customer, and he just looked at me and said, "sad," and wouldn't eat a morsel until I came around again. Yep, it's downright scary how they are so tuned in, gauging your every head tilt and gesture; there is no getting away with going through the motions of playing trucks for the thirty-seventh time that day without rousing up the proper enthusiasm. And you know what? I'm down there on the floor all the day and night and *it's hard*. Very hard to keep up the level of interest and fervor, and just when you think you may very well cry from boredom and isolation, your child does something magic. Like, while playing tea party for the umpteenth time, Oscar pointed to the marshmallows in our cocoa and said, "Look . . . tiny snowmen!" with total delight. And your heart and soul are thankfully and instantly healed and you can power on as you are reminded that this is the best part of life, no question.

Traded in eHarmony for Facebook, after much pressure from my best friend Kathy to get some semblance of a connection to the world by joining Facebook (since she well knows I'm not going to become a member of the local bowling league or square dance group). It was surprisingly cool to reconnect in real time with *real* friends in Paris and even receive "invitations" again to openings and parties in St. Germain that I, of course, could never attend. But it miraculously made me feel less forgotten and anonymous to have a voice again.

Then, after the initial thrill, I started considering what I would or could post on my Facebook wall. My European friends' posts are flurries of events such as, literally, "I'm off to the Cesar Awards in the South of France" and "Weekend in the U.K. at Elle MacPherson's son's baptism in 17th c. castle" and "Holidaying in Ibiza."

Whereas my status posts would be the following:

- Oscar made poop soup in the bath today . . . You can't imagine how it adhered to the Elmo nonslip bath mat. What a bugger it was to get out—I advise, after much trial and error, using an old toothbrush, *mes amies!*

- Realized I now have a larger collection of muffin pans than I do of sexy underwear!

- Polished off a whole bag of ghastly "Pizza Bites" as Oscar hates 'em and referred to them as "barfo," yet my budget demands I not let them go to waste!

- Actually got out into public today, if you can call taking the trash to the curb while child yells bloody murder thinking I was never coming back!?

- Day 3 of nonwashing hair and you know what? No one really cares!

- Spent my free time—*that is, the allotment given by beloved napping child*—sitting on ass in ripped jeans, embracing toilet bowl, scrubbing away at the calcium stains with a wire brush—*with as much focus, I might add, as I used to expend studying an old master's painting at the Louvre*—until, unfortunately, I chipped off the enamel and I wept.

- Elated to discover if I let Oscar whip 300 packets of Sweet-n-Low all over the floor, it buys me a full five minutes to do dishes without him climbing up my legs!

- I got a great Spam crescent roll (known as "croissants" to previous self) recipe off AOL when I checked my e-mails today. Glad to share it!

- In my lavish 45 seconds of "me time" today, I got to iron pillowcases. Not that anyone ever sees them, but trust me, they look really posh!

AS A NEW MOM, GOOD LUCK EVER GETTING
ANOTHER CHANCE TO

1. Have a normal phone conversation. It's no longer possible to decide when YOU actually feel like ending the call rather than having to make your usual apology, "Sorry (insert child's name here), is losing it, I better go." And forget having a phone call that flows and has a sense of continuity rather than barking bullet points like a loon as you try desperately to string together something resembling a conversation. Many times you will find yourself simply saying loudly, "I'm sorry I can't hear you over his screaming, really sorry, will have to call you back later," and just hang up feeling defeated to one's bones.

2. Ever really put yourself together with the same thoughtfulness as your previous self. You end up looking in the mirror twice a day, to quickly jam a brush through your hair and put in or take out your contacts. Brushing your teeth is something you do while picking out your child's jammies and trying to get them to submit to a diaper change. "Getting dressed" is simply picking up anything that doesn't have spit-up or Play-Doh adhered to it. Makeup? Ha! You're lucky if you can get chapstick on, and many a day passes where you have a craggy broken nail and can't even get to an emery board. In short, your physical self is now way down the list of "things to get to."

Chapter 18

"Designer clothes worn by children are like snowsuits worn by adults. Few can carry it off successfully."

—FRAN LEBOWITZ

Winter lingers on. How tiresome.

Paradoxically, I longed for snow, since you rarely see it in Paris, and now I *have had it* with the white stuff. Sick to death of shoveling. Hadn't considered this daily and monumental task back when making my big leap to get back here. Generally shoveling is just a pain, but try doing it with a twenty-four-month-old pitching a fit that you're just outside, beyond reach, "playing" in the snow without him. Like that speed lawn mowing I'M SUCH A FAN OF, snow shoveling is a task that adds a certain "I hate this place" spin to my life. And the funny thing is, after years, make that *decades,* of dreaming of what a joy it must be to bundle my own child in a cozy little snowsuit, putting on his first winter bonnet with a pompon and a matching pair of fuzzy mittens complete with mitten clips—how cute!—about one-third of the time, *it's a real pain in the arse.* Especially if you are in a hurry or when he is defiant and fighting you to the tooth. Good god, can it just go a little less treacherously than as if I were trying to jam a ferret into a Pez container?! When the planets are not aligned and beloved child is undressing one side as fast as you're dressing the other, you just want to grab duct tape and make that damn hat stay on once and for all! Not that it's really worth all the trouble, since after thirty minutes of getting Oscar into the full winter gear, he steps outside, feels the cold winter winds, and does an instant about-face yelling, "Home!"

Back inside, momma trying to fill the long days with activities and fun, is exhausting. And half the time after you carefully set up one toy or project, he veers off disinterested. I have found myself actually saying, "Get back here, you *will* play with the train set now and *enjoy* it!" How Nazi of me. He looked at me like, "You play with it, I'm off to jam Matchbox cars in that potty that I refuse to pee in." Argh.

Plus, I'm feeling rather worried that my handing him a bunch of crackers so I can make a phone call to the dentist without his crying or shrieking may be a nasty habit that will result in a fat little boy who never actually learns to shush ("the self-soothe"). Furthermore, I have been known to say, "too loud," when he is screeching, which has had the singular result in Oscar naming his teddy bear Too Loud. Lovely. No gold stars for this mom.

On the subject of the *tired mom struggling to keep up,* I also discovered that, as a new mother, I just don't have the interest in keeping in touch with the people who aren't able to understand the new world

I live in. Dashed off are those that I call "friends *lite*," the ones that I'd—in my previous life—just meet up with for drinks, dancing, or mindless dishing. Like hell there is any time to nurture any relationships with people who aren't able to get that your 8:00 P.M. is no longer cocktail rendezvous hour but *bedtime*. And, frankly, you don't want to hear all the details anymore, those inane long recaps of *this* party or *that* guy who looked so freaking hot. If you don't have the answer for how to get this kid to sit on the potty without his pants on, I have, like, two minutes to hear you rattle on about your late-night escapades.

And also set to sea are the moms that are preposterously, full stop into creating the illusion of perfection in themselves and their child. I'm so sick of the women who claim their child slept through the night from day one, learned to walk at nine months, and spoke Italian with the maid by two years. Oh, fuck off. Sometimes it sucks and anyone who can't say that should shut up. Which is why when I heard this American comedian Louis C.K. say, "Sometimes my kid is just such an asshole," I died laughing. It seemed so shocking at first, and I was taken aback, but then, I thought, "You know what? Yeah, sometimes this kid of mine is being a total jerk," and there's something freeing and cathartic in being able to acknowledge it and laugh.

To that end, recently a couple of neighborhood moms made a "pop by" visit. Oscar was sent into his usual flurry of elation to have a fresh audience, ricocheted around and zipped off while I threw together an impromptu buffet of snacks. Just at the moment I offer up a tin of my precious La Tour d'Argent madeline cookies ordered in from Paris, I notice Oscar has gone and raided the laundry basket and is currently handing my dirty gigantic MOM underwear out to all the guests. OHMIGOD. Talk about airing my dirty laundry?! How ridiculously embarrassing, but as I, red-faced, grabbed them by the handful, vowing to keep soiled undergarments under lock and key from this point

on, the mothers all kindly laughed it off and offered up their own kid-
die horror stories:

> "Our Ben took to dragging out my tampons and trying to use
> them as straws in his juice boxes."
> "When Ariana was five years old, she thought 'daddy's' box of con-
> doms were balloons and she took them to 'Show and Tell' at
> school! Or the time while cooking dinner, I said, 'Darn, we
> are out of oil,' and Ariana piped up, 'Isn't there some in your
> bedside drawer?'"

For this sharing of terrors, I was ever so grateful. Had the same event
unfolded in Paris, NEVER would French *mamans* have been so cool
and commiserating. One point for the Midwest!

Add another point for Midwest moms: they will talk freely about
the rigors of potty training and weaning, two things that French
mothers wouldn't dream of discussing and, from what I have seen,
have a rather harsh and rigid approach to both tasks. On my side, I am
desperate for tips, advice, and suggestions lately, since I cannot wean
this kid! I have valiantly adhered to the NIH, American Academy of
Pediatrics, CDC, and the World Health Organization's suggestions of
breast-feeding until age two. To quote WHO:

> Exclusive breastfeeding is recommended up to six months of age,
> with continued breastfeeding along with appropriate complemen-
> tary foods up to two years of age or beyond.

Not to mention, I stuck to Dr. Sears's Attachment Parenting at every
turn and promoted it like a religion, so faithfully they should anoint
me a patron saint. Thus with this boy's immunity and sense of security

and self-worth at off-the-charts levels, can I have my boobs back please? Not that they are all that great anymore, but it would be nice, after two years, to be able to wear a shirt that doesn't have to open down the front or have to worry about a possible milk stain expanding across my chest while I rattle on unawares. Even if said boobs are going to be returned to me resembling empty Glad bags with a few grains of sand in them, I'm okay with that. Not thrilled that you could pluck them up like a cobweb in two fingers, but OK.

I have read all the blogs, websites, and books for the miracle answer on this weaning dilemma. After poring over the studies and reports, I happened upon a report that revealed the vital and seemingly classified answer: rubbing lemon juice on your breasts was 98% effective for the leagues of frustrated moms hoping to wean successfully. Hurrah! I feel like I have been given the Secret Decoder Ring and can see the end in sight. Relieved and excited to have the final answer, I went out and bought a two-pound bag of lemons and set off with high hopes and firm determination. After sprucing up the girls with their citrus spa treatments, I let Oscar at 'em. He sniffed the air, just said, "Lemonade, mmmm," and attached himself for a lip-smacking session of nursing. Pulled away for a moment. Smiled and continued.

Oh bother. Maddening indeed. I have come to acknowledge full well (that unlike French moms and some moms here, I should add), I personally cannot bear to see this kid cry and because at the mere mention of "no din-din" (no more boob access), he instantly veers off into hysteria. (Rats, I guess nervous drama tendencies are genetic, after all.) I can't cut the poor kid off. So, here I am nursing this kid just the way I always said I wouldn't—he comes over with that look in his eye, pulls my shirt open, and demands, "din-din." Thank god I didn't teach him the slang, "tits," as that would be a lovely moment to hear him whining and demanding at the top of his voice at dinner in a restaurant, "I want teets, momma!" Sheesh. Frankly, in the midst of the mental dead zone of nursing, when you are held hostage and incapable of accomplishing any task, I have come to a theory. To understand the trauma of what it must feel like to be weaned, I imagine it is akin to, say, if you (the mom) were in bed next to Gabriel Byrne and he was naked AND he had caviar in one hand and a flute of Dom Perignon in the other, but he says, "Sorry, you can't have any! All off-limits here!" Seriously, because he is always right next to me, as we are locked into this cosleeping thing (promoted by that Antichrist Dr. Sears, who suckered me into all this), he thinks of me as a "warm tray of brownies" as in "oh what the hell, why not have some."

NEW MOM ISSUES

ISSUE #1. Okay, what's the story with aging? I woke up from a rare stolen nap and with a smudge of eyeliner around my tired eyes (said makeup is a new feeble attempt in trying to pass for a female buried somewhere beneath the shroud of winter layers), and I looked in the mirror and the face was familiar: I was a dead ringer for Alice Cooper.

This is not a good moment. I want to look like, I don't know, me five years ago, or Diane Lane would be great. But not this haggard old goon staring back at me. I'm going to hell. I always wanted my forties to be the time I really shined, as in, so very fine with my wrinkles, wise and mature with life experience, radiating life and health. Like Anne Bancroft as Mrs. Robinson: sexy and cool-headed.

I am not pulling that off terribly well and sometimes resent the living daylights out of all these celebrity moms we congratulate for the way they look drop-dead sexy fab. Everyone celebrates people like

Heidi Klum, Demi Moore, and Angelina Jolie, and how amazing that they look perfect after having kids. I think any one of us mothers, if given a team of nannies, housekeepers, cook, nutritionist, Botox, personal trainer, and financial security, could strut around like easy, breezy perfection too, fer fook's sake. Nevertheless, like all my big issues, I wake up with it slapping me in the face, knock it around all day in my head with as much pleasure as a fork jamming into my temple, and then cast it off, only to wake to it midway through a nice dream at night. Fair enough, I guess, I made my bed and now I have to lie in it . . . or more like, lie awake in it. Lovely.

ISSUE #2. Much more minor (I am happy to report)—I'm ready to set my diaper bag aflame. No matter how much you love your diaper bag, and I don't care if it's a $2,000 Vuitton or a $20 Target number, at some point you look at the thing—so chock-full of toys, a stray M&M, the odd broken toy, the dog-eared Handi Wipes package that accompanies your every outing—and you just want to rip the thing to shreds with your bare hands, fueled by that back stock of unexpressed frustration/anger *that never gets to get out,* since, as the mom, you have to keep your level-headed cool 24/7 or quietly torch the damn thing to ashes (*for those of you with calmer, more passive instincts*).

Sure, with the first child, you were the giddy mom-to-be, excited to shop for your very first diaper bag, all tickled to look at the "baby bottle pouch" and the "spit-up towel nook," thinking, "Yippie, how fun!" And then at some point, you just loathe the damn thing, heavy as hell, slamming into your hip or, in my case my-waist-used-to-be-here-somewhere area. I've tried everything to get over this annoying omnipresent satchel: switched to the chic oversized (*fashion victim much?*) Coach bag in pumpkin leather, the black-and-white houndstooth diaper bag for winter, you name it . . . and I just cannot bear the sight of them anymore.

Lately, I find myself looking longingly at my old under-the-arm clutches and tiny purses that hang on a thin chain. I ache for them, for they are symbols of my old freedom to saunter, spontaneously gallivant, or dash off at a whim—the antics of a previous life that ain't coming back soon. And I don't care who you are, sometimes you absolutely miss that feeling. It's not even that you want to live that life again, you just want to *feel* you could or that it wouldn't take massive prep, babysitters, guilt, clock checking, and anxiety to even get out of the house alone.

ISSUE #3. I'm getting fat. Full stop muffin top. The jumbo variety. Weirder still, after stretching my belly to within an inch of its life during pregnancy, now if I so much as sip a soda, it juts out to the same exact girth it was when I was four months pregnant. A big meal is six months preggers. Flabbeus Corpus for you Latin lovers.

When Oscar pokes my belly playfully, I'm like, "Careful there, darling, you could get your finger caught in the fat rolls like Chinese finger cuffs." Yet, I can't stop eating: neglected or undesired food cooked for Oscar that he deems "garba" and is destined for the disposal, I stand over the sink, eating it like white trash. Which almost answers the question, "What the hell am I doing eating corndogs?" And obviously, it's not like I am a fantastic cook. To sum up, I made a zillion cupcakes with Oscar the other day, doling them out to all our neighbors and family and my brother's reply to, "Were they good?" was, "Well, it was better than, say, not having a cupcake." *Top Chef* contestant I am not, though *Biggest Loser* participant I may become.

Indeed, despite the occasional sit-up (isn't it enough that I *thought* of exercising?), the aftermath of having a baby has given me a body that when I wake and stand up, it's like a gravitational landslide. Stand back, everybody! I try to tell myself it's all okay, Oscar loves to grab and pinch my belly and thus I keep it entirely for his sake. (Best rationalization ever?) And like any mom, you tend to hold your child on one side, and thus my left arm is now like supersonic in strength and hypertoned with its bionic appearance, but the right arm is a fleshy flabby flag. I always did want arms like Linda Hamilton in *Terminator 2*, but I wanted TWO of them. And I'm aware that my film reference is dated. When do you get to the movies with a baby or toddler? You can't even finish watching a DVD!

ISSUE #4. My once intellectual self who read a couple of books a week and kept up with the art world with passion and fascination has seemingly been sent off on a discovery mission or extended sojourn. I am only able to discuss or quote whatever news I can overhear on CNN each morning as I dress Oscar. I speed-read through *Time* magazine and get the gist of stories, which only qualifies me to suggest the topic for others to engage in. As in, at family dinners in restaurants, "Did you see the footage of the earthquake? Now discuss among yourselves as I leap up to go fetch Oscar, who is jettisoning off the walls."

It does kill me when I see those newspaper subscription ads on TV for people who speak of their love of kicking back and reading the entire *New York Times* on Sundays. I ache with envy. The other day, my super-cool neighbor, Jessica, called me, "Kiki, come over and see my new mudroom." And you know what? I was actually eager to do so, with the same excitement I once had for opening night at the opera. And to that end, not only was I really into what she had done, but I went out and copied her clever and colorful organizers by week's end. Is that 100% who I am now?

Note to self—figure out where previous self went and find her and bring her back!

Today, trapped inside for yet another regionwide, history-making snowfall, I failed to enchant Oscar with my attempt to resurrect a sweet tradition my mother created for us children: high tea every Sunday afternoon, with proper attire, homemade scones, and jams. Clearly too young still, he sniffed a scone, deemed it worthy of a hockey puck by kicking it, and split to go watch *Special Agent Oso*. By 4:00 P.M., having exhausted every toy and game, "Tired Mommy" tried to make sorting through old clothes a fun event. As I sat with Oscar sifting through the clothes he's outgrown and trying to sort them for donation piles, I got another good smack in the face—*take that, you sniveling martyr*—wake-up call of just how great it is to be a mom. Folding each jumper, onesie, tiny bootie, or pair of footie pajamas, I was stunned at how hard it is to part with baby clothes *or even a toy* since each is just loaded with dear memories.

"This was his first sunbonnet—he wore it to watch the parade of planes for his first Bastille Day in the Tuileries. His first polo shirt—worn his first playdate in the sandbox. And he wore this the first time he ate an orange, and these the first time he went swimming." Every piece is saturated with the first time he did everything. Both the really moving *and* the mundane events that are blazed like short films in your memory (complete with lighting, sound, and sets), fixed for ready replay, and brought to the fore by this tiny stained sock or that threadbare stuffed bear. Amazing! That these tangible keepsakes hold all of the experiences and they are so deeply rooted that your hand will not physically drop any first toy, blanket, or clothes into that donation pile. Finally, I truly understand why my mother's most treasured belongings were her children's keepsakes; her dozens of huge boxes of our drawings, baby shoes, blankies, and art projects. I remember as a seven-year-old saying to her, "We are all right here, why do you love all that old stuff, now we can talk to you and everything."

"You were all my babies. You will understand one day," she said, smelling my baby blanket with a poignant smile. That day is *now* and to not be able to share this all with her is so tragic. To only be able to go and hold her hand and caress her cheek is so hard. Oscar pats her knee and says, "Wake up, Gran," and we all look at each other, finding it so dear *and* so sad. Oh, how I miss her and wish she could give me her wisdom on so many things. I know in one phrase she could soothe these aches I have for Paris. Not in telling me what to do or feel, but in opening my eyes. Sometimes when Oscar yells, "Momma!" I'm thinking, "You got that right boy."

PRO PARIS POINTS

1. It was, you have to agree, chic and glam and that's always been a tiny, okay, fairly large part of life that I have enjoyed. What woman doesn't want to play dress up sometimes, and here that option is totally limited to Halloween.

2. Interesting close friends with whom I could identify; it's taking more than a little while here for my roots to grow back.

3. Culture and art at every turn. A sense of history and dynamic energy. The buzz of activity and people dashing about doing interesting things is not replaced well by the incessant clanging of neighbors' wind chimes and the rare sighting of a human walking a dog down my street.

PRO WISCONSIN POINTS

1. I love seeing family and Oscar just adores it! All these magnificent male role models for my boy, like his doting and loving

Grandpa "Ta," Uncle Andy in all his playfulness, and "Opa" (my father), with his warm smiles and tenderness.

2. I love that people here are just sweet, helpful, gracious, and open-minded. Oscar will be a far kinder and more thoughtful young man growing up here. In France, I so worried he would become a smidge misogynistic, elitist, or brash by sheer osmosis.

3. I, more or less, know what I am doing and how to manage getting Oscar through childhood here. Finding a great preschool is a snap. A great pediatrician—a cinch. In Paris, I knew how to do/handle anything and everything one needs to know as a single woman, from hosting a party to selling my artwork to galleries, but as a new mother, it was a sea of unknowns, uncertainties, fear, and worry. That can't make for a confident, effective parent. It's hard enough to raise a child, and you need every advantage and skill you can employ!

4. Financially, we can live like kings (well, deposed kings, maybe) in the Midwest, whereas in St. Germain we would be trapped to a diet of only ramen noodles while totally struggling to buy back-to-school clothes and the rare toy!

5. Being a single parent isn't a scandalous title in the USA. In France I certainly felt it was a role that was pitied or frowned upon. In fact, here more than forty percent of children are born out of wedlock.

Chapter 19

> "If there is anything that we wish to change in the child, we should first examine it and see whether it is not something that could better be changed in ourselves."
>
> —C. G. Jung

My current reality—Menard's (local hardware store). I'm there buying a snowblower (how chic! And for this price I could get a Hermès cashmere sweater set), in line with a herd of farmers and locals in full snowmobile gear. *Trust me, "herd" is the right word.*

I glance up and try to compute just what I am seeing. Really!? A "snak bar" (just the spelling says it all, *n'est-ce pas?*) on the mezzanine, ridiculously set up with nailed-to-the-floor plastic chairs and mustard-smeared laminate tables, along a wall of Miller Light neon signs amid the row of vending machines dispensing nachos with hot cheese, pork rinds, and beef jerky with the added ambiance of the nearby key copy machine shooting out splinters of metal.

Are you fucking kidding me? Who would say, "Yeah, that looks like a charming setting and a lovely bounty of items to nourish my ravenous palate. Let's go!"? Bizarrely, this bleak "snack with a view" reminds me of Paris. And I'm relatively sure I am the only one who is making the following comparison: The only other "eating with a view" I have in my mental files is the beyond opulent, nineteenth-century, three-star Parisian restaurant Le Train Bleu, which sits on the mezzanine at the Gare du Nord. White-jacketed stewards serve *fois gras* and three-tiered *plateaux de fruits de mer* under elaborate chandeliers to its impeccably clad patrons who quaff Pol Roger champagne as they watch the Orient Express arrive to the station in all its glory. It was positively mental whiplash to see this sharp and evil contrast. I stood paralyzed a moment, not hearing, "Ma'am, ma'am?" since I could not bear being sucked back into this rendering of my new life in the heartland. Heartland? More like heartbreaking.

In the car, heading home (finally got my driver's license—hurrah!), I thought back to the recent conversation I overheard in the local Piggly Wiggly between fellow shoppers decked out in Green Bay Packers jerseys, baseball caps, and sweat pants:

"Hey dar, doncha know, we be goin' after dis to go bowl a few lanes and have a couple brewskis, ya wanna bring da wife and kids and make a night of et?"

"Oh ya, that sounds like a real fun tang to do dare, we be comin' right away, ya."

It's damn hard to pat myself on the back for moving here when days are chock-full of this stuff. In Paris, you may be just heading out to run a routine errand to get printer ink at FNAC, but along the way, you grab a fresh warm croissant at the Gérard Mulot boulangerie that melts in your mouth while you trot the cobblestones, noticing to your right Catherine Deneuve at Café de la Mairie having tea on the terrace in front of the magnificent St. Sulpice as a wedding party pours out onto the square, festooned with its majestic fountain, attired in *prêt à porter,* top hats, and morning coats. You get it. Going to buy something like cotton balls is still loaded with transporting beauty and visual treats. Here, not so much.

Like a beacon in a storm, my dear family is helping tremendously, taking Oscar and me out to new restaurants, seeing art galleries, and assisting in skooching me toward adapting from extreme elegance to the good old souls in the Midwest. The saving grace is that, truly, the local population is just ridiculously nice and friendly. No more sneers and judgments from other moms, saleswomen, or waiters full of pretension. All the same, it's still a struggle, because dinner out ain't what it used to be—taking a two-year-old to dinner is like sitting on a ticking time bomb. You pack a big bag of snacks, juice boxes, toys, and games and hope EVERY TIME that you will be able to escape without a major tantrum where toys get flung and drinks tossed and eardrums shattered. So, to ease the pressure of arriving at a normal-person dinner hour, we end up going for a 5:00 P.M. dinner, where generally an early-bird special is offered—thus, once again, I'm hanging with an aging crowd of Golden Girls and their spouses.

Falling in with this geriatric-esque schedule I will obviously never happen upon a dateable man and, to that end, who the hell am I now, that I anxiously look forward to these dinners with as much anticipation as I once had for dinner at Joel Roubouchon. I'm almost giddy, "Dinner at Applebee's . . . Yippee!" (Ugh, I'm unrecognizable to myself.) Of course, I'm home before dark and asleep before the sun sets and when I wake the next morning, it's still dark at 5:55 A.M. as Oscar announces with joy, "Hello, moon!" Ugh!

More than once, it has occurred to me that my current life is like that of the farmers, *literally,* just a stone's throw over the hill: they milk the cows at 5:00 A.M. and 5:00 P.M., and with these boobs getting more of a workout than my ass lately, I'm sporting what could be mistaken for cow udders. Gajillionth note to self—keep Oscar from farms in fear he sees cows' udders all craggly and wrinkled and yells to all and sundry, "Just like momma!"

Rants aside, I love being a mom, even more than I thought I would, but every mother would agree, motherhood is simply impossible to imagine until you're living it. No matter how much prepatory reading you may have done or babysitting or conjuring, you don't have a real clue of the sacrifices and the self-imposed pressure that come hand in hand with all the touching moments of bliss.

It's forever difficult to gauge if you are doing the right things, employing the right balance of rules and freedom. I am constantly accused of being too lenient with Oscar, but while this seems to appear the case when we are in public, you get tired of defending your child-rearing approach of, "Well, I am not going to scold him for tossing his sippy cup, with such sternness here, in a filled restaurant, as I might if we were home. He would howl, shriek, wail, and ruin everyone's meal." In fact, it's a gesture to everyone else's benefit. (So back off.)

I also find that often Oscar is so excited to see family, to be out and about, that he gets all revved up and acts like a hyper whirling dervish. Of course, because of this, I look like I am a crap mom who has created a kid that's ricocheting silverware while bellowing, "Woohoo!" It gets tiring to feel like you have to keep apologizing for your child when he is just being *a child* or defending your approach with a line that has become like a mantra to me: "Well, if you read *What to*

Expect with a Toddler, chapter 8, page 4, you will see that his yelling like a wildcat while I'm on the phone with you is *actually* very common." Odder still, I never used to care what people thought of me, the way I live my life, but now, as a mother, I find I care a hundred times more than I ever thought possible. Suddenly, I'm hypersensitive to the slightest eye rolling from an onlooker or the tiniest of quips by family. My brother, who is as adoring and free-spirited as he is cool, casually said, "Ugh, Oscar's being a nightmare today," and I was so hurt and defensive. He pointed out, "You sometimes say it, why can't I?"

And that's the thing; parents can make comments about their own child like, "Oscar is the Antichrist today!" but woe be the idiot who would say that about *your* precious offspring. It just seems like there should be a global memo: "Thou shall not criticize the behavior of someone else's child AND certainly never question their breast-feeding, non-circumcising, cosleeping, or other child-rearing philosophies." *And all that goes twice over for people who don't even have kids!* I know it's human nature to judge others and be judged, but I am trying to tell myself, as I go about my own path, there is not just one way to raise a happy, healthy, and kind child. Admittedly, at first thought, the idea of homeschooling seemed odd to me, but as I learn more about and meet kids for whom it is "their way" I have come to think if you do it right (with structure and socialization), there can be advantages. All the same, homeschooling is not for me, but you have to allow yourself to be open, inquisitive, and educated to raise children, or you are going to stink at it and raise monsters.

And yet, ironically, one has to confess there is no time in your life when you felt such strong opinions about how children that you know, *or just see,* are raised. There are many definitions of what it is to be a good mother, and the masses don't have to agree on all of them. If we did, we would have troops of like-minded clones and no diversity and it's always the unique souls and characters that bring creativity and new perspectives to the world. Because we all waffle between feeling like experts and *feeling like failures,* it is off-limits for others to critique. And it's quite humbling. Reminds me of that Mark Twain quote, "When I was a boy of fourteen, my father was so ignorant I could hardly stand to have the old man around. But when I got to be twenty-one, I was astonished at how much the old man had learned in seven years." A terrific summation of how you think you know everything until you're in it, then after a bit of time you realize, "Holy cats, I don't know what the hell I am doing."

Somehow people think their unsolicited advice or comments are going to help; they rarely do. As a mother, you sure as hell are doing your best, making the innumerable decisions that you know will affect your child every day. And I don't know any moms who won't ask for advice when they want it. In fact, usually fueled by desperation, we will hit the Web, ask our sisters and mothers, even ask mothers at a playground. I have been known to ask moms I don't even know, "Your baby seems so content strapped in the grocery cart. My son's writhing to get out and run around—what's your secret?" (A snack bag full of candy Nerds was the self-soother.)

Oscar losing it in restaurants is nothing compared to what really embarrasses me: I am now captive to TV. You know your social life has really gone in the crapper (one, I think when you use the word *crapper*) when you plot your evenings around TV shows. I'm horrified and ever so reluctant to admit to the following: Too many an evening is booked around when *Top Chef, Rachel Zoe,* and *The Real Housewives of NYC* is on—in fact, I think it's the only time I've ever told Oscar to shush. Okay, I almost had a conniption fit when he chattered over the audio—how absurd is that?

One would think the following are additional reasons for concern:

- You see Siegfried and Roy will have a one-night-only special and actually think, "hmm, could be interesting."

- You have glimpsed the Rachael Ray show enough times to *not* be annoyed by her reference to EVOO (extra virgin olive oil). As the first time you hear her say it you think, "oh, shut the hell up!" To be fair, I guess, she is good at what she does. To be honest, I find her insufferable.

- You have fallen head over heels for former CNN morning host John Roberts AND anxiously await the days he chooses not to wear a tie whereby it is a guarantee that you will see at least one drop-dead sexy man that day. Further to that point, let's talk about Sanjay Gupta (be-yond sexy man!). There is some sadness to be found that I have fallen in with the millions of women who fantasize about him.

In good news, I am becoming a handywoman.

As a parent, your life is suddenly all about batteries and fixing things. I always wondered who was buying those forty-packs of AAs. I feel like I am forever saying, "I fix, I fix it" to my boy. With an endless stream of toys that "brake-ah" (break) daily, there are always at least two awaiting batteries, a new antenna, or a wheel reattachment. You can never get ahead of it. That goes the same for the laundry, the cleaning, a pedicure. I find often I am waiting all the day for Oscar to nap and then when he does, I am just so crazy in love with him, I end up watching him sleep, increasingly eager for him to wake up again. Which is bananas because then it begins all over again until nightfall.

But dear, oh dear, seeing the world through your child's eyes is pure scrumptious fun. Recent Oscar antics:

"The hoppacopta . . . he seeping." (The helicopter that went out of eyeshot is "sleeping.")

When the neighbor's cat, Snooks, trots over, doing figure eights on the front step looking for a visit, Oscar yells to me excitedly, "Momma, go get fun music, hamburgers, and french fries," as though we will be entertaining the cat all afternoon in a make-shift 1950s diner. What a riot.

When I say it's time for Snooks to go outside, he then offers his shoes to the cat. "Here Snooks, for feets."

Oscar's feet ALWAYS smell like warm sugar cookies.

He tells me my tummy "smell like candy."

He wakes me with a tap on the nose and declares the following random declarations in one breath: "Uncle Andy loves noodles. I love pah-corn ("popcorn") . . . Three! Where is a bucket?"

He says he wants to wear a shirt "with short arm pants" (sleeves).

He often laughs in his sleep, a tiny giggle that erupts into a hearty laugh. Adorable!

He thinks the billions of wood chips on the playground are "mon-eys." Jams his pockets full of handfuls to "get gumball candies" at the store.

When things don't go right, he shakes his head and says, "Oh, gawd."

When we leave the garage, he gets to push the open-and-close button, elated, "I in charge of the *garge*." *Garge* is catching on in the 'hood now—all the neighborhood kids call their garage *garge*—the neighbors even have a *garge* sale, to Oscar's delight.

Oscar looked up at me while I was doing the dishes and said to me, "You lovely, Momma."

The precious and unique way he runs, with arms paddling high at his sides and his scrumptious, chubby cheeks jiggling with each pattering step, yelling proudly, "I running!"

I almost cannot bear the overwhelming rush of love I feel when I gaze at him sleeping so sweetly. The wet lips slightly agape, deep sonorous breaths that reveal a fleeting passage into peace. The smell of his warm head after a nap is like an elixir for all my worries or stresses. To watch him delightfully gobble a jelly bean, the lip smacking and wet chewy nibbles—no other single person on earth has ever been so damn adorable to watch doing *anything*. Somehow one's child makes farting, chewing, sneezing, and a dribbly runny nose downright charming and intoxicatingly cute. Instantly the irksome endless chanting of his, "No! No," at every given option and the increasing refusals to take a bubble bath or even put on shoes is washed away with one adorably delightful hiccup. This boy hiccups so much it's a regular riot. He thinks it's just so much fun and, with the four freckles he has discovered, he thinks himself quite the chosen one to be so fortunate as to have "freckas and h'cups." Pardon my language, *but you live for that shit as a parent.*

Telling anyone who will listen and even those that won't. I have even fallen victim to discussing the unthinkable—potty training. It's surreal, really. Imagine trying to conquer this skill all over again. *Indeed,* it's not going very well—after years of never giving this process the slightest thought, I am now very much held hostage by this surprisingly frustrating task. Frankly, I am starting to become very much convinced that Oscar will never be toilet trained and I will be buying diapers all my life and swaddling this stubborn boy as he sets off on his prom night.

Hilariously, after buying every book, guide, and potty, I thought, *as I always naively do,* "OK, here we go, let's knock this out and move on to the next hurdle and task." I found myself skipping over the chapters in the potty-training book that seemed exceptionally long and unnecessary—"Anger Management Techniques" and "Controlling Your Emotions"—a barrage of suggested methods to keep calm as the potty-training parent. I was like, "Hello, what the hell, it's the kid's

job, and thus their own study in frustration, right? Why would *I* need
to be searching for ways to keep *my* cool? How weird."

Day 3 of opting for the "gentle method" of simply introducing the
potty for play and discovery while child plays diaper-free and gets ac-
quainted with his body—I hear Oscar chirping with euphoria, joy-
fully announcing, "I naked!" dashing about the bedroom while I take
all of 2.3 seconds to go and grab a polo shirt for him and turn back to
see him scooting out the door laying eggs of the poop variety, one . . .
two . . . three! They scatter behind him as he runs off.

"Oscar!" I yell out of autoresponse, which results in sending him
spinning around and running back to me, running *back* over one . . .
two . . . three poops, grinding them deeply into the champagne-
colored carpet while simultaneously seeping through his toes as he
tracks the new "poop-paint" in perfect footprints five steps up to me.
Motherf%&&$r!

Okay, I get it now. The calming bits of wisdom make sense and
would indeed be helpful as I am flipping out thinking, surely, in a
court of law I would get a reduced sentence for tossing him into the
yard by one of those stinky toes.

Day 4 was also a trial in keeping unruffled. As I was following the
rules of letting Oscar run around diaper-free (to ensure he under-
stands that the trickle of pee is coming out of his "privates"), he climbs
up onto my freshly appointed bed (with new splurgy 600-thread-count
linens), smiles at me, and pees in such quantity it can only be described
as an unbridled river, flowing all over bed, mattress, and staining the
seventeenth-century French cherry footboard. While skillfully funnel-
ing a self-created reservoir pouring onto that freshly steam-cleaned
champagne carpet.

Clever, clever me grabbed the first absorbent towel I could find
and soaked up the yellow wetness with my single remaining Yves

Delorme guest towel, normally reserved for pure aesthetic value on towel rod. Oscar falls into gleeful giggles as his momma does a dead-on cartoonlike frantic Speedy Gonzales cleanup skit. Dear god. This potty training is going to take forever, isn't it? And one of us is going to survive this . . . I'm not even guessing who—it's a draw at this point.

All that said, obviously, I am, make that we are, trashing this house as if it were a mission. The previous owners lived here eight years and left not so much as a fingerprint and within six months I have demolished everything from floor to ceiling—every corner has been nicked to an inch of its life by either Oscar careening around on one of his cars, trains, pedal cars, or rockets or, more likely, my dragging the high chair over from kitchen to Oscar's pee-viewing station at the bathroom door entrance. This is required because, if I try to dash to the loo for a pee for the decadent span of all of thirty-nine seconds, he wails for me, thus I must prep him for a full presentation of me peeing while he eats breakfast and makes comments like, "Momma pee, potty, to . . . toilet . . . make wa wa, Mommy!" This is less than my favorite recognition of my array of skills and efforts as a forty-year-old woman. Times like this I would marry any man, even the local troll, just to have him watch Oscar while I have a blessed private pee without stadiumlike seating, "theater in the round"–like critiques and reviews. Sheesh!

Of course, other times, everything falls into place and our lives seem full and rich. Like today, making a tomato–grilled cheese sandwich (with tomatoes from our garden, one more point for the USA) for Oscar just seemed like another task, when he called for me while giggling madly, "Momma, I tickle-eesh!" he announces, discovering he can tickle himself under the arm with his own hand. What a riot! There are so many unexpectedly charming and hilarious moments with this kid.

Walking along the neighborhood pond after dinner, his tiny warm hand in mine, he looks up at me. "Dance, Momma!" he chants, and we begin to dance among the pussy willows and tall grasses, taking turns swaying back and forth and going on tippy toe while holding hands. Both of us smiling from ear to ear, Oscar sings loudly, "Momma, *je t'aime,*" releasing my hand to clap wildly, as I realize that is exactly what I do whenever he says that wonderful phrase to me. With early fireflies darting in the light breeze and the last rays of golden evening light saturating every blade of grass and leaf to a faded hue, it all suddenly feels like I'm in a super 8mm family movie from the early seventies: hair in a high ponytail, wearing basic dumb khaki shorts, flip-flops, a tank top, and not a stitch of makeup. I feel like the way my mother *looked*— fresh, radiant, with that same internal light that she had all the days I remember. She was the guiding light, heart, anchor, and center of our lives. And now, I have come to understand, I am that for Oscar and it's no small honor to take for granted. It is humbling and my greatest gift.

POINTS FOR PARIS, AGAIN (LORD HELP ME!)

1. In France, virtually the entire population is literary, well read, and well spoken. There isn't a soul who doesn't know who Alexis de Tocqueville is or the year of the fall of the Bastille. Whereas in the USA, commonly known facts are much limited to sports teams' MVPs and where to get a cheap taco. Which makes me just shake my head and mutter, "Oh, bother," to quote my latest favorite protagonist, Winnie the Pooh.

2. In Europe, both college and attending university are free to all citizens. Sure, you pay two-thirds of your income in taxes, but you also get free health care. As I send off my enormous check

each month for my self-employed health insurance premium, I do tend to pause a moment on this subject and wince.

3. I miss the grandeur of the parks, fountains, museums, and city buildings. Christ, the *hôtel de ville* ("city hall") in Paris completely resembles a palace. In my hometown, it could be mistaken for a car wash. The architectural eye candy of Paris just lifts your spirits and exalts your soul—c'mon, it's hard to be too depressed sitting fountainside in the Tuileries with your back to the awe-inspiring Louvre, the shimmering lights of the Tour Eiffel sparkling like champagne to your right, the Arc de Triomphe majestically center stage and Place de la Concorde lying before you. (Had I never lived in Paris, perhaps this all wouldn't be like stabbing daggers to imagine. "Ignorance is bliss," as they say, and I can add to that, "experience and memories can be ROYALLY gutting.")

Chapter 20

*"We cannot fashion our children after
our desires, we must have them and
love them as God has given them to us."*

—JOHANN WOLFGANG VON GOETHE

My mental trauma about Paris versus staying put in the good ole USA has come to a head. Though I am still teetering on the fence about it, I have decided to put the house on the market and feel out the real possibility of returning to France. I know most families list their home with a conviction of wanting to sell, but as a single mother I haven't the luxury of having a copilot that hugs me and says, "Yes, we can *and should* move back, my darling. I will support you and make it happen." So, baby steps over here. The lingering question is, Do I just take the first offer and pack up and go, or do I take all advice on this matter and make a reconnaissance mission back to Paris ASAP to make bloody well sure this is the definitive right thing to do?

Lord knows I moved here with blind certainty and that's gone about as well as my clever self-mutilation haircut last year. Yep. You guessed it, inevitably and confusingly, the siren song of Paris, with all its perils, lures mother and child back to the City of Light and the legions of interested parties are lining up taking sides on the idea.

> *All for Us Staying*: family and neighbors
> *All for Us Returning to Paris*: Every friend I ever had, met, or knew . . .
> and every person I ever smiled at, walked past, met eyes, brushed
> past, or glimpsed at a distance, or so it would seem.

There is something almost disturbing in that all my friends are verging on adamant in their insistence I belong in Paris. It's like they can't and don't want to conceive I am anywhere else. It's a strange pressure.

Good lesson to have learned here—never be so judging of others as to where or how they want to live their life! Which brings me to an event that literally sent me into tears for days. I feel like the rug has been pulled out from under me and my little world is all off balance.

Backstory: Had a really great chat with Zola a couple weeks ago. I told her that I finally started having a babysitter come five hours a week so I could resume some time for working and also so that Oscar gains more independence (read, not so attached that mom can't leave room to get a glass of water). I expressed to Zola that, after much hemming and hawing—as she well knew—I was definitely, well, *sort of*, plotting Oscar and my returning to France. She was totally elated and instantly begged me to move to Saint Cloud where she, her new baby, and husband have moved to set up house.

Days later, she called all excited, having viewed an apartment in her building for us and made yet another very convincing PR push for the charms of Saint Cloud: the enchanting gardens, the many expats living there, and the surprisingly good buys on charming apartments. I was thrilled she was so supportive and we mused at how fun it would be to be neighbors again—this time as *mamans*! But I thought I'd better nip that hope in the bud, so I voiced that, being a single mother, I probably would stay in Paris so as to not be too isolated. She seemed quite deflated about it, but acknowledged it would be lonely and quiet compared with Paris *centre*. Along the way, I kind of admitted to her that I have been thinking maybe Gilbert is actually a possible potential love interest after all. (Which means I have, of course, envisioned us married and skiing in Gstaad with our children each Christmas. I do tend to get ahead of myself.) But truth is, I will need to shelve the solitude and date again, and single in Saint Cloud would be like trying to find a drag queen at a National Rifle Association meeting.

Then a week later, Zola rang one morning; she seemed tense and short-tempered but oddly passively aggressive about it. She made an odd comment, "I told my friend you were still breast-feeding and she said that's disgusting." (*BTW—the friend isn't a mom.*) I thought it not terribly kind but brushed it off without a word since she has never been anything but lovely to me and to Oscar. Then during the next call, more of that tension and this: "Another friend saw your paintings at the gallery and thinks they're terrible."

What the hell? But I still let it go since it seemed very possible people would be unkind about my work OR the fact that I'm still nursing. Understandable even if it did "hurt my feelers," as I used to put it as a kid. But the two comments together nagged at me, as so odd and out of character for her to relay, so I rang her the following day.

"Zola, I am sort of bothered that you chose to pass on these negative comments and critiques of your friends. What good does it really do me to hear those things, anyway? You know I endlessly struggle to do things as well as I can and I'm only doing my best. So, why the cutting remarks?" I say, remembering a mutual friend of ours who told me he had seen her pregnant and remarked she looked like hell, but I tweaked it to "she's never looked better" in my recount to her. That's what friends do—rally spirits!

She paused and then said, "I guess for some time now I have held some anger against you and your choices and, despite myself, they are creeping out."

"Anger? What the hell for?" I plead, racking my brain for possible events or reasons I could've made her upset. Was it that I couldn't help very much with the wedding?

Another agonizing pause on her end. "Frankly, what I have to say to you may ruin our friendship," she replies, in serious tones.

"What??! What are you talking about?" I cry, staggered by such heavy and shocking news.

"I can't say just now. I have to put the baby to bed. Speak to you soon, I guess." And the line goes dead.

As does my soul. Seriously. I am startled and stunned beyond words. Blindsided and completely at a loss what in the world she could need or want to say that she believes would destroy our deep friendship. Like a dumped girlfriend, I call her back insantly.

Her phone is off. I fire off a panicky e-mail asking her what's going on. Is she okay? What on earth did I do? I can hardly cope through the next twenty-eight hours as she refused to answer phone or e-mails. Which is really heartless of her as she can clearly tell that I am at wit's end and suffering.

She finally takes my call the next evening, and as my heart races I beg, "This is so unfair, why would you lay that bomb on me? What do you have to say that could end our friendship? I've been going out of my mind trying to figure out how I could've upset or offended you!"

"Kiki, perhaps it's partly due to my recent return to Catholicism for Roland's baptism . . . but I just feel the way in which you chose to become a mother is wrong."

My gigantic gasp almost inhales the phone and surrounding furniture.

She continues, "And I think this 'still nursing' thing is really off the charts. And cosleeping? I mean, really? What's with Attachment Parenting? Are you going to homeschool Oscar as well?"

"No, I have no intention of homeschooling. Jesus, there is no connection to nursing and homeschooling. How and why are you linking the two? I think you can argue that, unquestionably, the whole nursing experience is a marvelous and special time. Every baby needs this just once in his life, and I have had the privilege of meeting this need of Oscar's. He has and will continue to benefit in so many ways from it—higher IQ, immunities, nutrition, comfort, sense of security . . ." I pause, as her previous words finally penetrate and strike me at my depths. "Wait . . . what are you saying to me? Being a mother alone is wrong? And you don't even know or have ever read anything about Attachment Parenting, so how can you judge it? Arm yourself with the facts before you attack, girl," I say, thinking she is so lucky I am not slamming her with the fact I know she has read exactly ten books in her whole life. Eight of which were self-help dating manuals. Okay, I'm pissed now. Gloves off.

"Come on, Kiki, do you really think you're ever going to get a man in your life when you're sharing your bed with your baby? And to that, don't go thinking that Frenchmen are going to be so keen on you and Oscar as a package. They aren't. And you can't even afford to live in Paris again, so what are you doing? And are you drinking?" she shot at me in an AK-47 onslaught attack of venomous words.

"Holy Christ, what is your issue? Trust me, after eight years living in Paris, I know about Frenchmen, Paris, and all about finances. Hey, let's remember, *I* don't have a penny of debt!" SLAM. I did say, "Gloves off." "And who are you to be the judging, all-knowing, mother superior? What is your gig? What did you just say? You think my choice of going it alone with Oscar is wrong?" I demand, feeling my throat clinch at the sheer pain of arguing these issues with who I thought was my best friend.

"Yes . . . I don't like the way you have become a mother. It's selfish," she says, almost enjoying it.

"You know what? This is all madness and totally harsh of you. I don't know if it's religion talking or you have the baby blues or something, but there is no way I can forgive you for this nasty deluge of evil and critical comments. You have been a mother all of three months and now you are *the expert*? Please. I will never speak to you again!" And I slammed down the phone and burst into tears. My best friend just turned on me, with such blazing viciousness and hostility. How shocking. How terribly cruel. Zola and I are—make that *were*—best friends for years; she is the godmother of my darling boy, she was present at his birth, she was always so incredibly thoughtful and supportive. What's going on?

I felt like the air had been sucked out of my lungs for days and kept running it all by family and friends looking for answers. The general consensus from those that knew her was that anyone who lashes out so inexplicably is either very unhappy or jealous or both. I thought she was happy, but who knows. She never does divulge her interior life anymore. And yes, I always felt her quiet jealousy but she handled it well with humor when it sprung forth. Perhaps the big issue is that she and her husband had to move out of Paris (to afford to have a family) and it makes her jealous/angry that *I* would go back to fabulous

St. Germain—where she no longer can be. Which is still nowhere near enough justification for this betrayal. Not to mention, I thought we outgrew all that with the maturity that motherhood brings. Still, this all doesn't make sense. Is it that she has beome a religious zealot now and believes herself to be an authority on all issues? *Good god,* indeed!

After some days passed and the shock that she wasn't ringing back with heaping apologies wore off, I came to understand that motherhood changes everyone. And I guess some for the worse. It seems shocking that when Zola became a new momma, she didn't experience the healthy revelation that so many of us do—that you can't act like an expert at mothering as we are SO new to it, evolving, adjusting, and learning as each month passes while doing what we believe is best. I just can't wrap my head around her need to be so harsh and condemning. It was so out of left field; had she given me some hints that she was in diametric opposition to my decisions, I think we could've sorted it out. Hell, as a dear friend, you don't have to yes me to death and agree with my every action, just be honest and open-minded, not all grandiose as she was. Hey, I may play with pretension and act the snob, but I know—*and everyone knows*—I am the same as the locals here: same upbringing, schooling, core values, hopes for my child, and current zip code. So, as I sputter on, it's just my silly exorcising the demons of elitism that have held me captive for decades.

Ironically, a few days after that, the so-called friend of hers that "hated" my paintings, found me on Facebook and wrote me a note saying he adored them and was a "fan." The plot thickens. Did Zola make that story up, after he had told her that he, in fact, liked my work? How screwed up is this girl now? Fuck. I have lost a dear friend. And I don't have many. And she was one of two, maybe three, people that I poured my heart out to and this is the woman I thought I knew? Such a disappointment.

This too shall pass. Still, I keep finding so many gifts, photos, and cards she gave me over the years and they make me feel so sad. Poop. Time to suck that up, as Oscar's my daily anti-depressant with his feet like those of soft baby rabbits—I could just caress them endlessly. I treasure his adorable chirping and darling budding vocabulary; with a storm bursting at dawn, he woke and in a small whisper said, "Thunder guy, he busy. Loud and rain." Yep. Nothing sweeps away the storm clouds of one's mind like a tiny voice of pure awe and delight.

So, with this new FOR SALE sign jammed into the front yard, there's much to be done. As in, making light of it with my nervous family, "You are not really moving back, are you?!" "Just thought I'd see if I could flip the house and downscale, perhaps." Sort of true, since if we move back to Paris, I would have to sell half of all that I own: all the new yard furniture, washer/dryer, garden supplies, my bike with child chariot, all Oscar's trikes, Big Wheels, red wagons, train sets, and motorized cars. Really, back to Paris means back to the meagerest belongings, since I'd surely be leaving the three thousand square feet for seven hundred, if I am lucky! *The poor boy would be in a tiny room with only a Matchbox car and a pillow.*

FYI: Prepping for house showings with a toddler at home is a ludicrous exercise in futility. No wonder families stay put for decades— they wanted to move but couldn't get the house together to show it! It's freaking next to impossible as a single mother of a hyper, spinning top of a tot to clean, polish, vacuum, and dust to perfection a three-level house at the drop of a hat. In record time, the real estate agent has made my lifelong black list for continually calling with (essentially) the following: "I know it's last minute, Kiki, but we have a 'sure thing' buyer that's just in town for seven minutes, with cash literally falling out of his pockets and pen at the ready. Can we stop by in three minutes to view your undergarments hanging from the shower rod?" I mean, really. There is never a call asking for next week; it's always during Oscar's nap time or "the client is in the neighborhood, awaiting access if you say okay." *I want to say, "Go, f *&@ yourself," but visions of Oscar sailing antique wood boats in the Tuileries fountain sweeps into my mind and I find myself agreeing and leaping into action.* With Oscar heavily into his *deconstructivist period,* when one room is done and I'm zipping on to the next with my bucket full of cleaning supplies, he blows through and reacquaints all the books with the floor and all the bed linens with the bathtub. *Fouck.*

Guarantee: one floor free of fingerprints all over the windows means the other now looks like someone's been dusting for fingerprints. This is hell. And I am embarrassed to admit, I'm becoming a crabby bitch to him in these cleaning sprees and he just looks at me with a sad face, "Why can't I throw all my toys through the stair gate down two flights—you thought it was hilarious yesterday, Mom?" By my example, he is currently confused as to why, *sometimes,* I am such an obsessive-compulsive clean freak, losing it when crumbs hit the floor (showing days) and then letting clothes pile up on the closet floor (regular life). Not to mention, he has started to acquire a similar sense of frenzy to be uber-clean, demanding a "na-kin" when a tiny drip of yogurt gets on his finger and sneaking baby wipes to "polish" the diaper table. I guess the gifts of a toy vacuum, mop, and kitchen were a bad idea, since he is frigging obsessed with them and, if he could speak in coherent sentences, would probably say his life dream is to become a maid. Oh la la. Guilt, guilt, guilt. It's inescapable as a mother. You feel you just wake with a Holster-O-Guilt already affixed to your hip: Self-Doubt Wipes in this pouch, Maximum Panic Spray and Constant Worry in that loop—it all goes with the title Mom.

Toss in that my wanting to move back to Paris is now so real, I'm weighed down, feeling seriously foolish and so selfish. Shouldn't I be putting *his* total well-being first, always and forever? In the daily life of children—*a world where consistency is the law*—I'm aware this Mission Paris Return COULD be hell for him. If we leave Wisconsin, he will lose every damn familiar person, object, and sense of home.

But then again, wouldn't growing up in Paris be a total gift to a child? Wouldn't moving back to France be something he thanks me for when he is older and we return to visit Wisconsin and he looks around at all the dumb malls and fat folks and says, *"Merci maman, je deteste cette ville! Ce n'est pas interessant, pas du tout—sauf la famille."*

When I hash this out with Kathy or David on the phone, they always say to me (as no one does here in Wisconsin, I might add), "Living in the suburbs is just not you. You've tried it now and Oscar has reaped important bonds and love, but raise a city kid. They will be savvier and in this complex world there is no benefit in stacking the cards against a child by not making available culture, diversity, and the best education."

SPEAKING OF IDENTITY . . . WHAT MAKES A GOOD MOTHER?

Everyone always says, Happy Mom=Happy Child, so why am I still feeling it's self-centered to want to leave here? I want to be happy. Will I be deemed a selfish monster for taking Oscar back to Paris as I am going out of my mind here and, let's be serious, I know I can't find a father for him here. All the same, I already devote every minute of the day to him, so can we cancel out the title of my being a TOTAL selfish monster?

Foook! I am not some malcontent that's just never happy wherever I am; I loved NYC and Paris madly right up until day of departure. I am just not feeling it here. I do love a lot about being here—falling asleep to the sound of owls, frogs in the pond, crickets, and the like is sublime. And just as divine is waking to birds chirping wildly as you loll in bed listening to the wind rustle the leaves in the tree tops, and yet I miss the dynamic of a city as beautiful and compelling as Paris.

But there is so much to consider with this returning to Paris idea. It hit me—will my French even come back? My daily speaking to Oscar in French (to give him that bilingual edge) hasn't really been tested as we are both at age two French. Not to mention, I can hardly find the right English words for things now! I find myself slipping into Oscar-speak even with adults: "The coffee maker is *brake-a*, so I have to put it in the *garb-a*." Scaling the huge hurdles one must do all *en français* to get an apartment and set it up is a sea of work (tide against you, undertow guaranteed to drag you out to the reef of insanity) and I can hardly remember the French word for landlord. Ei yi yi, what am I thinking? Is this total lunacy? Why can't I chill out and just be happy here? Damnit, my take on everything is skewed after living in France. Expats on that message board in Paris warned me of this: "Home doesn't feel like 'home' again; you're split and straddling two cultures and identities ever after."

Let's talk about guilt for a second here. I obviously can't speak about previous generations, but it does seem to me that we mothers of this modern age have it great in many ways *and shit in others. Par example,* when I was still in Paris, dashing about doing errands, with Oscar in my Baby Bjorn, many a woman over sixty years old would stop and mention to me "Oh, how I wish we had those pouches in our day!" and I realized, right, they had to carry their kids everywhere or pop them in those old strollers; baby at a distance all day. But then again mothers today are saddled with a different set of issues, such as—depending on where you live—it's either frowned upon to be a working mom OR frowned upon to be a stay-at-home mom. I know a woman here in Wisconsin who is the stay-at-home mom of three (which is celebrated and so normal here), but when she moved to Denmark—where they are very child-friendly, mind you—she was looked upon as a slug not pulling her own weight. Ouch.

All I know is being a stay-at-home mom is a struggle of my identity—the loss of freedom, the stealthlike way it sneaks up on you and you realize you *do* mourn a little of who you used to be. For me, I spent my whole life becoming a person who I felt could be independent, savvy, and (occasionally mistaken for) sexy, well spoken, and well read, and now I rarely feel even remotely pretty, witty, or intriguing. Because, well . . . I am not. Unquestionably, what and who you used to feel like alters whether you want it to or not.

You get the feeling of wholeness and purpose from being a mother but you lose a lot of things you didn't think you would lose or *miss*.

1. I thought I'd be able to date by the time Oscar was two. Not happening. Though the e-mail correspondence with Gilbert is picking up speed. We have been exploring each other's passions, sharing quotes and excerpts from our favorite books, and discussing artists that move us with their compelling work. Frenchmen are true professionals at seducing through words and expressions. I know literally dozens of women who after even the shortest affairs during vacations in France cannot get over the dizzying intrigue of a Frenchman's charm. The crashing dullness of a line like, "Wanna come over and eat?" of an American man feels like a slap in the face after *les charmes d'amour des Pepé Le Pews*.

2. I thought I would be cooler (read, could actually do it) with leaving him with a sitter to attend a rare art event or drinks with a friend.

3. I thought I wouldn't be this tired. Strangely, it's easier to wake up at 6:00 A.M. with your baby than it is at 10:00 P.M. to endure a tantrum. Sometimes you're so drained, your whole being is so exhausted by *being on call,* you just want to fall into bed, not wanting to even brush your teeth and certainly feeling too tired to fight your toddler to brush his. BTW, what a new appreciation this gives you for your own mother! And for mothers you know with a gaggle of kids! I'm in awe of my neighbor Jessica and her cool-headed, tender love for her four clever kids that are just spilling over with curiosity, energy, and bouncing off the walls. I must utter, "I *don't* know how you do it!" at least once every day to her.

4. I thought I would be better at keeping my cool. I have lost it sometimes—in the name of safety when Oscar climbed up to a stand in his high chair for the tenth time that day, teetering five feet above the tile floor that would turn his brain into stew if he fell, all done while I turn around to grab a pan off the stove. I just had it with yelling "NO!" and getting a giggle and sly smirk as my reply. I gave a brusque tap to the top of his head and he instantly wailed. I fell apart and cried then, he cried more, and it was a massive failure all around. I never thought I'd do anything remotely aggressive but it is just maddening trying to train your child to be safe and see he isn't getting it and you are at a total loss about what to do next. Grrrr . . . you get it! Wee bit of coping advice—I have learned that you simply can't be angry at your child when you see him naked. Children are so darlingly scrumptious and sweet with their chubby little soft parts and dimpled bottoms, you're instantly the most loving and adoring mom on earth. So, anytime I start to get frustrated or mad, I either undress or imagine my wild man *sans*

vêtements et voilà, I am laying kisses on that butter-smooth brow that seconds ago I wanted to shout at.

5. I thought I'd be a Supermom. But a Supermom wouldn't serve prepared frozen food, would she? A Supermom wouldn't say "shut up" under her breath when her child is shrieking demands, "I want dat!" for the hundredth time at the hundredth toy in a store. I guess I have to come to terms with the fact that I'm not a Supermom.

6. I thought I would excel at maintaining an equilibrium of discipline and indulging my child. It's impossible and I have had it with trying to be perfect all the time. As if letting your child wear a pair of mismatched socks is really going to make a difference in the long haul. Come on. After months of changing Oscar's shirts after every meal, enough already. So he has a tiny spot of chocolate on his collar while he plays with the neighbor kids outside, fine. Where does one strike a balance, when you feel guilty if you give your child chocolates *and you feel like a crappy-meany if you don't.* You feel like you're spoiling him if you give him that unnecessary toy or snack he begs for and like a crappy-meany when you refuse him. Sometimes it feels like you just can't win. And can't win what, exactly? Your own approval and peace at the job you're doing, I think is that answer. Don't you wish you could be given a tiny peek into your child's future life and see he is a happy, kind, and well-adjusted adult with a generous heart and kind actions? Wouldn't that be so fulfilling and enable us to come back to the present and breathe easier? As in, just toss out the stress and worry that gnaws at your daily life and just be able to enjoy every second of the good.

PRO PARIS POINTS

1. Ironically, this old desire of having a yard has now slid onto the opposing list to a negative! I am so over mowing the lawn every week. As a single parent, I have no time at all for this task, and it's just tricky as hell with a toddler since I have to wait until he falls deeply into a nap, then dash out, pushing the ugly beast of a mower, dash back every ten minutes to make sure Oscar hasn't awoken and not found me there, dash back out again, sweat buckets, etc. Ugh. I am now considering letting the grass grow wildly and calling it my own prairie restoration project.

2. In France, there is none of this crazily intense competitiveness that is almost national religion in the USA. French people are quite content with their little lives, small apartments, believing their bodies are made for eating healthy fresh food and for making love, not as a vehicle for attention and uber-fitness punishment. "Go for the burn" only applies to a crackly toasted crème brûlée. The culture in Europe simply has a more accepting take on everyone contributing and utilizing their varied skills, talents, situations, and outcomes. In the USA, just look at the popular TV shows: *Biggest Loser*, *Design Stars*, *America's Next Top Model*, *Dancing with the Stars*, *The Bachelor*, *American Idol*, *Top Chef*, *Hell's Kitchen*, even *Cupcake Wars*, for god's sake! It's all about winning, being the champion, the best, the fittest, wealthiest—the most everything. And the celebrity worship here is just bonkers—what the hell has Kim Kardashian ever done to warrant praise or applause?

Chapter 21

"You are worried about seeing him spend his early years in doing nothing. What! Is it nothing to be happy? Nothing to skip, play, and run around all day long? Never in his life will he be so busy again."

—Jean-Jacques Rousseau

Paris

Shockingly, for once, I took the smart road and hatched a Fool Proof Master Plan. In my endless musings that I simply must return to Paris for my sanity and to offer Oscar a really special cultural upbringing, I strangled off my impulse to operate on my standard "I am outta here!" Fool-at-Hand-Plan of just continuing the house showings, accepting an offer, followed by immediate packing and moving. Sure, you can do that, as I did *as a single person,* but when you look at your child and see he is thrown off-kilter by your simply changing juice box brands, you sure as hell better slow down and operate with sensitivity and focused preparation, not to mention reality! Reality! Something, I readily admit, that I held at bay or made up as I went along until I gave birth to this dream of a child.

Master plan being, don't sell house without an exploratory exercise. Off we would go to visit and fall in love with Paris all over again, get back a smattering of the life I once had, and give my son a truly unique and rich childhood. This expensive operation was all to ensure that moving back was, indeed, the intelligent, if difficult, next step. I'm old enough to know people and places are romanticized over time and absence and there had to be an unequivocal certainty to the next move. So, I spent a month looking for a killer deal on flights on the Internet with an eye to the euro-dollar exchange and booked two economy seats on our Paris Reconnaissance Mission. And let's just state that it sucks *hard* to have to buy a seat for a two-year-old when he will surely spend most of the flight crawling all over your lap. Still, it felt smart and right *and* thrilling to imagine being in Paris again rather than just playing my Edith Piaf CDs and yearning for it like the perfect lover that got away.

So, I also book online an apartment in the fifth arrondissement, since I think you can't stay with friends when you have a toddler that likes to wake at 6:00 A.M. And, frankly, if I am going to really gauge how it would be to be living there, I better do it in an area I can actually afford, in an apartment *of that budget,* and do an authentic trial run.

Truth in my heart and mind—this is all just an act of reassurance and a transitional period to see what the whole deal will be like, so when I do relocate to Paris I'm not in the slightest way blindsided. And for Oscar, I need more than anything to spend two weeks away from my world here full of family, daily ease, and comfort and see how *he* handles it. If he just aches for family and familiarity, then the whole idea is just a wash.

For him, I would do anything.

A week to go before departure. I rang my real estate agent in town, "Let's do that big open house you've been pushing for, etc. March all the clients you wish through the house while I am away." So, if all goes well in Paris and Wisconsin, we will have a fabulous time in France and return to an offer on the house and off we go! (No, my raging optimism hasn't dissipated despite innumerable well-grounded reasons to do so.)

With a day to go before departure, I am seriously starting to get nervous . . . about *everything*. Flying with a toddler more often than not can be a total and complete nightmare. Lugging two huge pieces of luggage and a stroller *and* a child all by myself through two flights and two countries? Seven time zones and jet lag and *fook,* this is going to eat up my entire savings for the year, but what the hell? The alternative is staying here, dreaming, and missing Paris every day as I have been doing and not living fully present as I keep holding on to Paris as the answer to everything. I am compelled and, more than that, they are nonrefundable tickets!

Day of flight, my stepfather sends us on our way, with a massive bag of new toys and games for Oscar to entertain himself on the flight and kind wishes of "Have a great time but come back!" I know all my family feels that I actually won't come back! And I have even arranged a few things at home on the off chance I do decide to just stay and rip up the return tickets. At this point in my life, I know I am capable of doing anything, so one must do a few minor tasks to prep for this!

Amazingly, Oscar is fabulous on the flight, lo-oo-ving the seat belt that I have claimed we have to put on "to go fast," and he is even truly charmed by the terrible airplane food and the attentive stewardesses. Side note—I always used to fly Air France, since it's more posh; stewards are fun, gay, and chic; stewardesses are *très françaises* and snob; and there's free champagne, better food, and interiors. But this time I opted for American Airlines, because of other concerns (*as in $1,000 cheaper*), and was so glad I did; the flight team were all angels, so chatty and nice, offering up help with Oscar and zillions of compliments for his fine behavior. I should've seen this as symbolic at the time, but didn't. Was too busy losing Chanel sunglasses on plane and trying to anticipate the next two weeks. Funnily, losing the glasses would've killed the "pre-mom" me, since there is no way I can financially replace them, wouldn't ever be that carefree with money again, but when I discovered they were gone forever, I didn't care.

Arriving at Charles de Gaulle airport, I thought I would feel that old wave pass over me that I used to love—I'm home . . . listen to everyone speaking French . . . they all look so European and interesting . . . not like at the Wisconsin airport, where people are in sweats and tipping the scales at four hundred pounds wearing "Cow Tipper and Proud of It!" tee shirts. Now in CDG, I just felt like, "Fuck, it's so hectic and hot and there are like eighty million people smashing into Oscar's stroller and slamming into me. There is nothing cool or enjoyable about this!" Getting all the luggage on the huge trolley and pushing it with one hand and the stroller with another was like an absurd joke—both careening in opposing directions and everyone just merrily watching. Not a single offer to help. Crazy! Good Samaritans apparently are held in captivity in France or beheaded since I never found a one!

After the rip-roaring fast—as in hope you have made a will—taxi ride into Paris in the early morning traffic, everyone driving with a death wish and attitude to match, I'm carsick like hell but trying to put it out of my mind as like many moments as a single mother, it's all up to you to pull it off and there's no backup plan, so carry on! *Garf.* Noteworthy—I have to say, after a year in the midwestern suburbs, where a neighbor's lawn mower seems evil-loud and a popsicle stick on the ground seems an eyesore, to drive back into Paris through the northern arrondissements is jarring. It's like sad, filthy, kinda dangerous, in a word, grim, and not the tiny sleek Paris I knew . . . *and rarely left.*

We finally get to the Paris I recognize and I spot the Centre Pompidou on the right side. "Cool building, huh, Oscar? Great exhibits . . . I love their collection," I murmur, as I notice the line for the exhibit is, I kid you not, five blocks long; literally hundreds and hundreds of people waiting in a nonmoving line in the raging hot sun. Heat+long line=what hell! I am gobsmacked. Oh right, I can remember, going three times to try to see the landmark Matisse-Picasso exhibit and the freaking line was so long that after hours and hours of attempting to endure, I finally had to just give up the idea, buy the catalogue, and see it that way. Culture? Sure, if you can get the fuck in. And to try doing that with a toddler? Pfff.

Finally, the taxi driver finds rue des Bernadins, where my rental apartment is located. Cool surprise #1: it's just across the Seine and about two hundred feet from Notre Dame. That's fab. Notre Dame is precious to me, my mother took me there at age sixteen, and we sat for hours in shared awe and beautiful silence, holding hands and just soaking it in. Miss her so, she too adored Paris madly.

Despite my amazing timing of arriving at 11:00 A.M., just as I hoped and planned, no one is waiting in front of the building to give me the keys, as we had prearranged. That's France for you! Driver lets me dump everything on the street as I also fumble around to scrounge up a fare to the tune of 80 euros (when all is said and done with the fees for bags, stroller, and kid's seat). That's almost $120 and we haven't even got in our flat!

Eventually, after being visually assessed—not so favorably—by many passersby (as if I am a tourist . . . uchh, I am, I guess), a wackily dressed gay French man from the apartment rental company appears to hand over the keys. For some reason, he opens with *"Bonjour,* you know this meeting is on a holiday, thus an additional fee of 50 euros is incurred. I would like it paid in cash, now." Additionally, he is just the definition of passive-aggressively enraged to see he is pretty much *obliged* to help me carry my massive bags up to the flat. "Why of course I can help you with the bags," he says, scowling and snorting about the weight. Need it be said, this isn't the fun "triumphant return" welcome I was hoping for. Whatever.

The flat is in a nice enough building, a stone eighteenth-century with wrought-iron balconies, but our apartment is one of those set back in the courtyard, which is about another one hundred fifty feet. The strain of flying, stress, and keeping Oscar happy has me witless and exhausted, so when I learn the apartment is also not on the second floor as promised but on the fifth, as in five huge staircases to haul up and down all the time, I flip into bitch mode and skip tipping my nut job key holder. I tell him I have no more cash and will pay him the 50 euros when I hand over the keys when we leave. He announces a standard French line: "This just isn't done, madame." Yeah, well tough. The old NYC me has reemerged after a long dormancy in the friendly Midwest, a rebirth of "don't fuck with me" girl has arrived and she wasn't a-kiddin' round. So, good luck with that request, buddy.

The door opens to the apartment and, yes, all the components to the images I saw on the Web *are there* but jammed into a tiny dark room with a leaky exposed pipe above, dripping water onto the scuffed floors. I'm *so* disappointed. This small apartment, this area, this is what I could afford, to be honest, if I moved back. In Wisconsin, a three-thousand-square-foot home that's very lovely—and here, a six-hundred-square-foot old broken-down apartment with no AC, chipped plaster, no dryer, a toilet that would be spacious only to a rodent, and only a shower—what the f@ * k! It advertised a bath. Oscar only takes baths, showers terrify him. Ohmigod . . . maybe he will surprise me though again here and be a sport since he is being just the best little traveler ever and is already leaping about pointing to the CD player, "Music!! Pay pay ("play")."

I am overwhelmed. I try to tell myself it's because I am so tired, didn't sleep a wink on the plane since was hyper-vigilant to ensure I didn't move and wake angelic Oscar splayed across my lap. It all feels so small and dingy. Just a year back in the USA—a world of stainless steel, matching washers/dryers set in their own room, and rooms to run around with a toddler—this feels cramped, crappy, and hot. Did I mention the heat?! It's 35 degrees Celsius, which I think is like 94-ish Fahrenheit and I remember too well, *no one,* save Karl Lagerfeld, has an apartment with AC, or *climatisé.* I recall the hellish August 2004, where it was so hot for thirty-eight days on end that to go outside was to feel like putting one's mouth to a bus exhaust pipe, and I had to sleep with liter bottles frozen with ice, so as not to die of the heat. *Fook.* Hellish heat makes everything that much harder. People of France, you have Facebook, microwave ovens, and even Segway scooters in the Tuileries, get some AC and dryers!

I unpack the legions of luggage, laughing slightly that there is hardly anything here that I actually currently wear. It's just a trove of my old chic designer clothes and shoes that I hold in my memories of my Paris clothes and a heap of new Ralph Lauren kids' clothes that I splurged on for Oscar so he would look like a chic *petit jeune homme* to boot. I quickly realize I don't feel like putting on a chiffon sundress with straps as thin as hair. I'm probably going to spend days taking Oscar to parks and playgrounds and I'm not up for wearing the beaded mules and the array of strapless dresses. What the hell was I thinking?

Oscar zips about, opening cupboards in the shoe box of a kitchen. It is actually about as big as his Fisher-Price toy kitchen, which may be why he thinks it is his "cooking" as he calls it. Just as I'm thinking this, he swings open a low cupboard—that is hanging by one hinge— drags out numerous bottles of poisonous cleaners (though they clearly haven't been used in the flat anytime recently). MOM PANIC— lunging to this disaster in waiting, I sweep in and in one gesture, move all bottles and sprays to safety, while accidently managing to knock down a set of crappy pans that were lodged on top of the rickety cupboard. Oscar roars with laughter. (Somehow when he first knocked over some large object that made a big scary clatter, seeing he was about to shriek with guilt and fear, I made off like it was hilarious so as to nip that meltdown, but now, of course, my ever-clever example has him throwing muffin tins and teapots around and laughing like a hyena. Lovely.)

Gig is, I rented an apartment so I could cook for us. Experience that unique pleasure to make genuine French cooking with the spectacularly fresh offerings of the street markets and now, looking at this shit kitchen with its dirty hodgepodge of old appliances and a dish sponge that looks like it was from 1968, I am freaking out. Is this going to be fun? This is like camping in a trailer, not even a double-wide. Just then I hear Oscar yelling from the living room, "op-en . . . open!" and I glance over to see he is, indeed, opening the large double windows and scaling the wrought-iron barrier (crumbling under his weight—since it was constructed in the start of the Iron Age, it appears) with a leg shooting up toward the top.

"NO!!!!!" I scream, envisioning my worst and frequent nightmare of his plunging out a window. *Fook!* Again, we are five minutes into this and it is torture—dangerous, old, scary hell. Okay, I am just exhausted, we have got to nap and get our bearings. I used to rock this city, and living here was a dream realized, everything will come together with some sleep and a fresh perspective.

Post-nap and first 3 days. First day: it wasn't all that wise to arrive on a holiday, since the streets of St. Germain were so flooded with people you could barely inch along, let alone with a stroller. I guess the year in the Midwest where people are wildly polite and helpful has rewired my brain since now I just find everyone so rude, slamming into Oscar's stroller, not a soul offering to help me carry the damn thing up a stone staircase or curb. It's just staggering what a freaking pain it is to get around a city with a toddler—nowhere to change a diaper, nowhere to duck into when a downpour descends as they do, no exaggeration, four to five times a day this time of year.

It was a virtual battle to make it to my old fave grocery store, Monoprix, for general supplies, as there is not a shopping cart with a child seat to be found! So I am pushing Oscar in his stroller with one hand and carrying grocery basket with the other, filling it with just a box of diapers, wine (it's as imperative as diapers!), and some milk, as it's already too heavy to carry anything else, and then we had to wait in one of those classic long French lines to even pay and check out. Forty minutes later, with about one-twentieth of the things I needed to buy to stock fridge, I have to set off for "home," eleven blocks away, negotiating the labyrinth of traffic and crowds, and then arrive, finally, to *my* apartment building, where I must scrounge out the door code from a note card, push door weighing roughly two hundred pounds (people passing as I struggle to make the microsecond time frame of "door opening possible buzz," while I straddle to keep door open with a foot, which scrapes over my sandals and saws toes to the bone, simultaneously trying to push Oscar's stroller in and up over the step while wheels get stuck and won't pivot to allow forward movement, swearing under breath as I right the bag of groceries pinched in that door that's so determined not to stay open, finally enter sub-foyer and have to scramble to find and take out keys from purse slung on crook of arm now, as bending over, new sunglasses tip and fall on floor, Oscar chanting, "Whoopsie daisy" twelve times as I turn keys in lock and push open the second door as woman with chignon— *obviously a building tenant*—stands aside watching but only offering a scowl. I smile through clenched teeth as loath to appear the haggard mess I so clearly am—she *blows* me off and *blows* past. Frenchwomen suck! (And BTW, not *literally* I'm told. Redeeming features must be great accent, tolerance, skills at staying thin, and decorating self and home.)

Now, in actual building of residence, I must get Oscar out of his stroller, kick (with my raw, bloody toes) the release latch to close stroller, but I forgot to take grocery bag from stroller handles so as soon as Oscar's up standing, stroller collapses backward from the weight onto my legs, shattering bottle of wine that I could literally fall on my hands and knees and lap up every drop from the dirty floor tiles as am so desperate to acquire any soothing alcohol in system right now. I am entirely serious.

Fairly cleverly, I soak up wine with diapers from the new box, leaving me about half untouched while Oscar trots around in it, happily splashing me and ruining his new RL madras sneakers that cost me more than my own shoes.

Reeking of cheap wine and jet-lagged, take Oscar by hand, leading him to courtyard to drop wine-drenched diapers in garbage bin, where Mister Curious picks up stray cigarette butt and puts to lips as I open garbage can lid. "NO!" I yell out, automatically. He bellows a cry from the mere pitch of my panicked tone. I drag stroller and purse and remaining groceries and wailing child to back staircase to begin ascent. "It's okay. It's okay, honey, don't cry! You're getting a taxi ride!" I say, sweeping him up to my hip for a lift so we can get up the stairs as fast as possible.

"No, I walk. I walk stairs!" my newly independent guy demands as he kicks at my legs fighting his way down to the slant slippery staircase.

"Oh, aces, this is insanity," I say to myself as I hold his hand and all the other shit and we walk as slow as snails up every flight and every step. Oscar's in heaven and I'm about ready to fucking have a mental breakdown that just getting from point A to point B, the simple task of getting groceries, is such a struggle. I don't remember it being this hard! Clearly, it's a very different world when your child is no longer a baby but a spinning top, into everything toddler. Getting around with an infant in my Baby Bjorn was a cake walk. Not unlike carrying a— *sometimes crabby*—bag of potatoes, but now this little boy is Mr. Curious and zipping all over the place like a blur.

The stairs routine was a thrice-daily event and never got easier. Teamed with the added delight of having to give Oscar sponge baths since the shower was inexplicably terror zone for him. Not to mention, the yuckety bathroom was far too tiny a space to contain him while I sped through a shower, so I had to race through shampoo, shave, and suds at lightning speed while I could hear him putter around the flat doing a host of possibly dangerous activities. It was agony trying to keep him from cords, plugs, climbing precarious furniture, falling down stairs, off the terrace, or grabbing knives from the kitchen drawers. I never sat down, just hovered and blocked everything 24/7. Obviously, to stay anywhere, even glorious Paris, in a non-child-proofed environment is just pure nervous-anxiety and tension.

Possibly more annoying: there is nowhere to change a diaper in this city! Oscar is now old enough to feel embarrassed and freak out if I lay him on a blanket to change him in public—on the grass, *en plein air,* as they say—so this is becoming madness. I literally only found one place in St. Germain, on my *last day*; downstairs, by the loo, at the resto Le Rostand, by Jardin du Luxembourg. The only other diaper-changing option I found, *par hasard,* is in the Carrousel du Louvre, the inexplicably chic and expensive "Point WC."

A posh, if scalding hot (no AC), public restroom just to the right of the escalator created to sock it to the museum goers and shoppers whose bladders are about to explode. Where, after standing in a long queue, trying not to melt or pee down own leg, I discovered, for the equivalent of $1.50, I had a spacious venue to relieve myself in a very clean and very high-design private bathroom—and with a changing table all at my disposal. Alas, with my luck, dear Oscar wasn't even in need of a change and the extreme heat made my thirty-second visit a marathon in maintaining one's mental capabilities in the treacherously dehydrating temperature. Thus the large array of decorative printed toilet tissue (dollars, euros, Louis XIV, and the like) for purchase at 5 euros each didn't get me to crack open my wallet, but I would've gladly paid 20 euros for a frigging Dixie cup of water to drink!

Add to the list of unexpected nightmares of having a toddler in Paris the frequent rain showers that have you diving for cover under the scant array of alcoves and awnings, since don't think for a bloody moment you can just pop into a boutique to wait it out. Does the word "scowl" mean anything to you?

All of which means this is not a vacation! This is just one hurdle after another with a great setting and some attractive extras milling around. Worst of all, I feel like from all the stress, I am not being as patient or connected with Oscar; it's like I have less "face time" with my darling boy, since 75% of the damn day is spent getting to and from and around town. Frankly, the first two days were sheer torment to adjust and to realize it was, despite my massive efforts, going to be like a triathlon as a mom. The first night, jet lag seized us both, but on opposing ends. By 9:00 P.M., I was just dead-drained and after trying to feed Oscar, his Majesty, his fav hummus and pita chips, albeit without a high chair, he simply flung it to the four corners of the room and ran off to the bedroom requesting "toons" ("cartoons"). Thus, every meal was a study in frustration; without a high chair, he was just uncontained and like a wild man. I'd hoped the little rascal would just sit on a chair, high on a pillow, but that was laughably too much to ask; pillow always got instantly tossed as chair fell over and he wandered off to jam jellybeans in the CD player.

That first night, while I was so physically and mentally withered and dying to sleep, my boy was having the reverse effects and was like a raging bull, total insomniac! He was up until 3:40 A.M., while I thought I might die from the strain. Around 2:00 A.M. he sensed my fading kindness (to put it in nice terms) and started screaming and crying at the top of his lungs. No way, this is not happening. Here I was, fuck, having to not just deal with this loony tunes bellow fest but also, as we are in an apartment building where I heard the man upstairs drop his belt this evening, the walls are so thin and set in a courtyard that's like an amplifier. I have to get Oscar to shush . . . which as any mother knows, only freaks out said child and escalates the shriek fest. So, as he howled and ricocheted off the walls; I longed for our house,

our life as we know it, as I pretty much had, all day. I kept telling myself, C'mon, chill, you knew it would be hard, so it's senseless to reason
that Paris is too grueling and arduous, simply because you're struggling NOW in some rented apartment. Yes, the rain has soaked all the
shoes and clothes you brought and there is no way to possibly dry anything so you're compelled to buy *more* clothes . . . and the female clerk
at the children's clothing boutique made such a nasty slam at you when
you went to buy your two-year-old son a pair of pants and she noticed
he still wore a diaper: "I can give you the name of someone who can
potty train your son if YOU cannot manage, madame," she said with
an expression of pure disdain. So what?! Can't you endure the daily
snubs, jibes, long lines, massive pollution, traffic and noise, Kiki? This
is Paris, for fuck's sake! Everyone expects you to be here, raise your
son, and assume the life you had, so shut up and deal.

Wait a minute, pedantic inner monologue, maybe, just maybe, it's
time for you to fall silent and for me to just watch, study, and see how
this lifestyle here would really would play out. So I did just that. I let
go of all the pressure, preconceived hopes and ideas, and just took in
all the information. The week was cool; Oscar and I slowed our pace
as much as Paris allows and we had the best time ever. He napped on
a blanket under a shady oak in the Jardin du Luxembourg while I
read, we shared *poulet* baguettes and Evian and went for a Bateaux
Mouches boat ride at sunset. We watched street musicians while lap-
ping up Berthillon *glace* ("ice cream") on the Pont Neuf and watched
old men playing *boules* at the Place Dauphine until the rain came. It
was heaven and yet . . .

By the tenth day, after some great times hanging with old friends
and feeling my feet fill their old shoes again, I was thinking, "Okay,
this 'living here again' idea is possible . . . bonkers tiring, but I love
a challenge, right? Hmm. Not sure." Went with my dear *amie* Sabina

to an event I once loved terribly: attending the chic Carré Rive Gauche *antiquaire* soiree. A very fabulous and fun evening (in the seventh arrondissement—my old 'hood), when all the antique dealers literally roll out a red carpet and open their doors for an evening of flowing champagne, people watching, and high-end furniture viewing. Roving musicians play old French classics while the *haute monde* mingle with the likes of the President of France. All good, right? After attending eight years as single girl—generally on the prowl—it was phenomenal to be there with my two favorites, Oscar and Sabina. Cool to see so many old friends, present Monsieur Oscar to everyone, and, frankly, be remembered. All was a delight until I ran into a sexy artist I knew, Vidor, who, despite living with the mother of his child, was notorious for always being in hot pursuit of hot women. So handsome this man that, despite knowing all that, it still was pretty damn fun to be on the receiving end of his attentions. With an invitation thrown out to me to come see him at his atelier the next *après-midi* (read, unquestionably, for sex), it was all quite entertaining until he reacted to my decline with, "Nothing is so unsexy as a woman who is just a mother." Bam! Ouch. Needless to say, I am not his biggest fan of late and think he is mad as a sack of cats. (Men of France as seen through my new eyes—crystal clear 20/20 vision, finally!)

My perspective on life à Paris was veering off course, while, *sans doute,* Oscar was loving it. He was enchanted and amazed at the elaborate fountains and gorgeous parks—but are months and years of that worth seeing his extended family maybe once a year? *Je n'en suis pas sûre.*

And Paris just seems different than I remembered, less shimmering. The ghastly pollution and, with the new nonsmoking laws, the public has taken to smoking ALL THE TIME on the crowded streets, so that it's just a stinky haze. I was also horrified to see that there is now a Starbucks in the basement shopping level of the Louvre. Is nothing sacred? Equally notable, the financial crisis has sent prices soaring. Even stopping to get Oscar his first *pain au chocolat* was about four bucks. Yes, it was true that by day 5 and with some rhythm and acclimation, I was digging being back and seeing friends. It was amazing to realize the summer light has the sun setting at 10:30 P.M., which made for some glorious evenings of long walks by the Seine and catching up with friends at cafés.

Oscar was a jewel, just a true and brilliant little traveler, amazing me by exploding his social skills at the playgrounds and sandboxes. Gorgeous little girls in classic bob haircuts and red-check pinafores swarmed around my boy and had him swooning and, lo and behold, sharing his "scoop" (shovel) and sand bucket. He ran up and down the slides and jungle gyms and drove every car on the *manège* ("merry-go-round") by Bon Marché. I had never see him so constantly happy and delighted, and he already IS a very smiley, happy kid. It literally was freaking me out that, here he was in Paris, so much more adventurous, independent, and blissful than ever, that I was now feeling virtually *obligated* to move us back here. I seriously thought that he would miss family and make those fake phone calls on his play cell phone, asking family members to "coming over," as he would chirp. None of that. This was all so new, so vividly engaging, and so varied. It was starting to feel like I was expecting to love it madly and was afraid he wouldn't, and here it's the inverse. Now what?

All my Paris friends kept asking, "You're moving back, right?" and I kept shifting my answer, skewing the odds, "Yeah, probably, I'm about 70% sure I will move back." There was so much I was sure I would love about being back in Paris: the cafés, the well-dressed public, the food I so desperately missed, the architecture, the sky, the

sound of seagulls cawing by the Seine . . . and somehow the overrid-
ing feelings were about Oscar and if it would really be best for him
long run.

Most of the children his age are already jammed into spending
entire days at *crèches, maternelles, garderies,* and schools while the non-
working *mamans* swan about all day. When I peered out the window
from the rented apartment, I could see the asphalt enclosure that was
the neighborhood *crèche.* The howls of children playing started at 7:30
A.M. and were heard at intervals throughout the day for recesses and
continued all the way until 6:00 P.M. I could see the teachers and
dames de service ("helper/minders") while they stood outside smoking
as the kids had nothing more than the ground on which to play and
run. Too many children were ignored and standing alone while bul-
lies ran riot. It reminded me of a statement I'd read in an expat
mother's guide to Paris: "Teachers take a 'sink or swim' approach to a
child's development; they will not advise or intercede on school playgrounds as they would in the USA. It's customary in this culture to let
nature take its course, following more of a survival-of-the-fittest point
of view."

Ouch. In short, seeing the kids was like watching *Lord of the Flies,*
and it all made sense to me: if that's the way children, and primarily
little boys, are taught how to reason or react, *with no intervention rather
than impulse,* it makes perfect sense that the city and the country are
rampant with these testosterone-reactive men who scream at each
other vulgar insults when a car cuts them off, when a girl does something they don't like, etc.—they just criticize and move on. And lord
knows, after having eight years of relationships with Frenchmen who
tell me how they had to watch their mothers suffer in silence as their
fathers ran off to see mistresses, I get it. This is not how I want to raise
my son. Yes, the schools are more rigid and strict and thus the chil-

dren are getting a higher level of education, but at what cost? They rarely have art, music, or sports available at these schools. (Again, quoting the expat mom handbook, "Parents often arrange sports or artistic activities outside school to complement what is offered by the formal school curriculum.")

Sure, Oscar's loving the parks and the playgrounds, but in a year or year and a half, he will be expected to be at school all damn day, on some asphalt courtyard, surrounded by kids who may be apt to judge or taunt him because he has no French father, his mother's an American *and* single. And he would lose daily interactions with the treasure trove of family who do love and adore him and would buttress any nonsense. Is it worth it? We will have to live in a small apartment for this Parisian lifestyle: no yard, no family around, no fun money to spare as the euro exchange eats 40% of my money in dollars. Goodbye tree house, swingset, garden, trick-or-treating, BBQs, and hugs from grandparents.

And for me, along with the pleasures of having a social life again and feeling part of the fabric of a community I once aspired *and achieved* to my utmost dreams, I feel a palpable disappointment. The framework of my life has changed, and so much of what I loved about Paris doesn't seem to apply in the same way anymore. Of course, it's a staggeringly magical place to live, but life is magic now, in ways that matter, without needing to be in the hipster BCBG club-art-design world. I used to love and revel in being chic and dressing to the nines, but Oscar doesn't need a supermodel—he needs a *role model*.

Time to realize I am not even that interested in all that game playing and presentation stuff anymore. Plainly said, Paris can really tweak the most minor action, like say, going for a walk, into a heady ritual of presenting oneself (almost like that of a prancing poodle . . . *in heat*) in that, you get so much unspoken visual feedback—judgment, approval, sexual interplay with men, tension among women, and even self-worth from simply being a member of the arrondissement. Your identity, as many expats would confirm, isn't so much about your income or job as it might be in the USA, but is about all the aforementioned exchanges. Frankly, it's a lot of frivolity and I realize I am happier, for the moment, to be Oscar's mother and not partake in all that. As a single mother, with a few years under her belt, I am too busy and, *finally,* too mature to care. What a revelation!

As all my emotions untangled from the hopes of Paris, I could see with a fresh clarity that my current reality is richer than the reflected image that I had held to. Ironically—as though I needed any more evidence of the illusions of Paris—Gilbert did me a massive favor in allowing me to depart with an uncluttered mind and heart. After a year and all the communiqués, e-mails, energy, and flowery words between Gilbert and myself, he stood me up.

I know. So shitty. It shook out like this; I texted him the morning I arrived and he sent a fluttery message:

Paris is now in full bloom that its beloved Kiki has returned . . .
We have missed you and can't wait to see you and young Oscar—
any time any where, you only need ask.

Having just arrived, I was so excited to see him, it actually gave me butterflies. The idea of finally laying my eyes again on this charming wordsmith, who had so skillfully succeeded in intriguing me, made my heart race. Obviously, being one for taking such things to the furthest imaginable fantasy, I let my mind dance into the realm of falling madly in love, marrying him, and "happily ever after" in his château. It seemed *très possible,* even probable, given all the pieces were there and could have easily been slipped into place.

Since my schedule was pretty hectic, we kept texting and trying to set up a dinner, and we both shifted it around. As this unfolded, it all came back to me how Frenchmen act like it's all about you but it's often just a poetic exercise and dance of seduction to them. And it was starting to get tiresome. Gilbert and I had to ultimately set our long-awaited "date" for my last evening in Paris. By then I was already terribly convinced to abandon the Paris Project Return, so I chose to let him call me.

He never did. For once, it was almost a relief not to be swept into a *liaison dangereuse* with a Frenchman. I don't have the time, energy, or interest in playing out all the games and rituals of dating a Frenchman, as I once so adored. Oh sure, I was pissed for about an hour (make that two) and more than a little stunned. But then I thought it so poignant and telling. I felt it another great sign of fate at work and I went and savored that my last evening was spent with my favorite man, Oscar.

We retraced our initial path from Day One and said a lovely adieu to all his favorites: Notre Dame, Pont des Arts to watch the boats go "under!," Jardin du Luxembourg's fountain, and the vast courtyard of the Louvre, where Oscar sprinted about yelling, "I running!" It was such a beautiful night, the sky brushed with vibrant oranges and golds like that of a Gustave Moreau painting. It felt so marvelous to be there, to be happy, and, at long last, to have my answers and peace.

Slowly strolling back to the apartment, with Oscar gobbling up his last quiche from Boulangerie Paul, my fragmented thoughts finally all shimmied into a clear picture: returning to Paris and being in the heart of it allowed me to truly see my life anew and the beauty in it. And to finally acknowledge that our life back in Wisconsin is just what we *both* need—right now. To wake to birdsongs, fresh air, running in the yard with the neighbor kids, followed by grilling salmon and corn on the cob at lake's edge with the "pack" (my family)—*that is* exactly what Oscar and I find essential now. To take Oscar on a walk to the neighborhood nature conservancy, with its acres and acres of forests, streams, and wildlife galore (a mere two blocks away) and to glimpse raccoons walking on their back legs as they make their way through the underbrush or to happen upon a huge shiny turtle on the path— this is what excites Oscar and thereby *me*. He loves to wake early from his new big-boy bed in his room (Oscar bid a fond adieu to cosleeping and nursing—miraculously—just before Mister Independent set off for his Paris sojourn) and to race outside to putter around the yard that is his private domain and sanctuary. Still in diaper (still mastering potty training), barefoot, and bleary eyed, he saunters about checking on his sandbox and the blooming sunflowers that his grand amour, Lola the ravishing seven-year-old girl next door, gave him. Oscar frolics about in the grass while I water the herbs and vegetables, darting off now and then to dash after the neighbor's cat, Snooks, whom he adores like a sibling. When he's ready, he tells me, "Momma, time, for *say-say* ("cereal") or eggs," and we pop back in to make breakfast, retreating back to the deck to eat with a view of the pond and the geese flying overhead.

Life in Paris is a total contrast; it is such a long haul, from the moment one wakes, there is not one iota of this easy pace of our lives in Wisconsin. No longer the barefoot sauntering or peaceful whims of eating a leisurely breakfast on the deck while watching the ducks glide through the pond. Nope, just a hectic race to get him and myself fed, washed, and presentable to face the masses and *then* make the mammoth expedition to some garden or park with every conceivable, possibly needed toy or truck, sunblock, sunhat, spare outfit, umbrella, juice boxes, diaper bag, all *my* things, keys—the stroller packed to the hilt and then a lengthy walk to overpopulated city parks!

I know, big-city living has its wonderful advantages, especially if you have loads of money (say, if I could afford to send Oscar to a great bilingual school), help (family, nanny, or partner or all three!), or a country house (to have space, fresh air, and the ability to run free), but with none of those, it's tough and not so user-friendly for me or for Oscar right now. At his age, a hug, kiss, and flying a kite with Grandpa, is infinitely more memorable and satisfying to him than a tour through a museum or sitting at a café drinking a $7 Coke at Flore.

What I needed so much from Paris to "fill me" is filled by Oscar in so many ways. I can hardly put it into words, but it feels like there is more of my childhood self—*the centered, simpler girl*—in my spirit now than that "big city, I will conquer you" woman who often fell victim to insecurity and image.

I know raising a child in Paris was my dream and the way I always *thought* I wanted to do it, but I think now that I have tried it twice, I am fully informed, have lived and witnessed it all; it's time to cast off the remaining shards of my personal *image*-imagination-fueled fantasies. They were fabulous and fun choices to delve into as an individual, but not so based on my new reality. *And* what is being a good mother other than making choices to the advantage and benefit of your child? To that point, I found myself laughing out loud today as I uttered the total mom cliché: "Well, if you don't feel like eating the whole hamburger, just eat the patty." This is a riot. Despite all my lifelong attempts at being unique all the time, there is a certain freedom of realizing *you aren't* and you don't have to be and that there is a great strength in feeling a sisterhood with all other mothers.

Did it take this child to finally make me grow up? Clearly. That elitist veneer that I so eagerly embraced twenty years ago, and wore with unabashed pride, is getting stripped away by a life that, finally, has meaning and purpose.

Chapter 22

*"Having children makes you no more
a parent than having a piano
makes you a pianist."*
—Michael Levine

I knew as we left Paris, I was over the Return to France idea and, god, it was such an immense relief to have that haunting weight from my shoulders. I was free! No more comparing one culture to another, one lifestyle to another. No more worrying when the house might sell and how in heck (note, new nonswearing vow in place) I was going to afford Paris month after month, year after year.

After so much time spent struggling that Paris was the answer to every long boring day or frustration, now that it's solved, I feel like I've been liberated, content to be back in my own skin. The best way to describe it came to me, amazingly, in the middle of my last night in

Paris, as the bright light of the moon bathed me in its light and woke me gently. I no longer felt that somewhat *dread* that the next day was a Monday—which feels like a work day—but I had the effortlessness sense that all the days now feel like weekends. No longer the apprehension that with morning comes the grind and the longing for Paris while enduring the reality.

Remarkably, I woke that last morning of leaving Paris, despite all the exhaustion, feeling possibly more beautiful than I think I ever have. A scant month or two ago, I would catch my reflection and debate whether Botox, a diet, or a new haircut could possibly lift my spirits about myself and getting older. Though I'm hip-deep in middle age, etched with stretch marks and spider veins that very much resemble a topographical map, a belly that isn't so much a six pack *as a "snak pack,"* and boobs that fail even the jumbo pencil test, I feel happier than ever. Wow, I may not be able to take a vacation for another year, but hey, money well spent. I exorcised the demons and they scrambled off!

Arriving back to Wisconsin, it seemed like all the planets realigned to bolster my decision to stay, as our welcome home was quite touching and dear. My whole family came to the airport to see us arrive, warm hugs and kisses as Oscar et al. bathed in the love of family. Not even when I had been in Paris for a year and came back for Christmas had I received such a welcome. Truth is, living here has brought all my family closer. I love seeing *and being* a part of my parents' and siblings' daily lives. After so many years in NYC and Paris, I had become some far-flung alien visitor who popped in at Christmas and sent birthday presents, who had grand stories and quick quips but little else. Now, we see family almost every day; soccer with Uncle Andy is tops with Master Oscar, as is Sunday brunch at Grandpa Ta's or going to the zoo with Opa. *And* I get to connect to the people I really love and who will always be there for Oscar, which far outweighs the creatures like a Gilbert or a Jack who I seem to attract like magnetic filings in France.

It may have taken me twenty years or so, but I think I may have finally recalibrated my values to those that I can be proud of *and that my parents can appreciate.*

Amazingly, at age twenty-five, giddily telling your dad, "I'm so happy, I met Sean Penn and we are now dating, do you believe it?!" doesn't register as a reason for him to beam with pride. But I like to think that now his seeing me living a life of meaning and purpose and having that daily contact with his grandson gives him great joy. And while my mother surely wished for and encouraged me to live a glamorous life full of jewels, galas, art, and travel, I think she would applaud the two decades I reveled in it with a *coupe de champagne and* celebrate that I am also experiencing and embracing motherhood with the same pride that she did. She always suggested not to do anything by halves, and by her example, I innately seek to give each chapter of my life that same passionate commitment. All I know is, family was everything to her, and I am so grateful to recognize this—for myself—at this stage in my life.

That whole "it takes a village" expression didn't mean anything to me before, but I can now see it is entirely true. Sure, you can do it all by yourself, but it's infinitely superior to be with loved ones, dear friends, and in a wonderful community. And that was exactly what we came *home* to. As though on cue, stepping back onto Wisconsin soil, the sky was filled with the magical dances of the soft delicate Chinese cotton blossoms sailing on gentle breezes that come this time of year.

Seventeen hours after leaving Paris, we finally arrived back home, where, delightfully, the neighbor kids were all waiting outside, drawing,

"Welcome back K & O" on our sidewalk. Cheers were heard all over Shorewood Hills, as the clan rushed to give hugs, all talking at once with interspersed pleads, "How was Paris? You're not moving, right?"

Hardly out of the car, as Tony and my brother Andy got our bags, I so enjoyed stating, "Nope, we are staying!"

"Hurrah!" resounded among leaps and flinging of colored chalk sticks in the air.

With the delicate white blossoms undulating everywhere like a beautiful ballet, Oscar yelled blissfully, "We home! Look . . . snow!"

Everyone laughed, charmed and with shared happiness. And in that moment, I realized with Oscar still on hip and all these dear and precious people, this all felt infinitely more real, touching, and valuable than anything I ever felt in Paris. Though a scant few years ago, I would have bet you my slew of designer *it* bags Paris was the idyllic place to raise a child, I had it all wrong.

This is our utopia.

As my mother taught me well, through her actions and not just words, family is everything.

Everything.

Kiki's Bébé Address Book

PARIS CHILDREN'S AND BABY BOUTIQUES

Bonpoint, 320, rue St. Honoré, 75001

Tartine et Chocolat, 24, rue de la Paix, 75002

Petit Bateau, 1, rue Pierre Lescot, 75001

Petit Faune, 13, rue de Mézières, 75006

Miki House, 366, rue St. Honoré, 75001

Okaidi, 115, rue Monge, 75005

Printemps, 64, boulevard Haussmann, 75009

Du Pareil au Même, 1, rue St. Denis, 75001

Jacadi, 9, avenue de l'Opéra, 75001

Galeries Lafayette, 40, boulevard Haussmann, 75009

Natalys, 76, rue du Seine, 75006

PARIS KIDS' TOY SHOPS AND BOOKSTORES

Le Bon Marché, 24, rue de Sèvres, 75007

Chantelivre, 13, rue de Sèvres, 75006

Il Était une Fois, 6, rue Ferdinand Duval, 75004—Love this joint, a
   paradise in a cave.

Le Ciel Est à Tout le Monde, 7, avenue Trudaine, 75009

Les Cousins d'Alice, 36, rue Daguerre, 75014

Au Nain Bleu, 5, boulevard Malesherbers, 75008

Si Tu Veux, 68, galerie Vivienne, 75002

Petitcollin, in the garden of Palais Royal, 9, rue de Beaujolais,
   75001

PARIS KIDS' COIFFURES—HAIR SALONS

Au Pays d'Oscar, 16, rue Vavin, 75006

Vert Tendre, 58, avenue du Docteur Arnold Netter, 75012

Coup Kid, 3–5, boulevard des Italiens, 75002

123 Ciseaux, 10, boulevard Courcelles, 75017

La Maison de Tif & Cut, 73, rue des Vignes, 75016

FC Kid's Island, 38, rue Falguière, 75015

GREEN/ECO FAMILY OPTIONS IN PARIS

Bébé au Naturel, www.bebe-au-naturel.com—A wide selection of natural baby products.

Bambino Mio, www.bambinomio.com—Reusable cotton diapers and accessories.

Monde de Bébé, 03.88.40.00.95/www.monde-de-bebe.com—Mail-order company done by a mother of five who chooses only natural products. Call for a catalog. Great advice and a wide range of toys, organic diapers and products, clothes and furniture.

Fibris, 40, boulevard St. Marcel, 75005, 01.43.31.63.63—Clothes, socks, underwear, and baby clothes in organic wool, cotton, linen, and silk.

Naturalia, 11/13, rue Montorgueil, 75001—Organic food market.

Canal Bio, 300, rue de Charenton, 75012—Organic food market.

PARIS KIDS' SHOE BOUTIQUES

Petit Petons, 20, rue St. Placide, 75006
Six Pieds Trois Pouces, 85, rue de Longchamp, 75116
Na!, 73, rue du Commerce, 75015
Till, 51, rue de Sèvres, 75006
Tavernier, 99, rue Mouffetard, 75005
La Halle aux Chaussures, 12, rue Brantome, 75003
Il Court le Furet, 6 Bis, rue Fourcoy, 75017

PARIS MATERNITY AND NURSING BOUTIQUES

Euroform, 50 Bis, rue de Douai, 75009—Best selection of nursing
    bras, many very pretty with lace and with closures that aren't
    seventy-six hooks and eyes locking down your back like the
    nineteenth-century models. And found a massively comfortable
    thong for my über-bulging belly.
1 et 1 font 3, 3, rue Solférino, 75007
Neuf Lune, 42, rue du Cherche Midi, 75006
Véronique Delachaux, 69, avenue Ternes, 75017

PARIS KID-FRIENDLY RESTOS AND CAFÉS

Altitude 95, on the first floor of the Tour Eiffel, 75007, Métro-Bir-Hakeim, 01.45.55.20.04—Kids' menu, high chairs, and an astounding view to mesmerize the children.

Café de La Jatte, 60, boulevard Vital Bouhot, Île de la Jatte, Neuilly-sur-Seine, 92000, 01.47.45.04.20—Sunday brunch with buffet and entertainment for kids (crayons, face painting, children's show).

Café de la Paix, 12, boulevard des Capucines, 75009—Children's menus, high chairs, and changing tables available.

Café LeRostand, bordering Jardin du Luxembourg, 75006—Changing table available.

Universal Resto, Le Carrousel du Louvre, 99, rue de Rivoli, 75001—High chairs available. Some children's menus and microwaves to warm baby bottles.

Villa Spicy Restaurant, 8, avenue Franklin Roosevelt, 75008—Family brunch on Sundays 12.30–15.00, cartoons on TV screens, and a clown to entertain the children.

Chain restos: McDonald's (high chairs a plenty if you feel like feeding your child this fare!), Flunch, Pizza Hut, Chicago Pizza Pie company, Lina's sandwiches, Leons, Hippopotamus.

Slip into a new life with
KIRSTEN LOBE'S
decadent novels

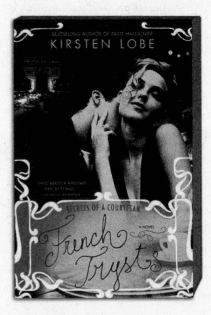

"Wickedly entertaining."
—*Chicago Tribune* on *Paris Hangover*

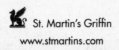 St. Martin's Griffin
www.stmartins.com